ISSUES OF BLOOD: THE POLITICS OF MENSTRUATION

Also by Sophie Laws

SEEING RED: The Politics of Pre-Menstrual Tension (*with Valerie Hey and Andrea Eagan*)
LIVING WITH SICKLE CELL DISEASE (*with Janet Black*)

First published 1990

Published by
THE MACMILLAN PRESS LTD
Houndmills, Basingstoke, Hampshire RG21 2XS
and London
Companies and representatives
throughout the world

Printed in Singapore
Filmset by Wearside Tradespools,
Fulwell, Sunderland

British Library Cataloguing in Publication Data
Laws, Sophie
Issues of blood.
1. Women. Menstruation
I. Title
612′.662
ISBN 0–333–48233–6
ISBN 0–333–48234–4 pbk

Issues of Blood
The Politics of Menstruation

Sophie Laws

Foreword by Margaret Stacey
Emeritus Professor of Sociology
University of Warwick

Consultant Editor: Jo Campling

MACMILLAN

'Taboo' – first published in the *Guardian*, 14 November 1983, reprinted by permission of Posy Simmonds.

© Posy Simmonds 1983

Contents

Acknowledgements

My thanks are due to the many women who have encouraged me in persisting with this book. I am grateful to those who read and commented on parts of my work, especially: Dena Attar, Celia Davies, Judy Greenway, Helen Gurden, Rachel Hasted, Hilary Homans, Liz Kelly, Wilma Laws, Fiona McCloskey, Esther Merves, Naomi Pfeffer, Jane Rosser, Lisa Saffron and Sylvia Walby. The Feminist Research Group at Warwick University (1982/3) gave me a supportive place to test out ideas.

Professor Meg Stacey gave me immeasurable help, concentrated attention and acute criticism, as the principal supervisor for the research on which this book is based. Lynn Alderson lived through the whole process with me and gave me essential support and good ideas.

Women who kindly shared the results of their own researches with me include: Catriona Blake, Heather Clark, Alice Dan, Andrea Dworkin, Suzette Heald, Esther Merves, Sandra McNeill, Nimmi Naidoo, Shirley Prendergast, Patricia Rouse, Hazel Slavin, Linda Torsani-Fatkin, and Anne-Marie Turnbull. Thanks to Posy Simmonds for her kind permission to reprint her cartoon 'Taboo', first published in the *Guardian*, as the frontispiece to this book.

I am grateful to the Social Sciences Research Council for a Studentship which supported me for three years, and to everyone who agreed to be interviewed for the research. Thanks also to librarians at Warwick University, Lancaster University, the Wellcome Library and the Fawcett Library who gave me a great deal of assistance, and to Jill Wilkinson who typed the thesis.

Foreword

I well remember the day when Sophie Laws, a graduate of a year's standing with an existing record of writing and publication, turned up in my office. She said she wanted to do a PhD on menstruation but had so far been unable to find a suitable home for her study. She needed a department which would accept the notion that menstruation was a proper subject for sociological enquiry, as well as accepting her, and also where she could find a suitable superviser. Menstruation seemed to me a proper subject for sociological analysis and I was prepared to take the risk of supervising the thesis – there was no doubt that it would be original – and to offer her an SSRC linked award.

My own interests were focused on the sociology of health, illness and healing and the insights which feminist theory could offer the sub-discipline. The research programme had special reference at that time to aspects of the health of children and women. I found analysis of how women and men handle the biological base, and the ideas and social arrangements they associate with it, both academically interesting and socially and politically important. Menstruation is clearly part of the biological base of our society and – in common with any other part of that base – likely to be endowed with different meanings in different times and places and subject to socially identifiable modes of control. Social anthropological accounts had already made that clear, limited though many were. Furthermore, menstruation was obviously an important subject for women with implications for their children.

I was all too well aware of the long-standing masculinist bias of universities in the selection of topics and modes of study. Sociology, historically dominated by the founding *fathers*, has been no exception. In these circumstances and bearing in mind the continued male domination of our subject and our universities, I was not in the least surprised that Sophie Laws had had problems finding a home for her proposed research. I was pleased to be able to offer her one.

I am delighted that she is now sharing her discoveries with a wider audience.

Sophie Laws has travelled a long and painful road to produce this book. She has had the courage to do what so few sociologists do – to research a dominant and powerful group. It is so much more common, as she says, to research the oppressed, the poor and the down trodden and so much harder to research the powerful, as I know to my cost. I have also been trying to do just that in another field – analysing the workings of the General Medical Council on which I at one time served.

Two premises, the one drawn from sociology, the other from feminist theory, formed the starting point for her research. Her first, sociological, premise was that the ideas of a dominant group in a society are those which will dominate, and therefore to some extent determine, the ideas of the oppressed. The second, feminist, premise was that ours is still a male-dominated society in which men act as a group to maintain their superiority. Taking the two together she concluded that the ideas of men are likely to dominate the ideas which women have about ourselves as well as about the social world in general. More particularly, she concluded that our ideas about menstruation, both ours as women and those of our society as a whole, derive from men.

This idea seemed theoretically sound but, given my socialisation as a woman born in the early 1920s, empirically unimaginable. Yes, obviously she was right, but how on earth did it come about that men's ideas were the source of the information and the social rules which women secretly shared with each other or kept guiltily to ourselves? What is more, if she was correct, as seemed theoretically likely, just how was she to get the data?

This book shows how rewarding her theoretical starting point was and how, by using a variety of methods and sources of data, Sophie has been able to uncover part at least of the male culture which, around the area of menstruation, sustains our thought and behaviour as women. Through it all she has arrived at the elegant and simple notion that the social rules about menstruation in our society are governed not by 'taboo', which she takes to imply the supernatural, but by etiquette – an etiquette which essentially dictates that women should behave as if the monthly cyclical changes of our fertile years do not occur. These fluctuations should not alter our demeanour in public life – and if pain overwhelms us it should not be publicly attributed to menstruation. In intimate heterosexual life the cyclical changes should be accommodated to men's wishes.

The rule which lies behind the detail of menstrual etiquette Sophie Laws sums up as follows: women may not draw men's attention to menstruation in any way, a rule which she argues is made workable because a man may decide to waive it in a particular, usually sexual, relationship with an individual woman. It was this rule that made her enquiry so difficult, for the rule forbids the investigation.

However, hers is no simple or static analysis. As you read you will recognise the many levels and the delicate nuances which she records. Her framework is social constructionist and radical feminist. That is to say her work is an analysis of male political power over women which regards such domination as socially rather than biologically created. Furthermore she does not rely on psychoanalytic explanations where explanations can be found in social relations – she does not need a notion of the unconscious to account for what she observes. The joking talk among men about menstruation is *of itself* enough to account for the sense of threat which we feel as women and which leads us to control our menses so carefully – indeed it is a better account than a psychoanalytic one would be.

Sophie Laws's study of medical writing about menstruation shows that attention is paid to 'premenstrual tension' to the exclusion of other problems women experience in the cycle and indeed overshadows menstrual pain, which has so far received little genuinely scientific attention. Interestingly, 'pmt' is the one aspect of the cycle which may be publicly discussed. The medical writings idealise the heterosexual nuclear family. Sophie Laws suggests that medical men, mediating as they do between women's experiences and the male culture, work as maintenance engineers to ease heterosexual relations.

Her observation that menstruation may be openly acknowledged in a heterosexual relationship but not elsewhere fits with her notion that sexuality is one key to women's sub-

ordination to men. Attitudes to and behaviour about menstruation in the sexual context have changed over the
lifetime of her male informants. She describes a new ideology of sexuality and menstruation developing. The new
ideology emphasises the sexual nature of women and makes
menstruation out to be sexual, whereas previously it was held
to be anti-sexual. This male ideology is different from that
which sustained the etiquette of former years and may
appear more liberal. However, the men's ideas about women
on which it is based are equally oppressive for women,
because the concern of the men is to free women to be
available to them, not that we should be freed to determine
our own behaviour.

Her study, based as it is on a variety of sources, has all the
strengths that derive from multiple methods – her methodological appendix is a mine of ideas and information. Her
samples are small, necessarily so to get this kind of information. Her men may not be typical either – she does not
pretend that they are, but they certainly demonstrate that a
male culture exists and shows variety within it. It is a culture
about which we need to know more. Her informants,
moreover, are the sort of men who are straws in the wind of
wider and forthcoming social change.

Sophie Laws has concentrated on one aspect of women's
fertile years. In doing so she has increased our understanding well beyond menstrual etiquette. What she has to say will
be helpful to those of us who are trying to explain the ageism
which falls more heavily on old women even than it does on
old men – the oppression which women past the menopause
experience – and how young and middle-aged women come
to play a part in it. It may also shed light on what seems to me
the increasing willingness of gynaecologists to do hysterecto-
mies and of women to accept them: 'you don't need it any
more – let's get rid of all that'.

Just as the research was painful for Sophie to do, so this
book is not always comfortable for women to read (or, I
imagine, for compassionate and thoughtful men). It is a must
however. If we remain deluded about the source of our
oppression we are unable to overcome it and, worse still, are
liable to blame ourselves and each other for its manifestations. In struggling to gain this knowledge Sophie Laws has

done a great service to us all. Furthermore, although she somewhere in these covers calls it a 'nasty book', it is really a hopeful book. She has after all done it! One more step on the way to liberation.

Meg Stacey
University of Warwick

1 Introduction

Why do women so often feel uneasy about menstruation? Why is it so thoroughly hidden from public view? Why do young girls still have to learn about it in fear and shame? Why are new products endlessly created to enable the secrecy to be yet more effective: now, the individually-wrapped sanitary towel!

How can it be that the powerful feminist movement of the last 20 years has not succeeded in changing these absurd, old-fashioned attitudes? Why don't women just refuse to be intimidated any more?

A number of studies have concerned themselves with women's feelings and views about menstruation, and these should, of course, be the only opinions that matter. But women develop their own attitudes within a culture, within families, with certain pressures upon them. This book is about one of these pressures, the attitudes of men, and the impact of patriarchal ideas.

British people nurture an image of themselves as tremendously tolerant and open-minded. Mention of social attitudes towards menstruation frequently produces discussions of vaguely-remembered stories about other cultures – behaviour and beliefs among 'other' people, seen as exotic and perhaps primitive. There is often a slight tone of self-congratulation, and British culture is seen as balanced and reasonable by contrast, since the stigma attached to menstruating women comes to be seen as relatively mild. This study concentrates on 'mainstream' white British culture.

Young people frequently see themselves as more tolerant, more easy-going than their elders. This study focuses on the views of younger men, those who might see themselves as developing the values of the future. How are men's attitudes formed? Are they changing for the better?

The most important issues for women themselves may be quite different. There can be pain, or changes of mood. How can a normal bodily function be painful? Does women's distress about how they are treated perhaps somehow create

1

the pain? Or is it the other way round, that women, upset because of the effects of their periods, have in fact provoked men's negative attitudes? Is the pain really physical, or might not a better attitude make it go away?

When women seek advice in dealing with menstrual problems, why do they so often feel that doctors do not give them the help they would like? How do doctors really see menstrual pain, and what has come to be called premenstrual tension? This book looks at medical textbooks as well as at ordinary men's ideas on menstrual problems. Does a scientific approach cut through traditional prejudices?

This is not a general 'book about menstruation': there is no attempt to 'cover' the variety of different understandings of menstruation which exist within this society. A very great range of different factors is involved in creating these understandings, and differences would be found between one school playground and another. Certainly massive differences exist between people of one cultural or religious tradition and another, of different age groups, of different social classes. To map these variations – differences and similarities – would be another project. I leave it to the reader to consider how her or his own experience relates to the particular male attitudes I describe. I am not trying to prove or disprove any specific theory – the work is exploratory, opening up new subjects to discussion rather than trying to say the last word on anything.

This book forms part of a political process, the process of women analysing their situation as women. In particular, women have been reclaiming their bodies as their own, redefining them outside of their principal meaning in patriarchy – as objects of men's gaze.

Women will determine for themselves how they can best understand their own experience of menstruation. I have tried here to provide some information worth taking into account. The spotlight is turned back, for once, onto the powerful, onto those who usually decide which questions will be asked and which will not.

2 Why Does Menstruation Matter?

Social attitudes towards menstruation are puzzling. Men's attitudes, in particular, are often puzzling to women. Trying to make sense of men's behaviour, women produce a number of explanations: 'they just don't understand'; 'it's because they can't have children – it reminds them that we can', 'it frightens them: it is blood, after all'; 'women use it to make men leave them alone'.

In this chapter I want to look at the arguments behind some of these ideas – and to explain how I hope that what I learnt from interviewing men can throw some light on these issues.

All theories related to social meanings of menstruation, however simple, are political by nature, in a gender-divided society. Because menstruation is experienced only by women, women and men of necessity understand it in different ways. This difference is vastly compounded and complicated by a social system which sets the category men in power over the category women, and which uses notions about 'nature' to justify this power.

Traditional theories about menstruation (and about women's bodies generally) are sexist in the sense that they take for granted women's inferiority to men, and they understand everything in that light – crucially, they deny and exclude women's own perspective. The problems some women have with menstruation, for instance, may be interpreted as a sign that women are simply badly designed (worse designed than men, that is); or that women are inherently sinful and being continually punished by a male god; or that evolution or some other abstract force intended women to be constantly breeding and that 'civilised' women's failure to do so naturally brings pain and suffering. Such sexist 'explanations' are banal and circular: they blend the social together with the biological into a smooth mixture of commonsensical ideas which ultimately explain nothing. I will not argue with them – rather I ask who benefits from these ideas?

3

The explanations which will be discussed in detail are
those which come in some way within the feminist project –
either they describe themselves as feminist or they have been
read as feminist.

WHY STUDY MENSTRUATION?

I chose menstruation as a focus through which to explore a
number of issues which concerned me within feminist
theory. The radical feminist impulse is to seek out that which
women have in common. More and more, though, when we
look at a subject in detail, we find new differences between
women emerging – differences previously hidden by ideologies which make some women's experiences more visible
than others, and which may also distort all women's experiences beyond recognition. For instance, in exploring issues
around women and our biology, many feminists have focused upon pregnancy and childbirth as the experiences
which define women as women. But while the ideology insists
that all women should become mothers, in the real world all
women do not, and even among those who do, the meaning
of motherhood varies a great deal – many do not regard it as
the core of their identity.

Neither is it the case that all women menstruate. Some
women never menstruate because they are born with unusual or incomplete reproductive organs. Others, affected
perhaps by environmental factors, disease, medical interven-
tions or malnutrition, menstruate rarely or irregularly, or
stop having periods early in life. Some women spend most of
their young adult lives either pregnant or breast-feeding.

But the largest group of non-menstruating women is made
up of women who have passed the menopause. A woman
who lives out her three-score years and ten will probably
menstruate for only half of that lifetime. Menstruation as
such is not positively valued. However, as long as the ability
to bear children is held to be the 'purpose' of womankind,
women who do not menstruate can be regarded by some as
not fully female. This view is obviously oppressive to older
women, but also indirectly to all women, for it is an essential
part of the thought process which justifies keeping women in

subordinate positions with the idea that this (compulsory) childbearing is 'naturally' limiting.

By choosing to study menstruation, then, I have been limited to examining the experience of some women for some years of their lives. However in so far as menstruation is understood by men as a marker of womanhood, men's attitudes towards it affect all women: they form part of their general definition of 'woman'.

Since menstruation is such a politically-charged area, various kinds of discourse around the subject have emerged over the last few years in and around the women's liberation movement. When I was first studying the subject, I came to feel quite bullied by people's assumptions about the approach I would be taking. I wrote in my research journal:

I am frequently offered research projects I could do by other sociologists. Invariably they see women as the core of the problem; usually they want to show changes taking place in the recent past. Very often the focus is on sexual practice – I have lost count of the number of people who have told me that many men and women do now have sex during the woman's periods.

The basic idea seems to be that I should be focusing on describing women's consciousness about menstruation, preferably showing systematic differences between groups of women with regard to this.

I want to start with a list of things I am *not* trying to say:

—I do not think that menstruation is necessarily important to women.

—I do not think that women should celebrate menstruation, unless it makes them happy.

—I do not think that women should even be interested in menstruation.

—I do not think that menstruation expresses our womanhood or our femininity or the dark side of our natures or any other 'cosmic truth'.

—I do not think that what we need is more sex education in schools.

—Nor do I think that what we need is more 'openness about these things'.

—I do not think that women's power resides in their reproductive organs, or in men's mystic fear of them. . . .

Men

One much-neglected issue is the relationship between individual men's behaviour and beliefs, and the social system of
patriarchy. In so much of the literature, men as men
disappear altogether – we have only 'society' and 'women'.
Menstrual 'taboos' are described as coming from the past,
from 'age-old' social attitudes and superstitious beliefs. 'Society' holds these ideas and no-one in particular is responsible
for this or benefits from it. It is often felt to be a little
mysterious that 'modern society' still holds such old-
fashioned beliefs.

This extract from the section on 'Society's attitude' in Judy
Lever's book on premenstrual tension is a classic example of
this kind of reasoning:

> Society, since way back when, has generally treated men-
> struation as something to be ashamed of and hidden away,
> in contrast to pregnancy (the other side of menstruation)
> which is a proud event to be announced and welcomed. In
> many early primitive societies, women were, and in some
> tribes, still are, banished from the main house and made to
> stay in a private hut during menstruation. They may not
> bathe, eat or touch their bodies, and have to remain in a
> crouched position the whole time. Above all, no men can
> come near them during this time, for fear of their lives.
> (Lever 1979)

This shows very well the process Mary Daly describes as
'deleting the agent' (Daly 1978).

Related to this kind of approach is the idea that men's
involvement in creating menstrual 'taboos' is unimportant,
and that women actually originated these practices. I will
examine the evidence used to support this idea later in this
chapter.

Another related set of ideas – that men more or less
spontaneously react to aspects of women's bodies in a negative way – draws on psychoanalytic thinking. Men's reaction
to menstruation is said to be unconscious, and social processes are said to derive finally from this 'deep' reaction. Men
are seen as out of control of their behaviour, irrational.

Shuttle and Redgrove's *The Wise Wound* belongs to this school.

Another close relation is the 'womb-envy' school of thought. Its feminist incarnation can be found in Adrienne Rich's *Of Woman Born*, but it originates with post-Freudian psychoanalytic writers like Karen Horney and Bruno Bettelheim. This group recognises that power is involved rather than simply reducing the question to one of sexuality, which is seen as non-political.

Women are said to have an important kind of 'natural' power in their ability to bear children. Men's devaluation of this ability is (re)interpreted as a reaction of awe and envy. Men are believed to have created a whole range of social institutions including the patriarchal family in order to assert and reinforce the weak connection of the male to his own offspring, and to bring reproductive power under male control. Often within these theories men are said to fear and therefore hate women and especially women's reproductive organs – this is how menstrual 'taboos' are explained.

There is a lot of evidence that men often use myths of male creation (such as the Christian one) to attempt to appropriate the power they see attached to reproduction (see Mary Daly 1978). But since very few men express any particular interest in childbearing, or much sense of lack of power in their own position as a sex, such theories when applied to individual men rest upon alleged unconscious motivations. Surely it is likely that a culture which values so highly men's abilities and men's creations, and which regards women as men's property, might give ample compensations for the inability to bear children from one's own body? The idea that men, even within such a culture, are likely to suffer great unconscious anxiety for this reason I find unconvincing.

It is not really possible for a sociological study to investigate claims about the unconscious. One need not resort to the unconscious for explanations of a behaviour, however, unless the behaviour in question makes no sense in more ordinary terms. Radical feminists say that men benefit from women's oppression, and that individual men often play an active part in creating that oppression. I would see relations around menstruation as part of this system of power rela-

tions between the sexes, and attitudes to menstruation as
explicable in that context.

In interviewing men I tried to probe especially questions of
how men themselves thought that they had acquired the
attitudes and beliefs they held. And in analysing my material,
I have looked at the sexual-political consequences of men's
ideas and behaviour. If my explanations seem inadequate,
perhaps we should turn to the unconscious – it is surely
illogical, though, to *begin* one's investigation with an assumption that such behaviours arise from the unconscious.

Methods

Research on attitudes towards menstruation is at an extremely undeveloped stage. The research I have done for this book
was aimed at generating ideas, exploring possibilities, not at
proving or disproving some sort of pre-established theory.
No claim is made that the men I interviewed are representative of other men, or that the texts used give a full picture of
medical views.

To gain a picture of the views of men from what might be
assumed to be a 'progressive', liberal section of the population, I interviewed 14 men aged between 21 and 40. All were
white and non-Jewish, 13 English and one Irish. One identified as homosexual; two were fathers. About half described
themselves as coming from working-class families, half middle-class; the majority now defined themselves as middle
class. I collected my sample largely by what is called the
snowball method, with one respondent encouraging other
men he knew to allow me to interview them.

I was concerned that by doing the interviewing and setting
the framework for the interviews, I might be inhibiting my
respondents, limiting them to what could be said to a
woman's face, if you like, so I also asked a 'men's group' to
tape a discussion about menstruation for me.

In looking at medical accounts, I confined myself to the
written word. Six textbooks were examined in detail, those
which the librarian of the Royal College of Obstetrics and
Gynaecology said were the most commonly used texts (see
Chapter 7 for more details). I cross-checked this with the

availability and level of use of textbooks in the local medical library. These texts could be held to represent what might be called the established belief of the profession, most having been through numerous editions, and all having been revised in recent years. Since such texts would presumably tend towards the conservative end of the spectrum, I also looked at more recently published articles in medical journals.

Feminist research?

I want to say something further here about my thinking in arriving at the unusual methods I have used. In trying to think about what methods to use in researching attitudes towards menstruation, I was influenced not only by the subject I had chosen, but also by debates around the question of whether a feminist methodology exists, and if so, what it might be.

Having set myself the task of describing the social meanings of a phenomenon like menstruation, I had to work out what could be used as evidence. Even the briefest consideration of the problem reveals that within even 'mainstream' British culture there is no single shared understanding of menstruation. The phenomenologist's view of the social world comes into its own – we can see that different people hold different ideas about it, see it as significant within different contexts, and that certain groups of people may share certain meanings that they attach to it. So whose definitions should we examine? What aspect of the social world could usefully be analysed?

What I tried to hold on to in finding a line of approach was my own curiosity. I was determined not to conceal my own specific perspectives behind the false style of objectivity which is so common in academic work. It seemed important to try to avoid what Mary Daly (1978:324) calls 'spooking with the passive voice', the use of a grammar which hides the agent, conceals responsibility. In the Appendix I discuss some of the difficulties this created for me – its strength as a way of thinking and writing has been that I could not stray far from working on what *I* wanted to find out into trying to fulfil others' expectations.

When I began my research I took it more or less for granted that I would interview women: I also found that there was considerable social pressure in the academic world to do this. I wondered whether the pressure I experienced was a manifestation of the dominance of survey research in sociology generally, for which my undergraduate education had not prepared me. But looking around me it was clear that surveys were far from popular in many fields of research within sociology, and indeed 'pure' theory appeared to be the norm in many areas. It was feminists, particularly, who were expected to avoid 'theory'. In my experience the assumption that a feminist researcher will interview women and the claim that there is a specifically feminist methodology to be discovered are interconnected.

I felt I was being pushed towards what I came to call the liberal feminist model of research. The best statement of this position at that time was Helen Roberts's collection *Doing Feminist Research*. I wrote in my research journal about my responses:

> Typically this form of research involves a woman setting out to interview some sample of other women, preferably women less privileged than herself, working class or Black women, but occasionally students or professional women, about some aspect of their lives. She does an unstructured or semi-structured interview, and tapes it, then writes it up, full of anxiety. The write-up may to some extent convey her own analysis of what is happening to 'her' women, but it must also categorise their responses. These will tend to be seen as different ways of 'coping' or of 'negotiating contradictions'. Women researchers often find that the women in their samples fail to analyse their situation in a feminist way, and are frustrated and disappointed by this.

I felt that such research, while essential, was seriously limited and the pressure to engage in it amounted to a kind of stereotyping of feminists, but also that it was based on politically dangerous assumptions. These stem from the underlying idea that 'we' do not know enough about how women feel, that the problem in whatever area we are dealing with is that women have not articulated their perspective. Women are then to be 'made visible' by being transformed into research findings. I felt that this was a misreading of the function of sociology: that informing the powerful about an oppressed group need not lead to any change on the part of the oppressor.

There is a worrying implication that 'ordinary' women do not express themselves adequately and need academics to translate for them. When I began to say that I was considering not interviewing women, one argument that was put to me was that 'you must let women speak for themselves', as if my refusal to *interview* my quota of women would prevent them from *speaking*.

I see the dominance of this anxiety as deriving from a common misunderstanding of the feminist practice of consciousness-raising. The original purpose of the process of consciousness-raising, where women speak about their own experiences to other women, was to discover what women have in common, in order to produce theory about women's oppression. Now this last stage seems to have been forgotten, and women speaking, whatever it is about and whatever they say, is seen as A Good Thing. Particularly it is supposed to be good for the women themselves. This is a liberal revision in that it focuses on the individual, rather than on ways of creating social change on a large scale. Originally if women found emotional release in consciousness-raising, it was a side effect: it was never the main aim (see Sarachild 1975). Much of the new 'feminist research' seemed to me to be about an attempt to simulate this revised version of consciousness-raising within the interview situation.

The interview itself was being given a priority over the whole research process which was problematic. Many writers emphasise the benefits to the interviewee herself as an important aspect of their research (Finch 1984; Oakley 1981). It is notable that in his textbook John Madge (1953) traces the origins of the sociological interview to the practice of counselling, psychotherapy; feminists seem to be returning it to its roots. Again the danger is that the problem is located within the individual. Such focus on the research process presents an idea that research can almost be justified by its spin-off benefits, without reference to how the results of the research may be used.

It seems to me that however 'reciprocal' an interview is

made, it remains an unequal situation if, when all is said and done, the research is the work of the interviewer and not of the interviewee. She has chosen to create the situation and will ultimately control what is used and what discarded from the words said to her. While of course interviews can be made into pleasant and where possible helpful social encounters for interviewees, I cannot see that they can be transformed into some kind of exemplary feminist practice.

Having my particular questions about menstruation in my mind, I was especially aware of the dangers of victim-blaming. So much of what is written about menstruation places the problem squarely in the minds of women. If many people in Western culture share one 'sociological' idea about periods, it is that women's bad attitudes are responsible for period pain. By interviewing women, especially if that was the only empirical work I did, I could do little to question such notions.

But I had other reasons for being less interested than I might have been in interviewing women. When I began my research I had been involved in the women's liberation movement for years, and had been present at discussions of menstruation in numerous groups of women – more than one consciousness-raising group, women's health classes, groups of friends. I had not found that my questions were answered in that process – indeed my questions in many ways arose from it. Contradictions may remain after women have engaged in introspection among themselves, and I could not see that sociological interviewing would be likely to generate better understandings than feminist consciousness-raising could. The best I could imagine doing would be to demonstrate systematic differences in experience or belief among women – a project I felt to be of questionable use. I felt, therefore, that I should use my particular status as a sociologist to attempt to discover things that women do not know.

I see myself as answerable to women, as do those women involved in the liberal model of research, but I would want to see the research process as a whole. The most important question for me is about how useful the research is to women as a group – can women learn from it? Whether or not individual women who are involved in the research benefit directly from their involvement, while of course an important ethical problem for the researcher, must be secondary to this consideration.

I must emphasise that I believe that research which reflects women's experiences back to women can be extremely useful: it is possible in this way to reveal aspects of women's condition which are not immediately apparent to the individual. A great deal of very useful work has resulted from this approach. But feminist research must go beyond the study *of* women to work out ways of studying *for* women if it is not to remain essentially a liberal rather than a radical, liberatory force.

The discussion around feminist research has been too broad for a full account of it to be relevant here (see, for example, Ehrlich 1978; Eichler 1980; Fildes 1983; McRobbie 1982; Roberts 1981; Stanley and Wise 1979, 1983). One problem with this debate was that it seemed at times to be as much about an attempt to define certain kinds of research as *not* feminist by nature of their methods, as about discovering what might be good approaches. Sometimes the claims made were clearly for certain kinds of theory within feminism, rather than for anything which could be said to typify feminism as such. Stanley and Wise (1983), for example, while maintaining that they do not want there to be a feminist 'line' on research, say in their introduction that 'Much of what we have written insists that feminism, for us, means accepting the essential validity of other people's experiences' (p. 8). They place 'experience' above 'theory' in importance, but fail to explore the extremely problematic nature of 'experience'.

My view is that, on the contrary, unless the term 'feminism' means nothing, feminist research can only be defined by its theory. To me, a minimal definition of feminism would be that it means a belief that women are oppressed and a commitment to end that oppression. Such a belief can only be called a kind of social theory. Within that, however, there is space for enormously varied theories about all the contingent questions raised by that first proposition. Thus different methods will follow from different theories within feminism. It would be wrong to attempt to close off the political debates within feminism by making some special claim for one, based on the methods of research it espouses.

Feminist research actually faces very much the same problems as all other research, particularly the central one of finding a way of discovering information which will genuinely shed light on the issue under scrutiny, rather than just describing the confusion in great detail. Therefore feminists cannot be expected to produce unique solutions to these problems, although a feminist perspective can form a basis for useful critiques of some traditional research practices. What does distinguish feminist research is that it asks feminist questions (Dickens *et al*, 1983).

Is menstrual etiquette natural?

A key question for anyone theorising about social meanings of menstruation is that of whether various social attitudes to menstruation are natural. This can be asked at several levels. Is menstrual blood inherently dirty? Is it perfectly natural for men to be repulsed by a physical function which they do not share with women? Does the social marking of menstruation follow automatically from the most obvious physical difference between men and women – that women can bear children and men cannot?

The same types of questions are, of course, asked about women's situation generally: basically, is it a natural fact, or is it due to social conditions, that women are constrained and controlled by male domination?

Those who accept the argument that such conditions are natural are referred to as 'biological determinist': believing that biology determines cultural, economic and social conditions, or as 'essentialist': believing that social conditions, such as etiquette surrounding menstruation, spring from the essence of the phenomenon, for instance that menstrual blood just *is* disgusting.

The great majority of theories about menstruation are deterministic in these ways. Durkheim thought that attitudes to menstruation derived from a 'primitive' fear of blood (1898); Mary O'Brien sees it as a 'negative moment' of reproduction (1981); Shuttle and Redgrove (1978) regard it as representing the active, non-reproductive, 'other dimension' of women's sexuality; Adrienne Rich describes it as a source of power, an act of transformation (1977); Paige and Paige (1981) say that menstruation betokens women's reproductive capacity.

While it is anti-feminists who are nearly always biological determinist, quite a lot of feminist theorists in fact share that approach to one degree or another. Certainly many feminists who have theorised about menstruation do, and it is these I will be addressing here. It seems to me to be crucial to avoid biological determinist arguments for the simplest reason – that they make change very difficult to hope for.

Most of the feminist work which has been done on menstruation comes from the psychoanalytic/matriarchalist and the essentialist radical feminist schools of thought (Weideger 1978; Culpepper 1979; Matriarchy Study Group undated (b); Delaney *et al*, 1976). Social practices around menstruation, being clearly about gender, and thus inexplicable to women generally, have been used as strong evidence that men the world over and throughout time are irrationally driven to oppress women, and/or that women universally seek separation from men at this time. It is this area of discourse about menstruation that I want to reconsider in detail. It is not an internally consistent set of ideas, so I will look separately at some of the propositions on which it is based. Chapter 5 on menstruation's relation to reproduction also addresses one of the assumptions often made by this school of thought.

I am concerned to contribute to the development of another kind of radical feminism – one with a social-constructionist basis. Radical feminism is characterised by its development of theories about the oppression of women which take that oppression to be unique and fundamental; that is, not deriving from some other social structure, such as economic class divisions. Women also suffer oppression because of class and race divisions, and from other causes, but these systems exist side-by-side: the one cannot explain or encompass the other. Radical feminists also see conflict as an inherent part of male-dominated society: women, like every oppressed people, resist their oppression, even where they do not do so in an open and organised fashion. I believe that radical feminism should, further, absolutely clearly reject the idea that sex conflict is a natural fact, and should

see it as a social phenomenon arising from power relationships.

In the rest of this chapter, I will look in detail at two of the
propositions which underlie much biological determinist
feminist thought – firstly, that menstrual 'taboos' are found
in all human societies and secondly (an argument which is
special to the matriarchalist school) that it was women who
originated menstrual 'taboos'.

IS MENSTRUAL ETIQUETTE UNIVERSAL?

One very common statement about social attitudes to menstruation is that 'menstrual taboos are universal' (for example, Weideger 1978). This idea is clearly tied to the idea that
relations between the sexes follow fundamentally the same
pattern in every human society. If change in gender relations
is to be held to be possible, this deterministic view must be
brought into question. It cannot be taken for granted that
people in vastly differing cultures somehow 'naturally' repro-
duce essentially the same gender relationships. Therefore I
wanted to investigate this statement further.

I approached this in two ways, neither of which has been
entirely satisfactory. Firstly I read a great deal of anthropology, seeking information about other cultures, and secondly I
attempted in my investigation of some men's attitudes in
British culture to look at the question of whether men within
one culture will react to menstruation in a consistent way.
One of my conclusions has been that 'taboo' is an inappropriate word for what takes place in relation to menstruation in
British secular culture, for it leads one to expect to encounter
supernatural beliefs which are in practice largely absent. I
propose to use instead the idea of an 'etiquette', since this
describes more exactly a set of social practices which express
and reinforce the distinctions between people of different
social statuses, without implying anything about supernatural belief. In this case the etiquette marks out the hierarchy
of power between men and women. This is more fully
discussed in Chapter 3.

Reading anthropology in search of answers to feminist
questions was a depressing experience. So much of the

evidence comes from such very questionable sources – male investigators whose main concerns were with quite other questions, and who were not sensitised to the sexual politics of who says what to whom.

Much of the material which related specifically to menstruation had been heavily influenced by psychoanalytic thought, and as a result paid little or no attention to what the people concerned believed themselves to be doing in their social practices (for example, Stephens 1961). Even writers who are attempting to challenge this tendency fail to free themselves from their own ethnocentric assumptions. Young and Bacdayan, in their essay 'Menstrual Taboos and Social Rigidity' (1965) do not consider the possibility that cultures exist where menstruation is not socially emphasised in any way. In their categorisation, those cultures with the least marked menstrual etiquette are described as those where 'concern for menstruation is informal' (p. 96). They suggest that this situation might involve couples practising informal avoidance during a woman's period or men being 'privately disgusted'. Perhaps Young and Bacdayan were limited by the sample of cultures they worked on (they give only pragmatic explanations, and no theoretical context, for their choices) – but if this were so, surely they should not generalise from such a sample?

But what evidence is there that not all cultures emphasise menstruation? I have discovered no ethnography describing a culture which does not do so. I have not even attempted the enormous quantity of reading involved in such a quest, for clearly the fact that an ethnographer had failed to mention menstrual restrictions would not be conclusive proof that none existed, especially when so many ethnographers are men. One would really have to involve oneself in another ethnographic study to check the evidence.

But some authoritative sources do encourage the belief that such cultures exist. Mary Douglas, in her essay on 'Couvade and Menstruation' (1975) writes 'I cannot think of any physical condition of which the ritual treatment is constant across the globe'. Even corpse pollution, she says, is not universal. Per Hage and Frank Hararay (1981), who have reviewed the literature on the New Guinea Highlands, write that 'Beliefs in menstrual pollution and more particularly in poisoning are not universal in Highland New Guinea'. The Etoro on the Papuan Plateau, for instance, hold no such beliefs (Kelly 1976). This is especially interesting since some cultures in that area have very intense pollution beliefs and practise strict menstrual segregation. Birke and Best (1980) cite another case: the Congo Pygmies, who are encouraged to 'sleep with the moon' in order to conceive, and who associate menstrual blood with life (Turnbull 1976).

Young and Bacdayan also, obliquely, acknowledge that they know of cultures where menstruation is not much emphasised, though they unfortunately give no details:

> Surely the most obvious interpretation of menstrual taboos is that they are institutional ways in which males in primitive society discriminate against females. While it is possible that women do not object to being so restricted, and very likely they become accustomed to the rules, it is probable that they submit to such customs only because the male-dominated system of social control leaves them no alternative. It is certainly a fact that, as Western standards have spread, menstrual taboos have been abandoned and not resumed.

This passage contains some extraordinary assumptions, among them that 'Western' society is not male dominated! These authors do not see any significance in the 'informal' ways in which their own culture marks menstruation – they seem to see that as normal or even natural. They seem to assume, also, that the impact of Western culture upon 'primitive' societies has tended to increase women's status in such cultures, something which cannot be so easily taken for granted (see, for example, Boserup 1970). This said, it would have been interesting to see an account of a particular case where the social treatment of menstruation has changed, and a close analysis of what the factors involved in such a change could be.

There is evidence, then, that 'menstrual taboos' may not be 'universal'. The fact remains, though, that a very great majority of known cultures do emphasise menstruation in some way. I would suggest that this may be because it is an obvious physical function for men in a patriarchal society to use as a marker of femaleness, to convey their view of a woman's place.

It is a physical event in women which has no necessary connection to men, but which is used to enforce upon women a sense of their being 'naturally' connected to men. The etiquette of menstruation emphasises to women that their ordinary existence can have effects upon men independently of their intentions. They are required to allow for this in their every action, to watch themselves carefully so as not to unwittingly transgress against the rules.

The one thing British girls at menarche are always told is that men must not know. In other cultures, for example among Australian Aborigines as described by Crawley (1902), women had to paint themselves red so that everyone would know and could avoid them. Women are held responsible for protecting men from being polluted by themselves. Carelessness in this can in some cultures get a woman killed. In the West, I have repeatedly seen young girls quoted as saying they would rather die than have the boys know (Whiting undated).

The female body is construed as inherently affecting men – this construction relates closely to the equally common cultural practice of enforcing heterosexuality upon women. Let us look from this point of view at the Arapesh ceremony of first menstruation: this account is simplified from Margaret Mead's description in *Male and Female* (1950:173–4).

The young girl is already married at menarche and living among her husband's family. She fasts for five or six days, staying in her menstrual hut, which her brothers have built for her. When she emerges, weak with hunger, she is prepared in various ways and then brought, supported by other women, to her husband. He has made a special bowl of soup for her, from which he feeds her. After the first few mouthfuls she is strong enough to feed herself.

So the girl becomes a woman in the same moment that her relationship to men is spelt out to her. She is isolated and weakened and then shown that her husband is essential to her survival. She learns her role, as Mead describes it elsewhere (p. 80); she is to be 'passive, dependent, cherished'.

I have tried, later, to look at how the practices of our own culture spell out to women messages about male superiority and about heterosexuality. Other writers have recognised the connection of traditional menstrual restrictions with heterosexuality – in this passage from her book *The MsTaken Body*

Jeanette Kupfermann defends them on this basis.

> Without religious values, menstruation can have no value
> either; at most a few *ad hoc* cults might be resurrected, but
> they, too, cannot be vested with any true meaning, as they
> will not be able truly to *relate the individual to the universe*.
> One such cult is described by Paula Weideger in *Female
> Cycles* where she rightly considers menstruation in the same
> context as the menopause and female sexuality generally,
> but still limits her view to a 'sexual' one rather than a
> cosmological one. It recounts a long letter from a travelling
> lesbian commune in which two women recounted the
> individual experiences and menstrual histories of the
> members and described the pattern of menstrual syn-
> chrony that evolved as they lived and travelled together.
> But the same feminist diatribe mars the otherwise valid
> suggestion that women attempt some kind of separatism
> when she suggests that lesbians can 'help heterosexual
> women to understand the extent to which fear of men's
> opinions and male power limits the search for self-
> knowledge'. Most women, however, do not live in com-
> munes of travelling lesbians, and their phenomenological
> stance is quite a different one. Most women would prob-
> ably prefer to know how they could experience their
> menstruation to help them relate to men and the world
> generally. (Kupfermann 1979:59; emphasis in original)

Clearly, different cultures have very different ranges of
expectations of what a woman should be. Forms of marriage
and family vary, as does the work women do, and the images
women and men have of womanly behaviour. Notions of
what is 'natural' are very variable, and attitudes to bodies
generally change enormously across different cultures. It is
not surprising then that among those cultures which do
emphasise menstruation, the form that this takes varies
greatly. I do not think it is useful to reduce this complexity to
general statements about 'taboos', for we can learn much
about how men's domination of women works in different
situations from a close study of such details.

Jessica Mayer (BMAS paper 1983) makes some very interesting points on this. She notes the problem that the
common focus of anthropologists upon pollution concepts

tends to bracket out consideration of gender distinctions. At the same time, though, she warns against 'reducing pollution to gender', for this closes off the way in which particular configurations of gender interact with other social variables. She discusses some specific examples of sexual pollution and points out how, among the Amora of New Guinea, such pollution rules only really applied between husband and wife. The people explicitly related the danger that men might be poisoned with menstrual blood to the fact that wives were held to be permanently angry with their husbands and husbands' brothers – they could also transmit illness by speaking angrily over their food. Mayer argues that since these beliefs pertain to a special relationship between men and women they should not be interpreted as a belief that menstruating women are inherently polluting.

It seems to me very important to distinguish between the various different social practices related to menstruation. As I. M. Lewis (1971) distinguishes sorcery (where a person, often a socially powerful person, is believed to be able to cause harm to another by conscious *effort*) from witchcraft (where a person, usually of low or marginal social status, is accused of being dangerous to others *in themselves*), we must always note the difference between a belief that someone can use a substance to cause harm and a belief that a category of people are polluting.

In the same way, it is important to make the distinction between rules of etiquette which are backed by supernatural sanctions, which can rightly be called 'taboos', and rules of etiquette which are not. Some cultures emphasise menstrual pollution to the extent that it could be called one of the central concerns of the cultures, at least *vis à vis* women, for example the people of Mount Hagen, New Guinea, described by Marilyn Strathern (1972). It makes no sense to conflate this sort of situation with *any* cultural marking of menstruation, however minor. The World Health Organisation's cross-cultural study *Patterns and Perceptions of Menstruation* (Snowden and Christian 1983), although it worked with large numbers and used methods of no very great sensitivity, found a very considerable variation in the beliefs and practices related to menstruation among the 14 socio-cultural groups it surveyed.

This is, of course, an under-researched field, but there is evidence to suggest that menstrual etiquette varies greatly from one culture to another, and that there may be cultures where menstruation is minimally culturally elaborated. The immense variety of cultural practices relating to menstruation suggests that it may be unhelpful to seek 'universal' explanations for such practices. The study of menstrual etiquette can teach us far more if we attend to the detail of each culture's ways, rather than reducing our picture of them to a single dimension, that which can be universalised.

In describing the views of men I interviewed, I have attempted to draw out a range of different sets of ideas which exist within British culture, and the ways in which these in practice affect people's behaviour. I hope it will be clear that what emerges cannot be adequately imagined as merely a mild, 'civilised' version of the practices of 'other cultures'.

DID WOMEN INVENT MENSTRUAL ETIQUETTE?

The idea that women originated taboos on contact with men during menstruation is one which has been put forward by a number of feminists in recent years: the Matriarchy Study Group, Elizabeth Gould Davis (1971) and Evelyn Reed (1975), among others.

One can easily see where such an idea comes from. The male dogma of this culture has it that men want to have sex with women at all times, in all circumstances: this stands in contradiction to the sexual 'taboo' of menstruation. Also men accuse women of using menstruation as an excuse to avoid unwanted sex – and some women are undoubtedly aware of having done exactly this. It is not immediately apparent how the sex 'taboo' serves the interests of men. In Chapter 6 I will look at these issues again in relation to what men actually told me, but now I want to look at the arguments presented for this explanation.

This line of argument goes hand in hand with a particular idea of human history – that all world societies have 'evolved' in essentially one direction: from primitive matriarchy to patriarchy. Matriarchalist writers use anthropological and archaeological evidence to assert the existence of widespread prehistorical matriarchal civilisation. This prehistory is taken to explain men's present-day treatment of women: men hate women because they were formerly subjugated by them. They retaliate against their 'former master' (Gould Davis 1971:148). There has been a good deal of debate about the adequacy of the evidence that such societies existed – a debate I will not go into here. It is enough to say that the case is far from proven.

What I want to look at is the evidence and the logic used in relation to the particular case of menstrual taboos. All these matriarchalist writers refer for their evidence on this issue to a very few sources, the most important of which are Robert Briffault's *The Mothers* (1927) and Ernest Crawley's *The Mystic Rose* (1902).

Both these books use for evidence anthropology and travellers' reports from the nineteenth century and sometimes earlier, but their conclusions seem to me to have little to do with the information they present. They have more to do with their notion of what 'Woman' is or should be. Briffault, for instance, gives page upon page of accounts of menstrual and puerperal taboos and menarche ceremonies from a wide variety of societies, not all of them by any means primitive even in the sense of using only simple technology. Here are some examples from the book of the kind of practices, relating to menarche and to menstruation generally, which he cites: specific examples are never given when later writers refer to these pages. The detail seems to me to produce a quite different impression from the usual generalisations.

> Among the Eskimo ... 'the women must live secluded for so many days, and it would be a great offence for her to enter any other hut during the time' (F. C. Hall, *Arctic Researches*). They are subject to special dietary regulations and ... they may have to go a week without eating, although the family may be living in the midst of abundance. (Briffault 1927:366)

> On the island of Kadiak, off the coast of Alaska, women ... had to retire to little huts, or hovels, built of reeds and

grass, which were about 4 feet long, 2.5 feet wide, and less
than 3 feet high ... their food was reached out to them at
the end of a stick. ... Among the Tlinkit, when a girl first
menstruated, she was immediately shut up in an isolated
hut. ... She was not permitted to lie down during the
whole period of her seclusion, but had to sleep propped up
with logs. (p. 367)

Briffault quotes G. H. Loskiel's *History of the Mission of the
United Brethren among the Indians of North America*:

When a Delaware girl is out of order for the first time, she
must withdraw to a hut at some distance from the village.
Her head is wrapped up for twelve days so that she can see
nobody, and she must submit to purgings, vomits and
fastings, and abstain from all labour. (Briffault 1927:369–
70)

Among the Guayquiry of the Orinoco, menstruous women
were secluded and a girl before marriage had to fast for
forty days. A Guayquiry chief is quoted as explaining to a
Father Gumilla that 'in order that women's bodies should
not contain this poison, we should make them fast, ... for
forty days. Thus they are thoroughly dried up, and are no
longer dangerous, or at least not so much as they formerly
were'. (p. 371)

Among many Brazilian tribes a girl at her first menstruation is suspended in a hammock under the roof of the hut,
and subject to the most severe fumigation as well as being
starved. Thus among the Guaranis the girls were sewn up
in their hammock in the same manner as those tribes sew
up corpses, only the smallest opening being left to allow
them to breathe; they were suspended over the fire in that
condition for several days. ... It not infrequently happens
that the unfortunate girls die under the severity of the
process of disinfection to which they are subjected. (p. 371)

Among the Ticunas the girls are shut up, when they
menstruate, in a dark hut, all their hair is plucked out, and
they are subjected by the women to a severe flagellation.
(p. 372)

Not long since there were in Parsi communities public menstrual houses where women resorted at their periods. The women had to remain entirely silent, and their food was handed to them with every precaution from a distance. . . . Among the Hindus, . . . it is laid down in the *Institutes of Vishnu* that if a women in her courses should touch an Aryan, she shall be lashed with a whip. (p. 376)

In Ceram a special hut is built for women . . . but on no account are they to eat any fish from the river. Not many years ago a young woman was solemnly tried on the charge of having eaten a fish while she was unclean; she was condemned and executed in the presence of the people, by being thrown from a rock into the river. . . . (p. 380)

Crawley tells many more similar stories, among them of an 'Australian [aborigine], finding that his wife had lain on his blanket during menstruation, [who] killed her, and died of terror in a fortnight' (p. 76).

Now I make no judgement on the accuracy of these reports – I give them here to show the kind of evidence these writers use to support their argument. It seems to me perfectly plain that these 'customs' are not ones which women would be likely to encourage. Considerable violence against women is involved in these practices. There are cultures (our own included) where powerful people, usually men, do submit to painful rituals as part of their initiation into a privileged group. The indications from the manner of telling of these customs are, however, that the concern is for the safety of other people, and not for the woman in question. The way in which punishments are reported for transgressing the rules of these customs implies that compulsion is involved, that women tend to rebel against them rather than regarding them as a privilege. We should bear in mind, also, that these stories were largely reported to men by men, so we do not have access to what the women might have told us.

But none of this is clear to Briffault. He believes that all these practices derived from the taboo on sexual intercourse during menstruation and that *that* derives from the female's natural instinct to refuse sex to the male. Female mammals, he says, refuse the male at all times except during oestrus ('heat'). Therefore, although men are always ready for sex, it is biologically necessary that women should refuse men at some time. Ernest Crawley, on a slightly different tack, puts it all down to women's 'subconscious physical fear of men'. So for them all this follows from women being designed to dislike sex. And this has been repeated and repeated.

What we see is the image of turn-of-the-century heterosexuality projected onto pre-history (or rather onto these 'primitive' cultures presented as the prehistory of 'civilisation'). Women do not *naturally* enjoy sex and they will use any trick they can think of to get out of it.

Our attention is distracted from the question of why it is during menstruation that sex was to be avoided – why women's fear of men or dislike of sex should overcome them at these moments particularly. We are also not encouraged to think about the systematic violence against women which these taboo practices apparently involved.

Crawley (1902) is explicit about the purpose of his project: he looks at the ways of people he thinks primitive in order to discover the 'past' of his own society. He refers throughout to the 'lower races', 'the savage mind', and sees them as child-like, as more subject to domination by instinct or the unconscious than 'those more favoured by descent'. The basic method that these writers use, of generalising across 'other' cultures about which they knew very little, is plainly racist.

The modern matriarchalist writers use very much the same line of argument. It is taken for granted that it is in women's interests to avoid sex. For example, Gould Davis (1971) suggests that taboos on women's blood were imposed in 'the gynocratic age' to protect menstruating girls and women from 'the brutal rages of their male relatives'. She rejects the idea that such taboos exist to protect men, for 'certainly intercourse during menstruation or pregnancy is fraught with more danger to the female than the male'. She compares the magical beliefs attached to rules against sex during periods to tales of hobgoblins told by nurses to instil fear into the children in their charge (p. 92).

But why were women in a matriarchy living in fear of men's violent tempers? Why did they have to invent stories to protect themselves? And in what way is sexual intercourse dangerous to women at such times? One can see that violent sex of the classic patriarchal kind is in one way more dangerous to women during pregnancy than at other times, for it can induce miscarriage, but why should it be any worse during menstruation? There is a failure of imagination here, for Gould Davis sees men and heterosexuality as basically having the same character in matriarchal cultures as in patriarchal. This is particularly odd since elsewhere Gould Davis would have it that women in such time enjoyed penetrative heterosexual intercourse to the extent that they could have influenced evolution by selecting for men with larger penises (pp. 95–6, 37)

Beyond the specific area of sexuality, I see this piece of mythology about 'primitive' society as reflecting the interest of some modern US and European women now in the idea of periodic withdrawals from 'society' (that is, men). Women who dislike or feel ambivalent about men are attracted to the idea that there is some 'natural' urge in *all* women to separate themselves from men. This they see expressed in the practice of menstrual segregation, menstrual huts.

Again, though, the popular image of such segregation bears little relationship to reported reality. Menstrual huts as described in the literature (Briffault, Crawley, Mead) are generally clearly uncomfortable and unpleasant to be in. They enact the 'special' oppressed status of women – either they are individual huts, isolated on the margins of the settlement, or they are placed centrally in the village so that the men can be certain that the women are staying in 'their place'.

Women of religious and cultural groups which practise menstrual rituals, such as Muslims and Orthodox Jews, are sometimes reported to say that they enjoy the process of segregation and purification. They do not, they say, 'feel oppressed'. Jeannette Kupfermann in *The MsTaken Body* argues that such women are better off than those of us living outside such faith. But what is quite clear is that the satisfaction these women refer to is that of feeling integrated into their community, their religion, of marking their commitment to their particular forms of marriage. That they should express this militantly as demonstrating the benefits for women of their way of life is entirely understandable given that all these groups are despised by the racist dominant culture.

Separation from men, when it is defined and enforced by men and when it forms part of the enactment of the inferiority of women, is an entirely different matter from autonomy, self-determination, for women. Being free to be alone or with other women when you want to be is not the same as being put aside at a particular time because you belong to the group 'women'.

It is necessary to stretch one's imagination to see beyond the confines of a discussion which compares one set of patriarchal restrictions upon women with another and tries to weigh up the costs and benefits of each system. There is no image to turn to of women unrestrained by patriarchy, but one must beware of therefore mythologising other women's experiences without fully understanding their circumstances.

A SOCIAL-CONSTRUCTIONIST RADICAL FEMINISM

As I have said, this book is in part an exercise in developing a social-constructionist radical feminism. I have been concerned therefore to look at the social treatment of menstruation as an aspect of the playing out of the social power struggle between women and men.

I have rejected the idea that one can discover a universal 'truth' about biology beneath social distortions, seeking instead to describe and as far as possible to make sense of the social meanings themselves and how competing social definitions interact. What follows is an attempt to summarise the way I have come to see men's definitions of menstruation in this society.

Men maintain their social power over women in part through an ideology which defines women as inferior to men, and as naturally fitting into the place men have designed for them. This includes universal heterosexuality and in many cultures universal motherhood. The sex hierarchy is also expressed and reinforced by an elaborate etiquette which regulates relations between the sexes, one part of which governs how menstruation should be dealt with and

spoken of. In our culture, menstruation is not especially
emphasised, but male definitions nevertheless prevent
women from generating positive self/woman-centred understandings of it for themselves.

Patriarchal ideology is produced and sustained in a variety
of ways. Male groups in this society produce a sexist culture
which contains reference to menstruation – jokes which men
see as 'sick', which centre upon sex during menstruation,
often linking it with violence (see Chapter 4). They accuse
women of 'using' periods to 'get out of things' – defining this
as an illegitimate use of power on women's part.

Medical men, especially gynaecologists, produce another
important kind of ideology about women. They emphasise
women's reproductive role as the only hope of health for
women. Menstrual disorders are seen as the result of refusal
to conform to the female role. Medical men institutionalise
men's failure to empathise with female suffering and justify
it with the notion that inconvenient women's problems are
'psychosomatic' – that is, imaginary. Doctors frequently
ascribe a woman's problems to her mother's influence, suggesting that mothers inculcate 'unhealthy' attitudes into their
daughters. They seek to persuade women to place their trust
in male authority, not in female support. Some female
experiences can be distorted to fit men's ideas about women's
inferiority – for example, women's experiences of physical
and mental changes during the menstrual cycle have been
used, named 'premenstrual tension', to put women down as
unreliable and out of control of their behaviour (see Chapters 7, 8 and 9).

Individual men are able then to use the various elements
within the ideology to manipulate individual relationships
with women to their own advantage. Present-day British
male culture on menstruation and sexuality gives men the
choice as to whether or not to engage in sexual intercourse
during menstruation – women are not so free to make this
choice since they must fear both on the one hand male
disgust and on the other the consequences of refusal to be
available.

The etiquette of menstruation decrees that women may
not make men aware of the existence of menstruation either
in general or in the particular. There is, however, no

sanction against men referring to it. For example women
very rarely mention menstruation in the workplace even to
excuse themselves because of menstrual pain. But men often
explain women's behaviour when they disapprove of it as the
result of 'the time of the month'.

Women on the whole do not draw attention to their own
periods in public, out of a sense of shame – behind which
subjective experience lies the fact that women who do so are
ridiculed, harassed or avoided by men. Women in this
country who have attempted to publicly challenge the discri-
minatory taxation of sanitary wear have been alternately
mocked and ignored, effectively kept out of the public
sphere. Men find reference to sanitary wear highly offensive.
One consequence of this etiquette is that in dealing with their
periods, women are obliged to be constantly aware of men.

Knowledge of a woman's menstruation becomes, for some,
something specially reserved for the heterosexual relationship: it must be kept carefully hidden from all other men
including one's father and one's sons. Thus the experience of
menstruation is reconstructed in such a way as to emphasise
an image of women's lives as circumscribed by men's gaze –
even while men themselves may be very little concerned with
the matter.

In setting out the sexist ways in which menstruation is
defined by men, I want to make it clear that I do not imagine
there to be some simple alternative, a spontaneous, 'positive',
female view of menstruation. Women's experiences of
periods vary greatly, and are of course socially moulded.
There is no need, though, for us to romanticise our physical
characteristics in order to see the possibility that we need not
allow them to be used against us.

Just as men are not spontaneously, biologically, driven into
certain attitudes towards women's bodies, so for women
themselves there is no single physical reality. In discussing
menstrual problems some of the consequences of women's
diverse experiences will be explored.

Written out so briefly, my vision of modern British culture's treatment of menstruation looks almost programmatic,
as if everything was very simple and clear – in fact, as will
emerge, I see the social meanings of menstruation in this
culture as a thoroughly messy area of discourse. If one

refuses biologistic explanations, it is also impossible to find simple theories to account for social phenomena. Complex though they will be, however, social-constructionist feminist understandings can help us to understand our experiences. There are many different sets of ideas which bear upon menstruation – on pain, on sex, on dirt, as well as on gender – and individuals (women and men) generally hold a number of inconsistent, overlapping notions about it. I have tried to make sense of some strands within this tangle of ideas, and particularly of the sexual politics which are attached to them.

3 Pollution, Taboo and Etiquette

This chapter draws some basic outlines of the way in which menstruation is dealt with in this society. When and where do women and men speak about menstruation? Who may raise the topic? More to the point, who may not? I will discuss the extent to which our attitudes can be seen as pollution beliefs, and will put forward the notion of an etiquette of menstruation.

This means looking at how women are required to hide any evidence of menstruation, and the difficulties which this creates. From a man's point of view different rules seem to apply in the private than in public sphere, and yet for women, concealment is expected within the family, often in the most 'intimate' settings. And what are the consequences of this etiquette: why is it at all important?

POLLUTION: DIRT AND POISON

Much of what has been written about menstruation in our society has placed beliefs about it in the context of pollution beliefs generally, those interactions where contact is associated with dirt and danger. To what extent could the men in my sample be said to see menstrual blood as polluting?

I would accept Mary Douglas's (1966) view that pollution beliefs should be seen as a continuum covering both danger beliefs relating to religious thinking and the ideas about dirt which we usually take for granted. Dirt is indeed 'matter out of place' and the treatment of menstrual blood as dirty represents a judgement on the 'place' of menstruating women. 'The prohibitions trace the cosmic outlines and the ideal social order' (p. 72), and patriarchal cultures very frequently regard menstruation as in some way anomalous.

In my interviews I asked a question about how the men saw menstrual blood – whether they thought of it as like other blood, blood from a wound. The most classic pollution-belief

I heard stated to me was in the following speech:

> I still think of it being sort of dirty or whatever . . . more
> like afterbirth or something like that . . . not something I'd
> like to be touching . . . whereas ordinary blood, I wouldn't
> bother at all. (*D*)

This association with 'afterbirth' is interesting: did he mean
the placenta, or the lochia, the bleeding which follows
childbirth (tabooed in many cultures)? Had he had any
contact with afterbirth? How had he come to see it as dirty?
Unfortunately I could not follow up this statement fully.

Other men made a variety of other connections. A number
of them did see it as like other blood. One said he had seen it
more as associated with 'sexual secretions' (*A*). A number of
them, replying to this question, referred to the lining of the
womb or the uterine wall. One remembered being alarmed
by this description, given in a Biology lesson at school: 'I used
to imagine all sorts of horrible things coming out' (*K*). It is
interesting how the feeling of horror can be attached to the
image of the lining of the womb, just as it can to menstrual
blood as such.

Some men saw menstruation as a kind of cleansing,
excretion process:

> *M*: I think, in all honesty, I would say it has a measure,
> something of a measure of impurity about it, which an
> ordinary cut, it doesn't seem, because it has the connota-
> tion of discharge.
> *SL*: Discharge, like vaginal discharge?
> *M*: Yeah, I think there is that about it, that sort of element.
> *SL*: Whereas ordinary blood wouldn't worry you?
> *M*: I don't think – if you use the term 'worry', I don't think
> menstrual blood worries me, if you see what I mean. I just
> sort of feel there is that element in it, in terms of the body
> functions [unclear] discharge [. . .] presumably therefore
> contains elements which the body is therefore rejecting, I
> suppose.

> *H*: No I don't [think it's like other blood] . . . it doesn't
> bother me so much but I think there are certain impurities
> which are . . . it's almost used as an excretory mechanism to
> get rid of certain impurities from within the body and I

believe that some women have heavier periods because
they're trying to get rid of more impurities.
SL: Oh.
H: . . . mainly because people I know who're on what I call
a pure diet, a balanced diet tend to have very little
menstrual bleeding.

He continued at length on this theme – 'the lining of the
uterus, the unfertilised eggs, are discarded because they're
not needed, and in a way they are foreign bodies, they are
impurities'. This man was presenting these ideas as if they
were scientific – he thought that chemical analysis might
reveal these impurities. As we shall see later in this chapter,
some scientists have invested considerable energy in giving
such beliefs scientific validity. It is fascinating how the
concern with purity of food and so on connects to the notion
that a pure/purified woman would hardly menstruate.

The sense that menstruation is dirty is also present in what
the men said about the smell of menstrual blood, and about
their feelings about sanitary wear. One man who seemed to
feel the blood was somewhat 'unclean', but also that it was
alarming by association with blood from a wound, said 'I still
flinch sometimes when I see STs' (*I*).

It can be quite difficult to interpret men's reactions – to
know how to decide what causes which response. Does the
following account demonstrate the presence of pollution
belief? Innate fear? Or just a hangover and adolescent
nerves?

The first woman that I had a really good sexual relationship with. . . . [. . .] I'd been drunk, I think, the night
before, and I was feeling sort of pretty vulnerable, pretty
edgy, sort of on the edge of nauseousness, and there was a
lot of blood in the bed. And I didn't even associate it with
her menstruating, I just remembered making love the
night before, and sort of drinking and nauseousness, and I
just puked all over the bed. . . . And she was really freaked
out, and I was really freaked out. . . . And um, yeah, it was
horrible, I can still remember the exact colour of the
dressing gown, actually seeing the blood, the pool of blood
and then blood all over her legs, and it was a really violent
sort of image, it wasn't just like the gentle image which I

now associate with menstruation. It was really violent, almost like a sort of shock horror murder stuff. [. . .]

In fact I didn't realise until a couple of years afterwards how much she could have been freaked out by what I did. (*E*)

I have not attempted to describe fully here the evidence that pollution beliefs of various kinds are current within out culture. This has been well-discussed by other writers (Shuttle and Redgrove 1978; Weideger 1978). Advertising for sanitary wear provides a rich source of data here, a kind of play-back of current attitudes (Whisnant, Brett and Zegans 1975; Slavin 1981; Treneman 1988), as it tries to key in to women's assumed anxieties about 'safety' and 'hygiene'.

There is one aspect which has not been much discussed, however (though see Birke and Best 1980), and that is the interaction of pollution beliefs and scientific endeavour: the fact that earlier this century scientists appear to have devoted a good deal of energy to the task of demonstrating the existence of a 'menstrual toxin'. As the most recent positive reference to this work that I have discovered, a letter to the *Lancet* in 1974, explains, the idea is that 'there appears to be a sound pharmacological basis for the ancient beliefs in the toxicity of catamenial (menstrual) loss' (Davis 1974).

A Dr Bela Schick is credited with, in 1920,

> reviving the interest of the medical world in one of these superstitions, namely, the wilting of flowers handled by menstruating women, and for carrying out some tests on flowers they touched, the results of which suggested that there was even more contamination in such contact than superstition indicated. (Macht 1943)

David I. Macht seems to have involved himself in researching this question for over 20 years, and his 1943 article cites 147 references to data which he claims support his primary finding, that 'Experimental data demonstrate in the blood and secretions of menstruating women the presence of a toxic substance or menotoxin, which is poisonous for plants and animals'. One section of the article is concerned with 'Absorption of Poisons through the Male Genitalia'; his investigations into this subject led him to conduct some nasty animal experiments.

M. F. Ashley-Montagu also surveyed the literature, and after mentioning various beliefs about menstruation, writes that:

Such conditions form a good foundation for believing almost anything of the menstruous woman, and would certainly lend some support to the suggestion that at such times she is capable of exerting a noxious influence upon the objects with which she comes into physical contact. (1940:213)

It is not clear how widely spread the influence of these ideas has been. I was relieved to find, when I traced one of the sources Ashley-Montagu cites with admiration, a survey article by G. W. Bartelmez (1937) in which she or he in fact states that 'There is little or no evidence that the uterus discharges a toxin' (p. 57). The complete history of scientific beliefs on this subject remains to be written.

Pollution beliefs can be read as statements about power relations in society. They define, according to the dominant ideology, what is 'matter out of place' and this in turn makes it clear who has control of such social definitions. Thus the idea that people with certain characteristics are dirty is very often found as part of the attitudes of a dominant group towards a less powerful one. It is a persistent feature of racism and anti-semitism as well as of misogyny. In relation to class, too, the upper classes have habitually made a distinction between the 'respectable' poor and 'the great unwashed'. Dirt represents lack of self-control, and those whom the powerful wish to control are expected to be eager to demonstrate their compliance. It is sometimes possible to observe the anxiety created in oppressed people by these beliefs, in their attempts to disprove others' beliefs about them.

These bizarre 'scientific' attempts to locate the poisonous element in menstrual blood, to prove men's beliefs about it to be rationally-based after all, capable of surviving the development of a rational-scientific culture in place of a more traditional one, give evidence that pollution beliefs about menstruation are present in British culture, as do some statements from my interviewees. But how important are they? The fear or religious awe described by anthropologists, where men truly fear damage to themselves from contact with menstrual blood, seems rare in this culture.

I tried to find out from the men I interviewed what conversations they had had with women about menstruation: I wanted to hear their side of the secrecy I knew about from the female point of view.

CONVERSATION ABOUT MENSTRUATION

When I began interviewing men, I was particularly interested to learn when men are likely to hear about or observe the existence of menstruation. Do women speak to them about it? In what contexts might the subject enter their lives?

In each interview I took the man over his life history, asking if he had ever been aware of his mother's periods. Two men were quite startled by this suggestion, and clearly had never thought of their mothers as having periods at all until that moment.

Most of the men were aware that women spoke more about these matters among themselves than they spoke to men. Within families, several men mentioned secrecy between their sisters and their mothers (Group; G):

> I think it was very much my mother looked after that side of it, she took them under her wing, and I mean obviously I don't know how they felt about it, but it was obviously a conspiracy of silence, if you know what I mean, it was totally . . . it was unmentioned, it was deliberately unmentioned at any time. (*J*)

One man recounted having asked questions of women friends, and their having avoided the subject. Others made more general statements about how women do not tend to bring up menstruation:

> No I don't remember any women apart from someone that I was maybe in a relationship with, not just someone I was working with, coming up and saying. . . . I mean, at times I've suspected that that's why they've gone home, or not feeling very well or whatever, but I don't remember

anyone ever saying that. It's not something that people openly come out and say, is it? (*D*)

A few men also said that they themselves would not initiate a conversation about menstruation with a woman – with the implication that it would be in her interests as much as in theirs that they would not do so:

> for instance in conversation, I've got lots of friends who are quite open about sexual matters, sexual politics, but still I don't, wouldn't talk to women about it. I certainly wouldn't initiate a conversation about it, I'm sure. [laughs quietly] (*I*)

> depending on the circumstances ... would need a bit of warming up to discuss that topic, it wasn't the kind of, walk in 'how's your period?' kind of discussion [laughs]. No, I mean it just seems ludicrous to.... And presumably would be quite rightly resented. But the other side is, I wouldn't initiate a discussion ... (*M*)

This is obviously a complex area, and people may be more or less conscious of their motivations and actions. These men are on the whole presenting themselves as willing to talk about, or even interested in, menstruation. One man, however, reflected that in the past he remembered preventing a woman from telling him about it:

> One woman I've known personally has found it very painful, actually said, this is painful for me. Either other women have not said it, or it's not been painful for them, and I suppose certainly the first couple of relationships I've had, er, I left it very much to them to get on with it ... it was something where I was conscious of the woman saying 'I've started today' or whatever. I would simply go 'Oh, sorry' you know, like, 'get on with it, then' ... almost 'tell me when it's over'. That certainly was the first response I remember having to ... still very much a private affair. You know 'sorry it's happening to you, but you *know* it's going to happen to you, and nothing you can do about it, so get on with it'. I was conscious of that. (Group)

It seemed important to compare what the men told me with some information on the 'woman's point of view'. Little research has been done in Britain. The best study I could locate to use for comparison was conducted by Esther Merves in 1983 in Ohio, USA. She interviewed 60 women in detail, and asked them, among other things, to whom they might mention menstruation. They told her that they were likely to tell their husbands or sexual partners and friends when they were menstruating. Some might also tell their mother or their daughter.

Four contexts in which menstruation might be discussed were mentioned by many women: communicating cramps or discomfort; as an explanation or excuse for a mood or behaviour; if relevant to sexual behaviour; and in reference to purchasing menstrual products. Married women, in addition, mentioned pregnancy, in the contexts both of wanting to conceive and of not wanting to. Merves writes that 'menstruation is not shared as an event in and of itself, but rather as an explanation for discomfort or negative feelings'.

I was very struck by this finding of Merves's, obvious though it may seem. The importance of men's attitudes on each of these subjects becomes clear when one realises that these are the most common reasons for female-male interactions around menstruation.

Esther Merves asked another very good question: 'Who would you not want to discuss it with?' Only eight women said no-one: 86.7% mentioned someone. Among younger women a frequent response was 'my father'. Other answers included: 'all males', 'adolescent boys', 'my boss', 'my mother', 'authority figure male', 'my son', 'parents'. The most frequent response was 'authority figure, strange men or older men' – 31.7%. Others said they would not want to discuss it with 'someone who thought it was vulgar, dirty or disgusting' – generally women did not want to confront those males whom they expected to have the most negative attitudes.

In my own interviews, many men emphasised how little they had thought about menstruation in the past:

> Once I got your letter I thought about it more than I'd ever thought about it before, which is a reflection of the fact that I'd never thought about it. (*J*)

Several men associated concern with menstruation with starting to have sexual relationships with women:

I don't think I really thought about periods until I started having sex. (*G*)

I don't think that. . . . I mean my major impression of what men think about menstruation is that they don't. They may use it to get at individual women, they may use it in their personal relationships . . . but I think they only ever think about it when confronted with it. . . . (*A*)

I think I thought of it in terms of, as a bloody nuisance, sexually, so it wasn't that it had any sort of, um, sexual significance, it was that it was obviously tied up with sexuality because it happened to women, because it happened to the women I was sexually involved with. (*A*)

. . . with men, other boys, finding out that way, gradually [. . .] but it was subsequently in terms of more, closer, closer and sexual relationships with women that I became – I began to understand menstruation in quite a different sense. That's an impression. But I mean the whole issue of menstruation didn't really have an impact on my existence, as you can see, from that kind of pattern: all boys' school, most friends boys, family . . . no immediate sisters. . . . (*M*)

How are we to interpret these accounts? An association with sexuality is certainly a theme which comes out in many men's accounts. But a sexual involvement can be the first close relationship of any description that a man has with a woman, so how important is the sexual element in fact? There is also the problem that in patriarchal thinking men tend to see women and sexuality as very much bound up together, so how could anything so clearly related to women not come within the sphere of sexuality from the male point of view? I will discuss more specific questions related to sexuality in Chapter 6. Catharine MacKinnon (1982) has argued that gender and sexuality are inextricably bound up together, and that the attempt to make an analytical distinction between them is misguided. This issue certainly looks like a case in point.

Women's attention to menstruation is compelled in a way in which men's is not – men's consciousness may consist of very different areas of concern depending upon their experiences.

So how did the men feel about being interviewed by me? None of them said they were embarrassed, or seemed embarrassed, at the time, although quite a few had expected to be:

I'm surprised at how comfortable I was. (*C*)

No problem, really ... no, I don't have any inhibitions about it. (*N*)

Many had found the interview 'interesting' and several said that they thought the issue important:

Actually I thought, oh, someone's doing research into menstruation, I thought, oh what a strange subject to do research into, but then I had to think about my reaction to that, why I felt that. Why is it such a taboo subject? And I was very nervous, very wary about being interviewed. ... I'm not sure why, I think it is because it is a very taboo subject. I mean something like sex, there's always been some sort of impetus for men to learn about it or find out about it. But menstruation has always been kept very much under covers, if you know what I mean. ... And then I realised that what is interesting is not the fact that you're doing research into menstruation, but the fact that it's very rarely done, that nobody does any research into it. (*J*)

This cheerful attitude to the interviews in retrospect, however, contrasts strongly with these same men's very first reactions to the idea of being interviewed. Many of the men I interviewed came into contact with the study through a list being circulated at an evening class they were attending on sexual politics. The first time it went round, none of them put their names to it, and it was only on seeing it again, at a later meeting, that some members of the group agreed to be interviewed. The men's group which taped the discussion for me, similarly, decided against doing so the first time they discussed it, and only later changed their minds. One of the men I interviewed individually mentioned that he was attending another men's group, and that they might discuss the issue. I said I would be interested if they would tape their discussion for me. He replied, laughing:

Well, it'd be a very polite discussion. They're watching
what they're saying all the time.

What produces embarrassment is very specific – not just what
topic is raised, but who raises it, how they speak about it,
what frame of reference the interaction is seen within. For
instance one man placed the interview in a 'scientific' frame
of reference: 'I thought I'd be embarrassed when I came
round to it . . . but, what with doing a lot of science anyway,
you can talk about rats and all that . . . scientific and all
that . . .' (*L*). It is also well understood by all the respondents
that social propriety in relation to menstruation is at present
in a state of crisis and change.

THE ETIQUETTE OF MENSTRUATION

The crucial idea in much of what has been written on the
sociology of menstruation is that of the 'menstrual taboo'.
This notion, borrowed from anthropology, has been used to
describe a very wide range of social practices. Very often it is
introduced by a passage beginning with a description of an
example of some very intense taboo practice in some 'other'
culture, followed by an assertion that such 'primitive' or
'old-fashioned' ideas still exist even in our society.

As I learnt more about the contradictions and subtleties of
the ways in which menstruation is dealt with socially, I
became increasingly uneasy with this formulation, this way of
approaching the subject. But it was also very clear that what
is most charged, most significant, about the experience of
menstruation indeed relates particularly to who may say
what to whom, to how various kinds of concealment may be
achieved.

One cannot isolate 'meanings' of menstruation in our
culture apart from the idea that it is *something which must be
hidden*. Any 'meaning' attached to it cannot be taken straight-
forwardly to explain any attached social practices. In short,
the meaning of menstruation for many people in many
circumstances relates only very dimly to biology, and derives

far more strongly from the intricate social rules that people in society attach to it. For this reason I propose the term 'etiquette' as a more accurate general description of the quality of these rules.

Etiquette is defined by Edward Norbeck (following Leslie White 1959) as 'rules of behaviour governing social relations among people of distinct social statuses or classes, hierarchical or non-hierarchical' (Norbeck 1977:72). In his article 'A Sanction for Authority: Etiquette', he argues that taboo should be seen as a special class of the larger category of etiquette, 'as rules of etiquette to which supernatural sanctions are attached' (p. 73). His article then concentrates on pre-modern Japanese and Polynesian societies with intensely hierarchical social systems. However, interestingly, he also suggests that etiquette is important in modern societies, perhaps especially in relation to defining and preserving the social statuses of men and women, where it continues to 'reflect and support formal and informal relations of authority' (p. 73).

This gives us an interesting perspective on the problematic way in which the term 'taboo' is used in much of the modern discourse on menstruation. It is frequently used to refer to *any* kind of social recognition of menstruation. This leaves one vaguely searching for the missing supernatural sanction.

This search for the fear, the 'reason', behind rules of etiquette is a real distraction from the consequences which follow from the actual practice of the etiquette. Etiquette is enforced, not by fear of magical reprisals, but as Leslie White puts it, by 'Social sanctions, such as adverse comment or criticism, ridicule, and ostracism' (White 1959:225).

So let us try to lay out the basic structure of white British culture's menstrual etiquette. For women, this is very much a matter of bringing implicitly understood social rules to consciousness. In looking at what men say, one must attend to the spaces in it: things not said, things not seen.

The rule behind all the others seems to be that women may not draw men's attention to menstruation in any way. This rule is made workable by a secondary allowance that a man may decide to waive the general rule within a particular, usually sexual, relationship with an individual woman.

Hiding

One obvious aspect of this rule is that sanitary wear must be hidden from men.

Some men, interestingly, mention seeing packets of sanitary wear which were not hidden as being important moments in changing their consciousness about menstruation:

> it was quite a shock for me in later years to walk into toilets and see packets of tampax and things ... before I had any conception, like, of the women's movement. ... It was a real shock, and then I thought, no point in being shocked.... (*E*)

> One of the big surprises of adult life, was going into people's houses and finding things openly displayed in places. I couldn't believe it, because at home these things had always been hidden away, and it was like a real shock to me, because it was like something that was not mentioned, never spoken about.... (Group)

Another tells of two incidents, one with a girlfriend:

> *I*: ... I used to see sanitary towels lying around, and I used to tell her to put them away....
> *SL*: Oh did you ... you thought they shouldn't be ... ?
> *I*: Well, yeah, I don't know, I just didn't want them to be hanging around, lying around....

The other was about a canteen where he worked as a very young man:

> there were about thirty women, and they did talk about lots of things, in front of each other, which I didn't, I didn't have any ... I used to get taunted as well, lots of sexual innuendo. ... The women used to talk about their periods, they're coming on next week, or ... and ...
> *SL*: Did you find that embarrassing?
> *I*: Um ... yes, because there were so many women together, talking about it and, it was an experience I didn't have, and didn't particularly understand either, really, and I'd usually walk out of the room or walk away from them, try not to listen.

SL: Would they be ignoring you, then, or trying to get at you?

I: They weren't particularly ignoring me, they were just talking about it.

SL: What sorts of things would they have said?

I: About running out of STs and things like that, and I once heard two women discussing whether tampons were better than STs and, er, I remember that one because I didn't know the difference between them. . . .

It appears that this man was threatened by the women's failure to pay attention to him, and attempted to change the situation by the only means available to him as a low-status male – by removing himself from it.

Notice that in all these cases above, where men report having been shocked by women's behaviour, the women had done nothing actively in order to cause this reaction. What they were doing was failing or refusing to take the trouble to observe the etiquette which the males had come to expect would be observed in regard of themselves as males.

Menstrual products remain a necessary part of life for women. Women are expected to buy, store and use them without men noticing. Even the language used is extraordinary. Who or what is to be protected with 'sanitary protection'?

Abraham's 1983 survey of 40 Australian clerical workers aged 16–35 years found that only 28 per cent of them said that they 'never got embarrassed buying menstrual protection' and that 20 per cent said that they preferred to buy menstrual protection that has been wrapped in plain paper.

We should bear in mind also that while no-one in Esther Merves's US sample mentions money as an issue, there are women in Western societies, as well as in less affluent countries, who cannot afford shop-bought sanitary towels and who therefore make their own, washable ones. Suzanne Abraham, a gynaecologist, mentions this in relation to Australian women (1983) and Snow and Johnson (1977) warn US doctors to be aware that poor women may be ashamed of not using bought pads and tampons. British women in this situation wrote to Denise Flowers of the Campaign against VAT on Sanitary Wear. The difficulty of concealment is yet more burdensome with home-made sanitary wear, especially as this will be understood as a sign of poverty as well as of femaleness.

Advertising for sanitary wear presents a particular problem to British culture, for to allow it is to allow public acknowledgement of the existence of menstruation. However the companies which sell these products are fairly rich and powerful, and have a very strong interest in persuading the authorities to allow them to advertise.

Advertisements for sanitary wear were banned from television entirely until 1979, when a series of experiments began, in which a limited range of advertisements were allowed for a set period. The Independent Broadcasting Authority finally decided to allow 'sanpro' (a trade term) advertising on both ITV and Channel 4 in May 1988, two years after it was initially allowed on Channel 4. Their press release explains:

> Viewers' attitudes were monitored during the two years both by the ITV companies and by the IBA. The research showed a significant shift in public opinion. In July 1984, 55% of those surveyed had said such advertising should be allowed, 38% that it should not, with 6% don't knows. By March 1988 66% said it should be allowed, 30% that it should not with 4% don't knows.
>
> A broad picture of increasing acceptance of the advertising over the period emerged. Nevertheless it is recognised that a minority, mainly of older women, remain opposed to it.
>
> A frequent reason given by those who object is embarrassment when watching with their families. The IBA received 889 complaints during the experiment on Channel 4.

Timing restrictions and guidelines on the nature of advertising to be allowed were instituted because of 'continuing reservations by part of the audience'. The guidelines (Copy Clearance Bulletin Number 9; August 1985) make a fascinating study in themselves, for they are obliged to set out in words social rules which are usually understood implicitly, without need to specify.

1. No commercial may contain anything likely to cause embarrassment or to undermine an individual's confidence in her own personal hygiene standards.

2. All visual treatments must be tasteful and restrained. No advertisement may feature an unwrapped towel or tampon. Pack shots, however, are normally acceptable [. . .]

4. Great care must be taken with any detailed description of the product, whether in sound or vision, to avoid anything which might offend or embarrass viewers [. . .]

7. No implication of, or appeal to, sexual or social insecurity is acceptable.

8. The use of potentially offensive words such as 'odour' is not acceptable.

9. Female presenters and voice-overs are generally more appropriate than male in commercials for sanitary protection products [. . .]

10. Particular discretion is required where an advertiser wishes to communicate a product's suitability for very young women, and girls shown in such commercials should not be less than 14 or 15 years old.

11. Overt references to relationships with members of the opposite sex should be avoided and men should not be featured prominently in commercials for sanitary protection products. There is no objection to male characters in peripheral roles in playlet-type commercials [. . .]

Breaking the rules?

An interesting sidelight is cast on all this secrecy in the fact that a few men I interviewed mentioned having bought sanitary wear. One saw this as a 'breakthrough', and compared it to what he found the greater embarrassment of buying condoms (C). This issue was also discussed in the men's group:

—Actually have you ever bought a tampax?
—yes
—yes

—it's quite interesting. . . .

—it is.

—yes, when I was living with someone, that was the first time I had to buy them. . . .

—a bit like buying contraceptives, but in a way it's even weirder . . . obviously not for you.

—it is, definitely,

—I'm very conscious of making a big play of buying them. I do, I do. You know what you were saying about breaking the taboo about sex, there's something a bit sort of [clicking sound], 'made it', sort of, you know. Well, whenever I go and buy tampax, it's the same sort of thing, I do the same. I do make a big thing about it, I suppose, I suppose I put them on the side, slam them down [laughter] here, say, how much are they? . . .

—the cashiers laughing at you (Group)

This account reminded me of a woman acquaintance telling me that her father used to insist upon buying sanitary towels for her and her mother, which she believed to be because he enjoyed the embarrassment he could cause to the female shop assistants.

In relation to these men's accounts it is interesting that Merves reports that many of the younger women in her sample said they found buying sanitary wear embarrassing.

It is disturbing to me that men in the men's group find buying sanitary wear exciting, when there are a great number of women who have to do it and who are embarrassed. The flouting of convention in this way seems somehow to reinforce the convention.

The public/private distinction

Some kind of difference between public and private situations was a theme which came up in the interviews. To recall an important point made in the group discussion.

when you first come across someone who is menstruating who you're close to. . . . Even though I knew all the mechanics of it, and I understood the thing, it seemed, you know, like a source of worry, because all the taboos had been about women in general, they hadn't been about a particular woman. (Group)

To look first at public settings, I asked the men I interviewed whether they had heard reference made to menstruation at work. Among all of them, with many years of working life between them, they could remember only three or four instances of women saying that they were off work because of menstrual pain. Where this had happened, it was in somewhat unusual workplaces: from students in a university, and from women in a particularly relaxed and friendly social work office.

One man described a work situation in a way which emphasises the silent nature of these interactions: we have to take his word for it that these interactions related to menstruation at all:

F: No, I've only . . . implied. I've got the impression that in some workplaces a few of the women, some of them more or less take it for granted that they can quite freely take a couple of days off about once a month, but there are others who, if they do take a couple of days off, do look quite shy when they return, as though it was common knowledge why they were away and as though it was something to be ashamed of.
SL: So it would be assumed that that was what it was?
F: Yes.
SL: What sort of places have you worked?
F: Well I had in mind a meat packing factory, where most of the men were operating band saws, and the people taking the meat off and putting it onto conveyor belts were women.

The men reported no instance of a woman referring to mood changes related to menstruation in a public setting. And yet several of them said that remarks about the 'time of the month' are commonplace among men in some workplaces. This is, of course, related also to ideas about menopause – it would be highly discrediting in most situations for a woman to refer to her own menopausal symptoms, and yet men will speak of older women as affected by the 'time of life'. In talking about their schooldays, the men again recal-

led boys joking about menstruation, not girls openly acknowledging it. We will look at men's talk among men in more
detail in the next chapter.

These impressions are confirmed by the results of a US
survey quoted by Merves, as reported in the *National Organisation for Women Times* (Sloane 1982):

> Sixty four per cent of the 1000 questioned said that women
> at work should hide the fact that they are menstruating:
> 36% said they should also hide the fact while at home; and
> 12% of the males and 5% of the females added that
> menstruating women should stay away from other people
> while afflicted.

On a quite different tack, I was fascinated to learn that
among naturists, some of the women in any group will always
be wearing bikini bottoms: they are menstruating. Even if
menstruation could be managed with internal tampons, the
women are expected to observe this practice (Odette Parry
1982). Nature can only be allowed so much freedom,
evidently!

On the whole it is women who must take care to avoid
public embarrassment in relation to menstruation. However
there are incidents when men do so, or are aware of acting to
avoid such embarrassments:

> The attitude in which it's held by men, I mean this man
> gave me a lift when I was hitching, in this lorry (carrying
> Tampax) and I can remember going into the transport
> cafe with him, and all the other drivers saying things like
> 'here he is, the daft bleeder . . .'. And this man was just
> mortified with embarrassment, you could see he didn't
> want to drive this lorry, he wanted to drive something
> respectable and masculine. [laughter] It's strange because I
> felt myself distancing myself from him in some way.
> (Group)

> Things like VAT being put on tampons and things like
> that, which, I mean I've been to political meetings where
> that's been raised as an issue, in the Labour Party, and men
> say, 'Oh, let's get back to politics', things like that. And I
> haven't backed them up, the women, I haven't backed the
> women up, even though I agree with them. (*I*)

The male group polices individual men with ridicule, much as it polices women.

Drawing together some of the strands, comparing male to female experiences of interactions relating to menstruation, one can see the public/private distinction running through the men's remarks. No equivalent distinction emerges from the women's point of view — Merves's respondents mentioned that they would prefer not to discuss menstruation with male members of their own families. It appears that there is no shared definition of what constitutes public and private between women and men.

I would suggest that for women there could be no clear distinction, as in one statement quoted above, between men in general and a particular man, because of the power inequality. The woman is not in a position to decide that she can ignore the normal etiquette in regard to any particular man without risking offending his masculinity. When a young girl is told about periods, she is told not to let men know about it — not that *some* men, or men in public settings, or whatever, should not know. Men *are* the public from her point of view. If couples negotiate to waive these rules, this is a matter of the man making a concession — women cannot expect it, as such. The split in settings, then, is maintained by men, who may simultaneously acknowledge menstruation's existence in their private lives and deny it in public. Thus the same interaction could be understood as a public one by the woman involved and as a private one by the man.

The campaign against VAT on sanitary wear

An interesting case in point, where women have tried to bring an issue relating to menstruation into the public sphere, is the campaign which has existed since 1981 to end taxation of sanitary wear. The low public profile of the campaign contrasts sharply with the very high level of active support from women. A petition delivered in 1983 carried 110,000 signatures, and many more have been added since.

Very large numbers of 'ordinary' women, who would not necessarily have seen themselves as feminists, have been angry about the tax, which was originally introduced as a tax on 'luxury' items, and not on food and other 'essentials'. Many women wrote to the campaign, describing the misery of not being able to afford the sanitary wear they need, whether because of very heavy bleeding, several grown-up daughters in one household, or just the poverty created by low pay or by unemployment and depending on state benefit.

I interviewed Denise Flowers, the main organiser of the campaign, about her experiences with trying to get press coverage. She summarised male journalists' attitudes to the campaign as 'hilarity and dismissal'. On one occasion, the Letters Editor of *The Times* decided to print a letter Denise had sent in, and his Editor forbade him to do it, saying that he was not having the words 'sanitary towel' in *The Times*. Often, for instance while speaking on radio programmes, women involved in the campaign were subjected to considerable harassment. Denise herself for a time received threatening obscene phone calls after an article about the campaign appeared in the local press where she lived.

During discussions in Parliament, where the issue has been raised several times by MPs Jo Richardson and Joan Lestor, arguments that the tax amounts to sex discrimination have been met with joking over-politeness and derogatory comments.

The response to this campaign reflects exactly White's (1959) description of the social sanctions which defend any system of etiquette: 'adverse comment or criticism, ridicule and ostracism'.

Family life

Only a few of the men I interviewed had heard their mothers mention menstruation – only one was told anything about it at home as a child. Most, too, had seen no physical evidence of its existence. As I have said, two of them were quite startled by the thought that their mothers must have menstruated – it had not occurred to them until I asked them about it.

Of the six men who had sisters, three had heard no mention of their periods – and this includes one with *six* sisters. One of the men who had been aware of its existence recalls a negative reaction from his father:

> when [my sister] started menstruating, that was a real trauma in the house. . . . It wasn't talked about, it wasn't, oh, sort of, X's had a period, in a joyful way, or a celebration of her having her first period or anything, it was all sort of . . . it was just a real chill atmosphere, you know, this means possibly confronting something to do with our bodies, everyone keep their heads down. (*E*)

This secrecy within the family appears to be reproduced to some extent in the next generation – the one man in my sample with daughters said that he thought they spoke only to their mother about it:

> To the extent that they dealt with it, they dealt with it with X, although I think that's probably the only thing they dealt with with her and not dealt with me . . . aspects of their sexuality and so on are referred to me as much as or perhaps more, for all sorts of reasons. . . . (*N*)

In contrast to this consistent secrecy in all other relationships, the men in my sample would generally know about it when a woman they had a sexual relationship with was menstruating. This knowledge in a sense marks off the heterosexual relationship from all other kinds of relationship between the sexes.

It would not be true to say, however, that no etiquette exists between lovers – in many ways the rules are very much the same. The woman may not *presume* that she will not be found offensive. As will be clear, when we look at sexuality in more detail (Chapter 6), the woman continues to be held responsible for managing the agreed boundaries for sex while she is menstruating whatever they may be.

Secrecy within the family affects women in various ways. Much of the literature on menarche places tremendous emphasis on the role of the mother, and the mother's personal attitudes, in creating the girl's experience of her first period. However it is clear that mothers are expected to police the etiquette and to somehow at the same time protect their daughters from the effects of it: surely an impossible task. Elizabeth Roberts (1984) writes that mothers in the

period of her study, 1890 to 1940, made menstruation a
taboo subject, that they 'undoubtedly gave their daughters a
feeling of repugnance about this natural function, as something which was shameful and to be hidden'. But when she
quotes an informant, Mrs Stott, we can see the problems with
blaming the mother:

> I always remember when I started she said 'Never let your
> brothers see this whatever you do.' She drummed it into
> me . . . and in those days things were a bit different to what
> they are today. You couldn't buy things to wash away down
> the toilet, they had to be washed, and she used to drum it
> into me, me being the only girl. No, she was most strict
> over anything like that. Strict over everything. She was a
> good mother. (p. 17)

Rosemary Lee (1984) recounts her mother's menarche story:

> When my mother was thirteen she came home from school
> convinced that, like her sister, she had a severe haemor-
> rhage. She told her mother she was bleeding and was
> bundled out into the kitchen.
>   'How could you have mentioned that in front of your
> father?' Her mother found her a sanitary towel. 'It's your
> periods. Put that on. It'll go on until you're forty'. My
> mother thought this shameful bleeding would continue
> unabated without reason for the next thirty years. She only
> discovered the full facts of life when in labour with my
> sister.

But such secrecy is not a thing of the past. Many girls
nowadays are told that men must not know they are bleeding
– many more, I suspect, like myself, do not even need to be
told. It is easy enough to observe the concealment which
older women practise. Several women have told me that their
fathers scolded them if they left sanitary towels in the
bathroom. One said that she used to do it to annoy him,
because he used it as an issue to impose his authority – he
would then tell her mother to tell her not to do it.

Whisnant and Zegans in their (1975) study of white
middle-class American girls' attitudes, found that while 24
out of 25 girls who had experienced menarche had immediately told their mothers about it, only one had told her

father. A somewhat larger number of pre-menarcheal girls said that they expected to tell their fathers about it. Generally Whisnant and Zegans note that the girls seemed to anticipate an openness which rarely occurred in the event. Fathers were told by mothers or not at all.

Neither does this problem cease after adolescence; when women have children of their own they are again confronted with these issues. After a talk I gave at a women's conference, a woman spoke of her anxiety about talking to her son about menstruation. She said that she felt that if she tried to give him information about it, she could only imagine him going off to his friends and whispering and laughing about it.

The most problematic aspect of the concealment of menstruation from everyone, but particularly from those with whom one lives, is the difficulty of getting rid of the evidence: used sanitary wear. Rosemary Lee describes her own experiences, showing how she used different strategies at different times:

> The towels that compressed after the first hour and thereafter leaked into your pants, starching them to sandpaper. ... The disposal unit that signalled your exit from the loo with bouts of black smoke, or was stuffed full, leaving you with a reeking packet and nowhere to put it. The desperate fear that an unfastened towel was about to work its way out of the back of your pants. The awkward questions asked by boys who 'must not know'.
> [...] I continued to cope until going to college digs, where there was no fire, boiler, or means of disposal other than the family dustbin under the dining room window. Crisis. I bought some Tampax, and with cold sweat running off me, and monumental efforts to relax, I made it in the third attempt, uninjured, and with the tampon in the right place.
> Since then I've changed to Lil-lets because their size makes them easier to conceal in the hand, or carry in a pocket. Why do I quail at openly carrying a towel or tampon? [...] I can admit to you that I bleed, that I hurt, that the mechanisms and inhibitions around it repel me. I can cope with my body but not with Joe Public's view of it.

In Whisnant and Zegan's interviews with pre-menarcheal

girls, they found that 'their concern did not centre about the
psychological meaning of menstruation, why it takes place,
or about the anatomy involved, but on the practical issue of
'What do I do when I get my period?'.

Suzanne Abraham (1983) reports on a survey of 40
Australian clerical workers aged 16 to 35 years. They were
asked 'Are you/were you concerned that a pad could show
when you are/were wearing one?' – 78% said that they were
concerned. Again, the other option is to use tampons, and
Abrahams finds that the vast majority of young women do
come to use tampons.

Some girls, of course, will learn this lesson about secrecy
within the family too well. Patricia Pemberton-Jones, in her
short story 'Tidal Wave' (1984) tells how when her anxiously-
awaited first period finally arrives, she associates it with
another coincidental new experience – sexual excitement.
She cannot bring herself to tell her mother, 'a distant elderly
deity', sure that she would be angry.

> So the weeks, then months, went on, always meaning to tell
> her tomorrow. I hid my stained knickers and the soiled
> towels in an old suitcase in my wardrobe. I didn't dare try
> and flush them away. When my underwear supply grew
> low I found a Saturday job in order to buy more, I learned
> all about bleaching sheets, and sometimes had to sleep on
> them wet because I couldn't dry them secretly.

> Summer came, my guilty secret in the plastic suitcase was
> bulging, it smelt horrible. Its presence seemed to fill my
> bedroom and dirty it, when I was bleeding this dirtiness
> seemed to cling to me and cover me.

When her mother finally found the suitcase she was indeed
very angry, and sent the girl to boarding school, on the
theory that her 'deceit' was the result of a lack of discipline.

I might be more ready to think of this account as fiction, or
a special case, if I had not been told a very similar tale by a
friend, who had been told something about menstruation,
but not what to do with her used towels, in a house where the
open fire was the focus of family life. She hid hers in a
bedroom cupboard until the smell led her mother to find
them.

'You can tell'

One of the consequences of the etiquette which requires women not to speak about menstruation appears to be that men become interested in ways of telling when women are menstruating.

Several discussions on this subject occurred in the men's groups:

—I don't know, I've noticed that you can almost always tell when a woman's having a period, because of the skin on her face . . .
—really, gosh, I've never . . .
—well, not always, but it seems to affect their . . .
—texture or colour? or both?
—yes, well, quite a lot of women actually start coming out a little bit spotty and perhaps cover it up, and they're women you know just aren't spotty, and this only goes . . . sometimes it's spots, sometimes the colour changes, things like that. . . . Particularly because make-up and so on just isn't used to the same extent that it used to be . . . in the past it would be plastered over. Or if sometimes women who don't usually use make-up suddenly start, for no obvious reason. It clearly does have some certain physical effect. (Group)

One man offered these thoughts on the smell of menstrual blood. In contrast to the fact that he had never in his working life heard a woman mention feeling ill or in pain due to her period, he remarks:

N: . . . Occasionally I've been in contact with women at work where I've thought they were having a period, and I think that's to do with a certain aroma, a certain smell,
SL: ah . . .
N: that I've associated with having periods. Now to be honest, again, I've never talked to anyone about this so . . . just a notion that I have that certain women, or women in certain circumstances, do give off some smell. It's different to a sweat . . . it's not a straightforward body odour in that sense, I mean I wouldn't swear to it . . . a mysterious smell.

The men's group serves as useful check here, for the fact that they were free to set their own agenda prevented me from avoiding topics which made me uneasy, but which may be very present in men's thoughts about menstruation. I was not very concerned with these matters, and I find the men's concern offensive. However it is useful to know about it nonetheless, since this sort of men's talk must partly account for the vague threat women perceive from men around the subject. It came up in the group in several contexts:

The only thing I do remember about menstruation in my childhood, was the smell of my mother's menstrual blood, because I'm sure she must have had very heavy menstrual periods. I know she was anaemic, and she was never very well, but looking back on it . . . I'm sure she must have had very heavy periods, and I was aware of the smell, that she wasn't very well at certain, you know, quite regularly. And I reckon that's what it must have been. She's not alive anymore so I can't ask her. . . . It's not exactly the sort of thing you can ask your father . . .
—[at the] Christmas dinner table!
—so, I suspect, I was sort of aware of that as a physical thing, but in a way repelled by it – I didn't like the smell and I found it a bit frightening, I knew my mum wasn't well and I was very close to my mum. And when this was happening, you know I could just sort of . . . a sensation, a feeling in the air, at that time of the month, I guess, that I didn't. . . .
—what age was that?
—Well actually I think it goes back quite young, to being eight or nine at least, if not even earlier. Being aware of the smell, not knowing what it was, but associating it with something rather tense and unpleasant for my mother. I may be imagining it a bit, but I know that I react to that smell with a certain kind of. . . . It brings back childhood memories of being rather unhappy. Um. . . . It wasn't until years later that I realised that that smell was . . . very distinctive.
—I don't know . . .
—you don't?
—I don't, no, I can't remember what the smell is. I can't remember a smell, particularly. . . . Can you?

—I can, yes . . . definitely my first memories of it, probably from that kind of age. . . . And similarly, I didn't know exactly what was going on, it was definitely a rather funny smell and I guess women just used sanitary towels then, and I think that's actually got a lot to do with it. And then the whole sort of build up after that as you get all these bits in Boots, like 'feminine hygiene' and all the rest of it, which kind of people lurk off to, and you sensed that it was an embarrassing subject. . . .

—mm . . . I still, I can . . . maybe I've got a very sensitive nose, but I mean when X is having a period, I can often, you know . . .

—mm

—I'm aware of that smell, I don't know why, in the loo. And it doesn't have the same effect, but it recalls the effect that it had on me as a child. And I don't feel. . . .

—really?

—yes, it's just a curious echo. . . .

—Could you describe it, what the smell is? I've got a feeling it's an almost metallic smell, but I couldn't really explain that.

—It's the smell of blood. I mean it's got a slightly acrid smell . . . the way I could describe it, sort of bitter, slightly . . . I don't know . . . acrid is part of it.

—Yes, I don't know exactly how you'd describe it either, actually

—metallic, yes, slightly metallic, yes.

(Group)

The *Collins English Dictionary* says that 'acrid' means: 1. unpleasantly pungent or sharp to the smell or taste, 2. sharp or caustic especially in speech or nature.

Another man in the group also speaks about childhood memories of his mother in somewhat similar terms, although he is not speaking about the smell of menstruation as such, but about other 'female'-associated smells:

Did I tell you about finding in my mother's bedside cabinet. . . . Do you remember those tubes, Pansticks, the sort of make-up foundation, and they're an oval tube, about six inches long, like a big lipstick, and my mother used to use it as a foundation. . . . I mean it *stinks*. If you think of smells that conjure up memories. I remember going into her bedside cupboard, and finding what I thought was one of those pansticks, and in fact, when I opened it up, it was a plastic container for two tampax, no, lil-lets ... and I had no idea what they were, again it was only later ... when I realised what they were, and then went back to it. But I distinctly remember, you know, I had a real bad association with this Panstick, and opening up this plastic container, and finding these two large, thin, paper-covered things which were ... which I didn't know what they were. . . . (Group)

The interesting thing about this account is that it should caution us in taking the unpleasantness of the smell of menstrual blood for small boys as some sort of natural fact, for here is a man apparently attaching a very similar significance to the smell of his mother's make-up, to a synthetic perfume, in fact.

Esther Merves asked her sample of women about the 'scent of menstruation': 18.3 per cent said that it does not have a scent. 35 per cent felt that it did, but could not describe it. The majority of the remaining 46.7 per cent responded that menstruation smells like 'blood'. Other adjectives included: 'heavy, sick, earthy, musty, normal, sweet'. Merves notes that 'many women prefaced their remarks by saying "not unpleasant"', although 25 per cent of her sample found the smell unpleasant.

It is striking that the adjectives given by the men here are not only different but actually opposite to those mentioned by Merves's women. The men say bitter where the women say sweet; the men say metallic where the women say earthy; acrid implies sharp where the women said heavy. The association with sickness is present in both accounts.

These assertions from men that they can tell when a woman is menstruating, by smell or by appearance, are interesting for several reasons. They seem to set some store by the ability to 'tell', in effect to undermine women's efforts to hide the evidence of their periods. I would see this preoccupation as part of an attempt to exert some control over one process which they perceive as out of their control. Even if they do properly observe the etiquette, women are held to 'give themselves away' – they cannot entirely escape the discredit which attaches to menstruation because their attempts at concealment can be seen through.

In another way, these discussions overlap with another broader subject, if possible still more offensive to women, that of men's beliefs about the smell of women's genitals generally. One man mentions liking the smell of dried blood on his hands, as a reminder of an earlier sexual encounter. This leads to a discussion about the smell of sexual secretions generally, revealing different feelings about it among the members of the group.

> —you go to work the next morning having not washed
>   after making love? [laughter]
> —why not?
> —fucking hell!
> —I wash immediately afterwards
> —I almost always have a bath afterwards . . .
> —yes, yes
> —it stinks!
> —it's not the blood, it's just . . .
> —And X always wants to have a wash . . . always wants to
>   wash herself afterwards
> —stinks!
> —because to spend the rest of the night, or hours . . .
> —what's that smell like fish-o-bake? [laughter]
> —yes, yes
> —it's a very strong smell like fish [laughter]
> —well, it's true
> —yours doesn't I suppose? (Group)

Shere Hite discovered a strand of preoccupation with smell and generally with the dirtiness of women's genitals in her studies of men's view of women (1981). In her research, as in the discussion in the men's group, this came out especially in response to questions about oral sex. A few comments among many are these:

> 'How does one ask a woman politely to wash?'
> 'Cunnilingus stinks! The smell is horrendous!'
> 'You can rub and scrub and clean it well, but you can't get
> rid of that codfish smell.'

'If I want to have oral sex with a gal, I am saying to her "You are clean".'
'I like oral sex done on me only.' (pp. 688–9)

Some of Hite's respondents refer directly to cunnilingus during menstruation:

'I like the warmth and moisture of my partner's genitals, and I enjoy the very pleasant odour of them. The only time I do not like cunnilingus is during her period, although I have done it and was surprised that I could not tell the difference in taste or odour. That was early in her period.'
'Menstruation makes little difference to me. Oral sex with a tampon in place is just the same as when she is not menstruating. Without a tampon, I reserve the right to refuse but that is unlikely. . . .' (p. 693)

It seems to me to be difficult to analyse these ideas about smell, for of course we generally think of smell as a straight-forward sensation, unaffected by social relationships. Ideas about smell are, however, clearly part of the complex of beliefs about dirt discussed earlier in relation to pollution beliefs; ideas which people often hold about people they see as inferior to themselves. Thus the idea that Black or Asian people 'smell' is part of British racist thinking, and this statement is sometimes made as a racial insult. It emphasises a supposedly natural difference, and implies inferiority.

Because bodies and bodily substances do undoubtedly smell, it can be difficult to separate out and make visible the social meanings of saying someone or something smells. Bringing home Mary Douglas's ideas about pollution fully would involve comprehending the meanings of cleanliness in relation to sex, race and class in our society.

In terms of women and menstruation, then, what does it mean that we find disagreements between Merves's women and the men I interviewed about the nature of the smell, and yet in Sharon Golub's (1981) study, 57 per cent of the males and 56 per cent of the females agreed that 'a woman smells different when she is menstruating'? Golub's formulation is a particularly neutral one – the women and the men could mean very different things when they agreed with it. Shere Hite points out that 'While the fact that all bodies need bathing rather regularly would seem to go without saying, no men mentioned the necessity for brushing teeth regularly to make kissing pleasant' (p. 692). I am inclined to see this insistence on the need for washing to be an observance of menstrual etiquette: men's manhood in some way requires that women acknowledge their possible impurity before coming into contact with a man.

Shirley Ardener (1975) has written a very interesting account of African cultures where there are ritualised forms of sexual insult to women which, if made to a woman, are followed by fierce protest from women acting as a group. In some places it has recently been given the force of law that these insults should not be made. The form the insult takes is for a man to assert that 'the lower part of women' smells. Ardener draws an analogy between female militancy of this sort in Africa and the women's liberation movement in this country.

Teaching the etiquette

Like all etiquette, that relating to menstruation must be taught to the young. Shirley Prendergast (1988), having studied girls' experiences in relation to dealing with menstruation at school, points out how the process of learning to manage menstruation and the shame attached to it can be seen as a pattern for the way young girls are trained to manage their bodies as women.

Advertisements for sanitary products have been much studied, to 'read' the messages they give about gender (Hazel Slavin 1981; Ann Treneman 1988), and Whisnant *et al* (1975) looked at the 'advice' literature produced by the same companies. These last have the most explicit training role. Whisnant *et al* describe the ideological messages delivered to young girls, such as the emphasis on a close connection between womanhood and motherhood, but they also note the laying down of rules of behaviour, some of which they refer to as ritualistic in their 'irrationality and dogmatism'. Girls are exhorted to take special care in 'grooming', to sleep more, eat 'properly', drink water, do special exercises, and so forth. They are told especially to 'LIVE AS USUAL'. Concealment is the paramount virtue: 'Your attitude and lack of good grooming give it away'. 'It's absolutely impossible for anyone to know you are menstruating unless of course you act stupid about the whole thing'.

Girls are to be shamed into not avoiding exercise or work during menstruation – pain is attributed to 'other factors'. Especially they must manage their emotions – they should 'take their minds off themselves'. As the authors point out, 'a girl achieves a positive mental attitude in part by not attending to her own sensations'.

There is tremendous emphasis on appearance. One of the first questions one of the leaflets proposes to answer is: 'how to keep smiling everyday'. Girls are told what they *should* feel – negative emotions are simply to be denied.

This material shows very clearly how menstrual etiquette is tied up with general prescriptions for feminine behaviour. Orientation to others, to one's appearance rather than to one's own feelings, are of the essence. Adult female self-respect is equated with calm secretiveness. Whisnant *et al* found that girls did in fact pay a great deal of attention to these materials, and in some cases followed instructions to the letter, for example about how often to change sanitary towels: 'They stressed the importance of "acting natural" and appearing "cool", and agreed that menstruation ought to be kept secret and that symptoms could and should be concealed by will power.' Premenarcheal girls anticipated complying with the suggestions about what they would feel, for example that they would 'act more ladylike'.

But we cannot regard these materials as the *source* of menstrual etiquette. As Whisnant *et al* emphasise:

> their materials are readily available through schools, churches, scouting programs, and physicians, or are directly available to the girl or her mother by mail. A great deal of research and market testing goes into the preparation of these booklets, and they are revised frequently. Accordingly, the content is influenced by what is deemed acceptable to a broad spectrum of consumers, and its shortcomings (which will be discussed) most likely reflect limitations imposed by that fact. (p. 815)

The focus so far has been on what might be called the normal manifestations of menstrual etiquette. In circumstances where women's lives are under especially close control, these matters take on a different significance. Women in prison often complain that menstruation is used to punish or humiliate them, for example by the prison authority's withholding adequate sanitary wear. Any bodily function may become an arena of struggle in such circumstances, but menstruation lends itself also to specifically sexual degradation.

Teresa Thornhill (1985) describes the experience of a Republican woman prisoner in Northern Ireland, during her interrogation by the Royal Ulster Constabulary, being made to sit in front of them all week, bleeding into the same pair of jeans.

Menstruation could also be used to make women special targets in Nazi concentration camps:

> many women in concentration camps ceased to menstruate. The rumour was that in concentration camps something was put in the food. But it is unlikely that this happened in places such as Treblinka (an extermination camp); the number of girls kept alive didn't warrant such precautions, and anyway this particular aspect of life only afforded the Ukranians and the SS one more opportunity for sadistic humour. There were, of course, no sanitary napkins, or even newspapers, and the girls used large leaves – burdock leaves if they could find them, to protect themselves. But any blood showing on a dress meant death; it was unaesthetic, and the SS were very keen on aesthetics. (Sereny 1977)

It is also said that the women who were forced into concentration camp brothels for use by the guards had to go to great lengths to conceal menstruation, and that if blood was detected, the woman would be killed.

I have concentrated my own work on ordinary everyday life, where concern with menstrual etiquette is generally at a low level of intensity. What does it matter at all?

From a conservative position, Leslie White spells out nicely for me the importance of etiquette:

> many persons who do not understand the nature and

functions of systems of etiquette are inclined to rail against them as being irrational, senseless and therefore unnecessary. They fail to understand that society must have some way of assuring itself that men will behave as men, women as women. (White 1959:226)

Using the example of a male student who arrives in class wearing lipstick or earrings, he emphasises 'the significant and important point: we do not know what he will do next' (White 1959). It is interesting that White uses examples from sexual politics to illustrate his general point, though he does not remark on this. Etiquette is clearly a particularly characteristic feature of the social hierarchy of the sexes – we take it for granted so much that it is difficult to see it for what it is.

While feminists have only rarely used the term etiquette (though see Rich 1977:57), they have in practice challenged the etiquette of menstruation in a number of ways. Some of the women anti-nuclear protesters at Greenham Common have tied tampons to the wire of the perimeter fence. A friend told me that her father had been so shocked by this that he could hardly speak about it. I found another interesting example in a review of Gloria Steinem's book *Outrageous Acts and Everyday Rebellions*:

Despite her book's title, Gloria Steinem's talent is not for outrage. That she should leave to Germaine Greer, who she remembers taunting a talk-show host by demanding as he laid down the law about monthly emotional changes and female unreliability, 'Can you tell me if I'm menstruating right now – or not?' (Conrad 1984)

No-one is telling any stories about the outrageousness of the talk-show host, who raised the topic.

In her more subtle way, Posy Simmonds draws attention to the absurdity of the exact limits of menstrual etiquette among the liberal middle classes, in a cartoon titled 'Taboo' (frontispiece). An intuitive connection is made between refusing the etiquette of menstruation and refusing male domination generally when feminists call a magazine *Red Rag*, a cartoon book and a local (Bradford) women's newsletter *Heavy Periods*, a theatre piece *Female Trouble* and a rock band *PMT*.

Since I have been working on menstruation, I have been to

a number of evenings of feminist entertainment in different towns in Britain. As often as not some item in the programme refers to menstruation: a poem about bleeding into one's trendy white boiler suit in a restaurant; a skit where the period appears in vampire form to disrupt a woman's tidy life, and is held at bay with crossed tampons. In my own town one of these events included the demand being made of the all-female audience that those menstruating say so, and the distribution of red ribbons for them to wear.

This attention to menstruation can be embarrassing to women, even among women – one is confronted with one's internalised conventionality. Just as men's jokes are not remotely amusing to women, I suspect that the point of these events, which can be satirical or serious, would be entirely lost on men. Making all our private embarrassments public is an attempt to exorcise the shame we carry, to bring to full consciousness also the extent to which we are still obliged to comply with etiquette in our daily lives.

This chapter has described some of the rules of etiquette relating to menstruation in British culture – the silences and secrecies that are required from women, and the consequences that has for men's ideas about menstruation. I have argued that taboo is an unhelpful term to describe these social rules. I was myself very anxious about the idea of interviewing men on this subject, partly, I think, because of some sorts of feminist theory about 'menstrual taboos', as well as because of my basic training in menstrual etiquette, of course. I was influenced by analyses such as that of Paula Weideger, who says that the 'menstrual taboo' is

> a means of keeping the fear of menstruating women under control. As soon as women succeed in overthrowing the taboo, these fears will no longer be comfortably contained. What is now covert may well become overt as male anxieties come to the surface. (1978:102)

She explicitly links the menstrual taboo with the threat of rape – or at least with women's 'fears of reprisal' (p. 123) – she slips somewhat in her writing between an acknowledgement of men's real actions to retain their power and an idea that women are unreasonably afraid.

In retrospect it seems to me that while in one sense

Weideger's analysis is correct in its linking of male power with menstrual etiquette, it can also in some ways reinforce that which it sets out to challenge. Men must be dealt with as individuals who are in control of their actions as well as being seen as members of a group who must be expected to act to retain their power as a group.

Social rules are within the power of human beings to change – but if they are understood as resulting from deep unknowable psychic horrors rather than plain politics, they are made to seem inevitable, *beyond* change.

The next chapter looks at talk among men about menstruation – joking talk belittling women which to me accounts for the sense of threat which many women feel around menstruation much better than psychoanalytic theorising. Chapter 5 looks at the ways in which explanations of social rules around menstruation tend to depend on taken-for-granted ideas about its relationship to reproduction, and Chapter 6 examines talk specifically around sexual relationships. Subsequent chapters consider the ways in which the medical profession has functioned like a male group in constructing theories about menstrual problems which ignore and deny women's experience.

4 'A Sick Joke': Male Culture on Menstruation

What do men really think about menstruation? In Chapter 3 the men I interviewed reported discussions or lack of discussions with women, what they had seen or not seen in their families. However the interviews also uncovered a whole set of ideas, mainly in joke form, which exist among men and are not usually repeated in interactions with women.

I began my research with a sense that I did not have all the information I needed to make sense of my feelings about menstruation. The accounts in this chapter not only throw light upon men's experiences in relation to menstruation but also upon women's. Women are interested in what men feel about menstruation, understanding at some level that their experience is conditioned by men's – much of the writing on the subject, however, implies that what we do not know about men's consciousness is beyond reach, existing at a deep, perhaps unconscious, level. What my interviews showed is that there is much that is perfectly obvious to many men, but which male groups ensure is kept from women. Its absence from the 'literature' is part of this same process.

The interviews took a life-history approach, asking the men to recall how menstruation had entered their consciousness as children and how their knowledge of it had changed subsequently.

BOYHOOD

About half the men in my sample reported boys at school joking about menstruation, the most common phrase mentioned being 'jam-rag' (or its variants 'jam sandwich', 'jam roll'): terms for sanitary towels. Some, echoing the stories in Mahoney and Prendergast (see Chapter 3) of girls being teased about periods, reported that:

For years and years, I'm not the only person I'm sure, we

used to . . . kids used to call, used to taunt girls, we used to say 'well, where's your jammy rags?' and things like that [. . .] people never knew what it was until I was older, but it's one of the things you just say; a way of getting at girls was to do that. (*I*)

This knowing/not knowing is shown also in this sequence:

SL: Can you remember when you first learnt that there was such a thing as menstruation?
M: No. I can't.
SL: But at some point you knew?
M: At some point, yes.
SL: Do you remember a stage of knowing there was something, but not what it was?
M: Um, I don't . . . it's very difficult to say . . . only in the sort of schoolboy sense, you know, adolescent, schoolboy [unclear] reference to girls, periods, menstruation, that kind of thing, but not in any serious way.

In some schools, the boys would make this an issue as a tactic in a dispute with the authorities.

then I suppose the only other instances is from recognising this is what happens to girls when they don't come to school, and that kind of thing [. . .] And why girls are let off doing certain things like PE and that, or, you know, certain allowances were made, and I think. . . . Boys at school used to think it was unfair [. . .]

A lot of it is connected with girls crying, I think, premenstrual tension I suppose, but a lot of it was to do with . . . if girls cry they get let off, get allowed to do certain things and . . . like we used to have to read out of books, in the English lesson, and girls used to be let off reading out a passage, taking a part, if they didn't want to, if they weren't in the mood for that kind of thing, but the boys were always pushed to do it. I suppose that's connected with other things as well, but [. . .]

There was a big row at school about whether you could bring your bag, certain kinds of bag to school, and it was really telling the boys what they could bring, bring sports bags and nothing else, and the girls were let off this, and there was a spate of the boys saying, oh, you know, taunting the girls about what they've got in their bags, and grabbing bags off them, and things like that, just to have a look. (*I*)

Another theme relating to menstruation is of a general 'put down' that 'she's on', referring to ideas about hormones altering women's behaviour. One man said that he thought the girls at his school used this about each other: certainly the boys said it about girls (*G*).

More men only remembered it being talked about among boys, not used against girls directly (several had gone to boys-only schools). In that context it would be referred to 'in the kind of dirty joke manner' (*M*). One man referred to 'jam rag' being used as a term of abuse to another boy, which he explained conveyed the same as calling someone 'you prat' (*F*).

A lot of men, a lot of the boys, used to have jokes, a pattern, a section of jokes about menstruation, like 'sunny periods' and all sorts of connotations about, um, there was a whole sort of part of the vocabulary of, like, jokes which were menstrual jokes, and about women, about women's blood, in a really sort. . . . I can't remember a lot of them, but there was one like . . . jokes on the word period, sort of metaphors and things of the word period.
SL: Would they say that to the girls?
E: No, that would be boys' jokes [. . .].
E: But I can't really remember men's jokes being geared to persecuting one girl in particular, it was more sort of 'it's us and them, and they have periods, so we've got a few jokes about that sort of thing'. Bit like Irish, Pakistanis . . .

Other men said that menstruation was not joked about in their schools:

things like sex were regarded as fun, as things to joke about, but something like menstruation wasn't. It was considered taboo by us . . . I don't know how far – I mean I certainly didn't understand it, and I don't know how far people that I went to school with understood it. Nobody was quite sure enough to make a joke about it, if you know what I mean, because nobody quite knew what it was. (*J*)

> No ... you see one of the things ... having periods was always something that wasn't very nice, basically, and people didn't tend to mention it, even young boys, very rarely would it come up. (*K*)

Girls also use slang and make jokes about periods – but I would argue that even the same words have a rather different meaning in female mouths. I certainly do not want to imply that taking an entirely solemn attitude to periods would do girls any good. Laughing at one's own bodily functions and the inconveniences they bring with them is a healthy sign and is quite different from the 'them and us' joking of boys. That the man quoted above did not even know what was referred to by 'jammy rags', but knew that it was something he could say to 'get at girls', demonstrates my point. He understood the sexual politics without understanding the subject matter.

I was very interested to find that this same phenomenon is reported by Marilyn Strathern in relation to the people of Mount Hagen, New Guinea. They regard menstrual blood as poisonous, and the men say it is disgusting, smelly. Small boys are told that when their mothers are menstruating, it is as if they are smeared with faeces, or have poison on their bodies. Children make this association of dirt and danger with women before they know the facts of menstruation. Men relate not having known until they reached adulthood that it was because of bleeding that women had to go into seclusion (1972:173)

The men's group discussion explores the differences in their memories further:

> —what about at school then ... there were some whispers down the corridor at home, which didn't particularly give me any sense of, er, nastiness or uncleanliness ... but somewhere along the way obviously, as well as reading these articles about Hells Angels, I obviously picked up something which allowed me to enter into the sort of school thing of ridiculing and joking, and er, really being very abusive about women. You know, the jamrag ... is it called jamrag? yeah
> —yeah
> —that sort of term, that came from school, didn't it? Again

I don't remember much about [. . .]

—I remember finding a sanitary towel occasionally in the woods, and things like that, and the jokes that were made about it . . .

—I don't remember that – it was a boys' school . . .

—no . . .

—I vaguely remember jokes about jamrags that I didn't understand but . . .

—they were very few, I mean it was pretty bad taste joking actually . . . a boys' school . . . a couple of allusions, not much. I think on the whole the taboo was pretty solid. And a joke about jamrags was breaking the taboo if anything, and that was in bad taste on the whole, most people didn't do it. One or two jokers who made jokes about anything in bad taste that they could possibly think of, would come out with those jokes, but then they'd come out with the most bad taste jokes on anything you'd care to think of anyway [laughter]

—mm, yes, I remember those characters. I found it quite distasteful, I must have had the taboo quite strongly [laughter] [. . .]

—you're reminding me now, when it was mentioned, it was pretty much frowned upon. I didn't go to a posh school or anything like that, but even there it wasn't something that was particularly widely joked about at all. There was a sort of hidden quietness about it . . . (Group)

This idea of bad taste recurs in the data about adult men. But menstruation as such is not central to 'dirty joking' – sexuality is the main theme, for adults and for older boys.

That's what you're told, isn't it? [. . .] I mean, yeah, looking back at school, that's the kind of jokes you would make, if you ever sort of managed to get off with some girl it would be just your luck that she'd be having her period or whatever. So yeah, I mean, that idea was definitely there, not that it was physically impossible, but just, like, you know, just that it was kind of . . . almost a bit freaky, I suppose. (D)

Equally the same man says that recently he has not heard such joking but

I suppose at university blokes were still kind of making those jokes, still come out with really crude terms like jamrags and things. But not since then. (*D*)

The following conversation in the men's group shows how adult male culture may be transmitted to younger males:

—the first memory I've got, the first thing ... about actually talking about menstruating was, I think it was being aware of these rituals that Hells Angels went through. Do you remember . . .
—yes . . .
—. . . reading stuff like that? There was a big
—the wings thing?
—yes, right, and that, the thing was that they were, all these Hells Angels got their wings by various things like you know pissing on their jeans until they stood up, and they're so dirty . . . and one of them was having sex with a woman who was menstruating. Do you remember that?
—yes . . .
—I definitely remember that as being one of the first times I was really aware. And it was in that sense, one of my very earliest memories, were very much linked up with, it was some strange, er, almost perverse ritual. You know, sex and menstruation were really a bad thing, that bad people did, [laughs] in order to get accepted in a really heavy group of people [. . .]
—. . . I can remember at school, reading those books, and remembering, and presumably what you were supposed to do was to share the horror of the author in writing about this, and I can remember thinking, gosh, ugh, no, you know . . .
—my god, yeah,
—no way [. . .]
—Mm. The first time I had sex with a woman when she was menstruating I definitely remember feeling, thinking back to these articles about the Hells Angels. Absolutely definitely. I mean not, I hope not in any sort of conquering [. . .] It was almost as if I'd sort of knocked down one more taboo. I felt a bit cocksure of myself . . . (Group)

ADULT MEN: SEXUAL ACCESS

Rather more than half of the men I interviewed had heard adult men joking about menstruation. This had occurred in a variety of settings, from workplaces (in heavy industry but also among scientific workers) to male leisure situations such as football changing rooms. One man recounts how he passed from one male group to another:

> in my adolescent years there was always jokes about women having periods, and knowing you might as well stay clear of them at that time of the month because there's no point normally, you know. Because you can't do anything [laughs] you know. And that, I suppose, it went through a long, you know, a long age range, right from, I suppose ... what? 16, 17 right up until mid 20s and I think even now men in general do think of, you know, make jokes about, you know.
> *SL*: What's it about?
> *H*: I'm thinking of the expression 'rags', you know, 'having the rags up her' is a very common phrase. And so, you know, you'll get nowhere with her she's got the rags up her. It's all to do with sort of having sex with them ...
> *SL*: not being able to have sex with them ...
> *H*: Which is not, in their thoughts, in our thoughts, it's about not being able to have sex with them when they're menstruating, therefore there's no point in having any relationships with them [laughs] [...] ... and at that time of the month they can't have sex so therefore ... you look elsewhere.
> *SL*: So you've heard that from men, over the years in all kinds of ... ?
> *H*: Yeah,
> *SL*: at work?
> *H*: Yes.
> Yeah. Probably not so much recently but there again I haven't worked ... for a long time. The last sort of job where I can remember it happening was probably ten years ago where the boss was, he had a particular sort of hang up about it. He really was a bit weird. He still is [...]
> *SL*: So what does he say?

H: . . . he's a married man but in a hospital situation where
there are a lot of young girls around, young nurses, young
women, who are eligible, if you like, and it's funny, but in
the hospital where we worked, and he still works, there was
a toilet – I used to work in the laboratories – there was a
female toilet just outside the lab so we could always see the
women going to the toilet and he actually used to time
them and if they were taking a long time he used to say 'Oh
well, they've got the rags up, there's no point in chatting
her up' . . . It's like trying to impress people by being that
weird, I don't know . . . There are a lot of jokes that go
around about women who are menstruating. Not jokes but
. . . sort of perversions, if you like. I remember, er, this
particular guy, and the group of us at the time were very,
almost turned on by the fact of suddenly being . . . menstruating. And the fact that it's a bit messy, you know if you
have sex then there's blood everywhere, you know that sort
of thing, it almost became . . . sensual. And there was this
thing about grabbing hold of the tampon string with your
teeth and dragging it out [. . .] [laughs] . . . the sort of, er,
almost nauseous feeling about making love and having oral
sex when someone's menstruating [. . .] And it was really
sort of getting high on . . . on the perverted, well, trying to
make sex during menstruation look perverted and therefore get high on it [. . .]
SL: would he talk about his wife like this? [. . .]
H: O yeah. If the wife's menstruating then he's obliged to,
er, well, there are two things [. . .] One he's obliged to, I
mean I'm particularly thinking about this guy but it is
because he's a very typical example I think. A man whose
wife is menstruating is either obliged to go into this . . . er
sort of nauseous act of making love and having sex in that
taboo situation, or he's got to look somewhere else for sex,
er, yes.

This sort of joking seems to be the most common type. One
man said he thought he was not representative of men
generally because:

I think a lot of men will use it as a derogatory term . . . from
previous experience, they'll say 'well she was fucking
having her period, wasn't she?' meaning they didn't have

sex. 'She wasn't feeling very well', as though she did it on purpose to spite him or something. A lot of men think in those terms . . . (*G*)

Another echoes the point made by *H*:

When I was younger, you know, you used to say 'oh, hard luck', kind of thing [laughs] 'picked the wrong one', that kind of thing [laughs] (*I*)

Women are useful only for sex, and therefore are inter-changeable, disposable. Christabel Pankhurst called this the doctrine of sex slavery: 'That woman is sex and beyond that nothing' (1913).

It is spelt out in the following account, from a man who had worked on an all-male shop floor in an engineering firm.

it was all men there, it was a much more divorced reality . . . the women were at home doing the cooking, and they were there, so they'd talk about sexual conquests if they had any, or they'd talk about how inadequate their wives were if they didn't. And that's where I first got sort of experience of pornography, and the way men make sex out to be dirty, and associate sex with violence, and domination, that to have sex, there was some sort of suffering involved and it was mainly the woman that did all the suffering and the man that did all the raping. I can remember a lot of rape fantasy going on in the pornography and in men's con-versations when I was working there [. . .]
SL: in the pornography, were there any reference to menstruation?
E: No, that's totally unerotic in male conceptions. Yeah, I mean the idea of that . . . you know? It's just a turn off, for men. The jokes that men make about it are sort of like sick jokes you'd make, about Thalidomide dogs being taken for a drag, or something, the same sort of inference that it's a sick joke, you know, menstruation is a sick business, you know [. . .]
SL: it isn't exactly that the women are sick, is it?
E: No, it's more like women, in a group of human beings, are redundant, when they're thought about in association with menstruation. That women and menstruation aren't erotic, you know, you don't sort of talk about them to

stimulate a conversation, like. I can remember one conversation I had with a good friend of mine, and I always
felt like he was different from the norm, like a lot of men,
because he didn't used to make really sick jokes about
women, and he didn't make racist jokes, and he was quite a
gentle man [. . .] He said to me one day, that he knew this
bloke, a friend of his, and he was in the same position as
me, he had friends in different cultural circles like, he
knew bikers, that were real sort of lads, and he knew men
who stayed at home and played chess and he said that he
knew of a young guy, he said he knew that he made love
with his girlfriend, and he said he was a really dirty little
fucker, because she was on, having a period, and he just
pulled the tampax out, and they made love, and like the
idea that he could do that, and not be sort of turned off,
still get a erection, meant that he was so dirty . . . [laughs]
. . . associations that, god, you'd have to be a real mental
case to be able to do that. Like, he's mad, but you know
men say, 'he's a real nutcase', when it can be a quite an
endearing thing, you know. He did used to get down to the
nitty gritty of things, the actual talking about tampax and
periods, but it's such a sort of violent imagery that goes
with it, connotations with sickness, and violence . . .

Julian Wood studied 'boys' sex talk', among some 'disruptive'
London boys and found that 'the reproductive and ex-
cremental aspects of the female body were constantly referred to by the boys in that fixated-disgusted tone edged with
nervousness and surrounded by giggling' (p. 22). In analysing the sexism of this kind of talk, one aspect he describes is
that 'Women are presumed to exist primarily in and through
their bodies as opposed to their whole selves. These bodies
are there to provide pleasure for men but, at the same time,
these bodies are alien (to men) and therefore weird, dirty,
and even sinister' (1983:9).

The ambiguity about whether or not sex during periods is
desirable for men should not be allowed to obscure the
central message of all these 'jokes', which is about control. In
this world view, if sex is to take place, the *man* pulls the
tampon out, he relates only to the woman's vagina, not to her
as a person with her own feelings.

There is an accusation within much of this talk that women 'use' menstruation – one man told me about this in relation to menstrual pain:

I can remember feeling irritated, feeling annoyed, feeling there was nothing ... that I didn't have any control over the situation, and that it was something that women used to exert control. (A)

Women are, I think, felt to be likely to want to avoid work as well as sex. The consequences of this for how menstrual pain is seen are discussed at greater length in Chapter 8. Interestingly, women are in one sense held to be using menstruation to control men, indeed almost to be in control of menstruation itself, while at the same time they are seen as controlled *by* it.

The other major theme of male talk in addition to the pre-occupation with sanitary towels and sexual access, is that women are unreliable, out of control, at 'that time of the month'. I will discuss this more fully elsewhere in the context also of medical ideas about 'premenstrual tension' and menstrual cycle-related mood change generally. It seems to be so, though, that male groups may support a particular set of ideas on this. One account is explicit about this, that 'it was not discussed with the women' (*H*). Another shows how one set of ideas runs into another. He has just been discussing jokes about jamrags, and has said that he hears less of this now. I asked:

Do you think that's because you've got different friends, or because it's an adolescent thing?
D: I think it's because I've got different friends. Still get people, sometimes at work and things, who just seem very intolerant of ... I don't think they actually know that women are having a period or anything, it's like I said before, women don't tend to say, but you do get men who kind of, if a woman comes out with some sort of, if someone seems a bit on edge or uptight, they'd sort of start saying she must be having her period, and stuff like that. Not actually joking about it, just saying 'Oh my god, you know, bloody women, having periods and things, you know' ... But no, the joking bit seems to have gone out, I

think that is because I've got different friends. I'm sure if,
like I've had summer jobs and things, on building sites and
stuff like that, the same sort of thing goes on there.

A man who said he had not heard adult men speak about
menstruation produced this statement of what he might
expect to hear:

No, I mean, I can trade in stereotypes a bit, but I'm not
sure I've actually heard them used ... about women's
behaviour being in some way either stigmatised, or justified or excused because ... being touchy, or inward-
looking, or whatever, but I'm not sure I've actually heard it
done. I don't think so. Not that I remember, oddly
enough. (C)

LANGUAGE: EUPHEMISMS AND TERMS OF ABUSE

Although there has been very little research of any sort done
on men's talk about menstruation, there is some evidence
that my material is likely to be fairly typical of Western
cultures.

It was a study of menstrual euphemisms which first drew
my attention to the possibility that men and women actually
have two quite separate vocabularies and hence ranges of
discourse about menstruation. The first studies of language
about menstruation merely collected terms from informants
of both sexes and recorded them as 'of' the culture (Joffe
1948; Boone 1954; Larsen 1963). But in her article 'American Menstrual Euphemisms' (1975) Virginia L. Ernster
sorted contributions to a folklore archive into those coming
from women and those from men, and further enquired into
where her informants had learnt the terms they contributed.
She found two different sets of terms – the ones men used
having 'sexual and derogatory connotations'. A wider range
of terms was contributed by women, these being used partly
so that women could tell other women that they were
menstruating without any men present realising their meaning, and partly to communicate to male partners with less
embarrassment.

When I asked men in my sample what words they had

heard used for menstruation, they generally volunteered terms they had heard from women. Most of them felt that 'period' was the most commonly used term, followed by 'that time of the month'. Variations on this, adding a negative tinge, are 'wrong time of the month', 'her funny time of the month', 'bad time of the month'. Two mentioned women referring to it as 'being on' and another stressed the use of euphemisms:

> it's more [whispered] 'it's that time of the month, you know, it's the monthlies'. Or even more it's, if someone's been a bit annoyed, or a bit irritable, and you say 'ooh, what's wrong with her?', they say [whispers] 'you know' . . . If you're lucky you cotton on straight away so you don't make a fool of yourself. But they usually use safe words, they don't relate to it exactly, nobody likes to say . . . you have to try and guess what it is if you want to know. (K)

Only two men had heard 'the curse' used – this was a term I suggested to several men, thinking it fairly common, and some were quite startled by it. One man said 'tummy pains' would be used in his home to refer to menstrual pain.

'Menstruate' was mentioned as never being used in ordinary speech (I think Americans use it more), though one man said he and his wife refer to it very clinically as 'day 28' – a usage learnt through paying attention to her menstrual cycle while she was trying to conceive. Two other idiosyncratic usages were mentioned – one man's mother called it 'little girls', and a woman friend of another referred to her periods as 'giving birth'.

The variety of terms which the men in my sample had learnt from women is not very great. The contrast with women's language is striking. Jane Black has informally collected terms from women who attend her women's health classes in Manchester. Her list goes as follows:

> Has it come?; That time of the month; The friend; Lady in the red dress; I've got a visitor; Monthlies; Are you on?; Unwell/ill; Issue; Jam and bread; Grandma's here; Aunt Susie; The reds are in; Are you seeing red?; Poorly; Curse; Redlight; The red flag's flying; The captain's aboard; Star period; United's playing at home today (a Manchester football reference!). (Lee 1984)

Women explained to Ernster that one purpose of women's terms is to avoid male attention, so it makes sense that many men would not necessarily recognise them.

Terms learnt from men were usually not mentioned when I asked about euphemisms, but came up when I asked directly about talk about menstruation in male groups. The majority of terms refer to sanitary towels: 'jam rags', 'jammy rags', 'jam sandwich', 'jam roll', 'having the rags up'. One man said that terms from men 'would have been more derogatory' (*M*); one called saying 'jam rags' 'really crude' (*D*). The words might also be used in name calling among boys – one man explained that it meant 'you prat' (*Collins English Dictionary*: an incompetent or ineffectual person).

The only other terms mentioned as used by men were that one man's father called it 'women's troubles' if he mentioned it at all (*B*), and that another recalled a dispute with a female supervisor at work where afterwards another man had consoled him by putting her behaviour down to 'the monthlies' (*K*).

British men's terms parallel the American ones in many ways. Ernster found the term 'on the rag' to be the most common, accounting for 16 out of the 31 expressions contributed by men. Her informants explained several different ways in which the terms might be used, including as a derogatory term to other males. If said to another male, it might imply that his being angry or upset was due to his girlfriend being menstruating and his not having sexual access to her. Or it might simply be an analogy: 'if used in reference to a guy, it is highly insulting since you are saying that his moodiness is like that of a girl with menstrual cramps' (1975:11).

Only one other set of terms was mentioned more than once – 'flying the flag' and its variants 'flying Baker' (refers to a Navy warning flag), 'The red flag is up' or 'riding the flag'. Other terms contributed by males that Ernster mentions are 'Too wet to plow', 'riding the cotton pony'. 'manhole cover' and 'coyote sandwich'. These last refer to lack of sexual access to the woman, as do all the terms mentioned, although 'on the rag' seems to have stronger connotations of being 'high-strung', irritable, moody.

The emphasis on sanitary wear in US and British men's

talk is striking. There is, further, a common term of abuse in Afro-Caribbean slang 'ras claat' or 'tor ass clot', from 'your arse cloth' – yet another reference to sanitary towels. This language draws attention to the very thing which women put such energy into hiding. Other shared themes are the preoccupation with sexual access and the accusations of emotional instability in women.

Some menstrual 'jokes' are recounted in G. Legman's unspeakably nasty book *The Rationale of the Dirty Joke* (1969). Legman fails to distance himself from the joke-tellers he discusses, and we may take his work as more 'of' than 'about' male culture. He categorises these jokes within a section entitled 'Sex Hate' as dealing with 'Menstruation and other Rejections' and under 'Displaced Aggressions'.

One joke he reports emphasises the impact upon men of lack of sexual access to their wives during periods:

A super-salesman is being watched from behind the door by the territorial manager, who is stupefied to see the salesman run up a customer's request for a fishing rod into a whole fishing kit, hip boots and hunting clothes, an outdoor barbecue set, a new automobile, cub airplane ('for those whoppers in Canada') and a country home to match. 'How were you able to do it?' asks the manager, when the sucker has gone. 'Oh, I knew he was in the right frame of mind,' says the super-salesman calmly. 'He originally didn't even want the fishing pole. He just came in to buy a box of Kotex for his wife.'

In another case, it is Legman's own comment which reinforces my analysis – that he himself perceives references to menstruation as 'sick':

The following burlesque skit was seen in a Florida night-club, 1946: 'The master-of-ceremonies' stooge pretends to be drunk and confides that there is a slot-machine in the ladies' toilet. 'Sure there is', he insists, when the master-of-ceremonies disagrees: 'where do you think I got this collar for my tux?' (Pulls out a woman's Kotex pad and hangs it around his neck, bringing down the house. Then as topper:) 'Well, maybe it isn't a collar. I could use it as a simonizing rag for my car, except for these two pins.'

(Dangles the pad and belt-pins before the audience.) 'I only went for cigarettes anyway.'
People who think that 'sick humour', or shocker nightclub acts began with Lenny Bruce in the 1960s have never been around.

Two jokes on the same sort of theme place menstruation within the context of the rapist mentality – it is seen as provocation to violence:

> A bride refuses to let her husband consummate their marriage the first night because she is menstruating. The second night she has nervous diarrhoea (or a head-cold). The third night he appears at her bedside in hip-boots and a raincoat, carrying a storm lantern, and announces 'Mud or blood, shit or flood, McClanahan rides tonight!'

> A man takes his girl out for a buggy ride. He drops the reins and begins to hug and kiss her, but she refuses, saying that she is menstruating. 'You know, there's another way you can satisfy me', he says, but she explains that she has piles. He drives a little further, stops the horse, gets out, picks up a rock, gets back in and says, 'Now just you tell me that you got lockjaw, and I'll crush your skull!' (pp. 278, 279)

PORNOGRAPHY

There are levels of male culture where menstruation is not even mentioned. Andrea Dworkin considers the derivation of the word pornography:

> The word pornography does not have any other meaning than the one cited here, the graphic depiction of the lowest whores. Whores exist to serve men sexually. Whores exist only within a framework of male sexual domination. Indeed, outside that framework the notion of whores would be absurd and the usage of women as whores would be impossible. (1979:200)

The valuation of women in pornography is a secondary theme in that the degradation of women exists in order to postulate, exercise, and celebrate male power. Male power, in degrading women, is first concerned with itself, its perpetuation, expansion, intensification, and elevation. (p. 25)

Dworkin wrote to me (1982: personal communication) that 'There is no doubt that there is a general refusal to show menstruation – I don't know why' and further:

The only specific reference (that I can remember) that I found in the pornography I read to menstruation was in Sade's *120 Days of Sodom*. As I remember, somewhere towards the end (after a thousand or so pages of unmitigated atrocity), Sade's imagination for horror spent, he mentions menstruating women and blacks. There is in pornography a lot of slicing of female genitals – obvious references to menstruation, I think, though in the peculiar code of the woman hater; there is also one special kind of lesbian photo-layout that recurs constantly, which is two women smearing paint all over each other – at first I couldn't figure out how this was a sexual act in any sense (let alone one so common that porn. mag after porn. mag has it represented) but then came upon a comment from Freud to Jung that menstrual blood represented excrement, after which the endless smearing of paint seemed obvious – paint representing menstrual blood (woman with woman equals essence of woman) representing filth. The other imagery related to menstruation in pornography is simply the enormous overload of instruments near, around, or in the vagina that are knife-like (vagina means sheath). Larry Flynt, publisher of *Hustler*, has published at least one picture of supposedly female genitals overflowing with pus.

Elaine and English Showalter also mention Sade's reference to menstruation as notable for its restraint and as unusual among Victorian pornographers (1972). Note that Sade mentions menstruation and Black people at the same time. In my own memory of hearing, as a young girl, the story about the Hells Angels' initiation rituals which the men's group mentions, there was this same connection made. The men won 'red wings' by having sex with a menstruating woman, and 'black wings' for having sex with a Black woman.

When I write 'having sex' I am aware that rape is quite likely
what is actually meant. This kind of male discourse makes no
distinction between the two, for the woman's point of view is
irrelevant. The element of pollution-belief, of disgust, which
forms part of white racism, appears to be sexualised into a
form which has something in common with the male view of
menstruating 'women', seen presumably as menstruating
white women.

It looks, then, as if menstruation has no place in the pure
male-centred world of pornographic 'sex'. It cannot be
recruited to enhance male power. The joking among men
may therefore police the periphery: control male anxiety
(and any real threat from women) that women's bodies as
they actually are might violate the men's fantasy world. We
might see this as in a sense a low level of male culture, where
the tacky realities of life meet pure male fantasy. We have
seen how obscenity was used by men to bully women trying to
raise the issue of taxation of sanitary wear in the public
sphere, a good example of how the periphery is policed to
maintain the masculine purity of the body politic. A report
on media and sexism in *Spare Rib* (O'Sullivan 1984) mentions
another interesting case. It quotes an article in the printwor-
kers' magazine *Print* (February 1984) which used typog-
raphical errors in anti-women obscenity. The piece is titled
'Study groups to aid women'. It reads:

> The WEA over the last few years has made women's
> studies a priority. These curses are available throughout
> the cuntry, and are aimed at questioning the role that
> women are expected to play in society.

To summarise the messages male culture conveys about
menstruation: women's inferiority to men lies at the back of
it all, so much taken for granted that it need not be spelt out.
Two specific aspects of this are (a) that women's genitals are
disgusting/produce disgusting substances (this is expressed
in the attention to sanitary towels), and (b) that women are
ruled by their hormones. Menstruation is also sexualised – it
is most often joked about as if related to men, to heterosexuality. Male culture sees women's bodies as existing to serve
male sexual desires – menstruation is dealt with as female
resistance, justifying either violation or the man going else-

where for sex. Menstruation is thus used to express the idea that women are interchangeable – if they are sexually useless to a man, they may as well not exist. There is nothing erotic (as in sensual) about this joking – in so far as it is sexual, the sexuality is entirely about power and control.

The male culture portrays men as absolutely in control of sex with women. When it is confronted with menstruation, which has nothing essentially to do with men or sex, it perceives this internal female phenomenon as somehow threatening to male power. Therefore male joking attempts to bring menstruation within the arena of sexuality – under male-centred heterosexual control.

Sanitary towels seem to crystallise in one idea everything that men find offensive about menstruation. Since they have nothing whatever to do with men, they seem to symbolise women out of control to men. A friend described to me having seen a group of young boys run through Boots the Chemists' supermarket in Lancaster, spitting on the packets of sanitary towels as they went.

MUST WE LISTEN?

But why should we concern ourselves with this? Why is joking among men important to women? Conspiracy theory tends to be used only as a term of abuse in sociology, but the fact remains that there exist in our society a whole spectrum of men-only groupings which exclude women and within which male supremacist ideology is unchallenged. This must affect relations between the sexes, and if we are to under-stand the gender order we must look at every part of the society, not just those which are easily made available to our eyes.

Mary Daly calls this male talk 'spooking from the locker room'. She writes that:

> most of the time this language is used in all-male environ-ments. Yet it is the common male view of all women and, although most women do not hear it directly, we receive the message in a muted way. It is conveyed through silences, sneers, jeers, excessive politeness, paternalistic

praise and disapproval, aggressive physical contact (an arm around the shoulder, a pat on the behind), invasive stares. Since women often do not *hear* the messages of obscenity directly, we are spooked. For the invasive presence and the intent are both audible and inaudible, visible and invisible.

Moreover, women are conditioned to pretend not to hear/see the constant and violent bombardments of obscenity, for we have been taught the lesson that since verbal violence is a 'substitute' for physical assault, we should be grateful for such seemingly mild manifestations of misogynism. Thus, spooking from the locker room, the unacknowledged noise of omnipresent male obscenities, constitute the 'background music' which continually confuses and fragments consciousness. Exorcising this invasive presence requires acknowledging its existence and refusing to shuffle. This has the effect of bringing the spookers out into the open. (1978:323)

Paradoxically, Legman comes up with the same sort of analysis. He sees dirty jokes as a sort of 'verbal rape' – 'a vocal and inescapable sexual relationship with other persons of the desired sex'. He suggests that such joking also has a secondary function 'to absorb and control anxiety' (pp. 13, 14).

Women anthropologists who have studied life in English villages have found this sort of behaviour important in maintaining male domination at the local level. Imray and Middleton (1983) write about Audrey Middleton's experience when she violated the rules about a woman's place in the village cricket club and challenged the men's authority. She was at once subject to obscene joking, placing her as 'an object to be screwed'. Anne Whitehead (1976) witnessed pub life in a Herefordshire village which hinged around men vying for superiority in constant joking and teasing. She observed that women were used as 'counters in joking currency' (p. 192), having no existence in that culture as human individuals. She reports that women appear in the joking in at least three ways: firstly, there is obscene, vulgar language; secondly, there are contemptuous and degrading stereotypes of women, part of the ideology of sex differences; thirdly, jokes are sometimes concerned with control over specific wives. We can see that each of these three types

of reference appear in the range of male talk about menstruation – there are obscenities: 'jam rag', 'having the rags
up her'; there are stereotypes of female unreliability and
emotionality; and there is concern over control of individual
women, in this case focusing on the issue of sexual service
from menstruating women.

Whitehead writes that 'It is difficult for men to treat their
relationships with wives as relationships with people when
wives are used as objects in another arena' (p. 195). We may
then consider what effect male joking about menstruation
has upon men's individual relationships with women, especially given how difficult it is for women to initiate discussion
with men on this subject.

So what is the nature of these male groups, this male
culture? Where and when do they tend to occur, how can we
characterise them? As a woman, I cannot answer these
questions properly, for my access to the answers is too
limited. I feel some embarrassment in presenting the data in
this chapter for I know it to be incomplete, but am unable (or
perhaps unwilling) to complete it. No man I have spoken to
about this has denied knowledge of it – none has volunteered
to tell me anything more. One or two have suggested that
there is 'worse than that' – in such a tone that I have not
pressed them for details. There is some absurdity in my
situation – one of a minority of women in a social science
profession dominated by men striving by roundabout means
to discover aspects of 'our' culture which are common
knowledge among men.

During my work I was often made aware that I was asking
to be told things women are not meant to hear. Two men
themselves became aware of this. One said at one point
'Sorry I'm being so upfront about it. Do you find that
offensive?' (E), and the other also almost apologised for what
he told me: 'I have to be frank' (H). These were the two men
quoted above who gave the fullest accounts of male culture. I
noticed that several of the other men said that while they had
heard such talk, they could not remember jokes or words
they'd heard used. This further reinforced my impression
that these are sexual insults which are meant to be kept
among men. The telling of these created unease within the
interviews. Several of the men told me quite personal details

about their sexual experiences, and, for instance, their feelings about blood – but this did not create the same kind of awkwardness. One responded to my prompting him to tell me about men's talk in more detail like this: 'Yes. Not sure if we can talk further about that. I don't know what sort of area you're interested . . .' (*M*)

When I was asking about joking among men, several of them would refer to 'the sort of things boys say', 'in the schoolboy sense', or just say 'you know', appealing to a commonsense knowledge that I did not have, and one man flatly refused to spell it out for me. I came away with the general impression that what they were ashamed of (if shame is the right word) was not their personal feelings, but their participation in male groups which talk about women in this way.

Some men reflected further about how they saw their participation in such groups, relating this to their relationships with women:

> Again I was fairly conservative, and I never ever talked to anybody else about our sexual relationship [. . .]
>
> Now in the last few years, obviously I would, and think it was rather stupid that I didn't . . . I might sort of go along with all sorts of sexist remarks, dirty jokes, the whole gambit, without, particularly, thinking there was anything terribly wrong with it, but when it came to our own sexual relationship, then that was just not on. (*N*)

> Yeah because at the same time as realising menstruation wasn't a bad thing, I began to stop being involved in those sort of situations where those sort of jokes would be told, so I never really did communicate to women that those jokes were being made about them . . . because at the same time as not wanting to be offensive, or hurtful about it . . . but I mean my relationship with X is close enough for us to be able to talk about things like that, say, oh, the boys at school used to say so and so . . . but I never really did, I don't think I communicated to her what they really were. (*E*)

Not all male groups discuss menstruation or for that matter anything to do with women. For instance boys in single-sex schools seemed to joke about such things far less than groups of boys in mixed schools. And in adult life too it would seem that male groups which co-exist closely with mixed-sex situations are the most actively unpleasant about women.

The essential point seems to be that the men are moving individually between the family where they have contact with women, and the male group, whether it is a work group or a leisure one. One man describes how this relationship works in one situation:

But I think it's very much connected with bravado . . . you know, it really is tied up to that. And therefore references to women become commonplace, but it's as sexual objects . . . you know . . . Well, I play football Sunday mornings, so 'what were you doing last night?' kind of discussion, they predominate . . . and even at a sort of mildly serious level, a serious joke, no sex before the game kind of discussion, so feeling [unclear] sophisticated comment, I suppose, rather than just the crude thing, club rule. Um, I don't think within that there is a great deal of discussion about menstruation, I think there's reference to periods, I wouldn't exaggerate it . . . Because it's not, it doesn't seem to be the most attractive way of expressing it . . . (M)

Many of the men who told me about jokes about menstruation emphasised that menstruation was not a central topic of such joking. What is central is 'sex' – meaning the sexual degradation of women.

However this kind of male talk must certainly be partly responsible for men's attitudes to menstrual etiquette between women and men. If the male culture regards menstruation as purely discrediting, entirely digusting, then it is only to be expected that well-intentioned men will tend to avoid talk with women about it, assuming that they might easily give offence. Young girls can grow up hearing no mention of menstruation, discovering the 'taboo' when they discover menstruation itself. Young boys may have the same experience, but they are just as likely to grow up hearing talk about it which conveys men's belief in the inferiority of women, rather than any 'information' on the physical facts of menstruation. The silences and the obscenities are intimately connected.

Although I have referred to 'male culture' in a general

way, my evidence relates to white English culture of the
1980s specifically. One would need much more data to work
out what would be the limits of this kind of ideology in terms
of social structures which would support it. It is clear from
the contents of the men's talk that how men speak about
menstruation is strongly connected to surrounding sets of
beliefs held in society.

5 Interpreting Attitudes Towards Menstruation: Is Reproduction Central?

Menstruation is sometimes described as 'the weeping of a disappointed uterus'. (Sir Norman Jeffcoate, *Principles of Gynaecology*, 1975)

Both menstrual segregation and male segregation practices can be interpreted as elaborate public expressions of the belief in the polluting nature of fertile women. [...] our theory of ritual politics argues that these practices are a response to the dilemma that a woman's fertility creates for her husband. (K. E. and J. M. Paige, *The Politics of Reproductive Ritual*, 1981)

Menstruation ... is the time when the healthy woman may draw upon abilities and capacities that are not related to the values of ovulation and childbearing, but that are instead related to that other side of her nature, of independence of thought and action. It is the exact counterpart, but in an opposite sense, of the ovulation. At ovulation she wishes to receive, accept, build, if she desires a child. But from menstruation there is a different set of energies available to her of receiving, accepting, building the child which is herself. (Penelope Shuttle and Peter Redgrove, *The Wise Wound*, 1978)

Whether or not woman was actually the originator of taboo, the mere existence of a menstrual taboo signifies, for better or for worse, powers only half-understood; the fear of woman and the mystery of her motherhood. (Adrienne Rich, *Of Woman Born*, 1977)

The writers quoted above include feminists and anti-feminists, rationalists and mystics — what they have in common is that they all attempt to explain cultural attitudes to menstruation by reference to the reproductive process. In their view, social behaviour around menstruation arises more or less directly from its place in biological reproduction. This is a very popular way of looking at menstrual etiquette, the one most people will draw on if pressed for an opinion about why people behave as they do.

Interestingly, there are great differences between the different theories, because each writer has a different view of the meaning of the whole business of conception, pregnancy and childbearing.

Gynaecologists like Jeffcoate tend to take the purpose of a woman's existence to be childbearing, and calmly attribute intentions along these lines to parts of her body. Menstruation may then be treated as evidence that a particular woman is not fulfilling her proper function. Other theories are rather more subtle, but they too tend to read the theorists' beliefs about reproductive biology into people's behaviour without reference to any specific individuals' own account. Paige and Paige take menstruation to represent the fact that a woman is potentially capable of childbearing, while Shuttle and Redgrove take it as some sort of anti-reproductive statement or state. They would have it that women's entire being vacillates monthly between preoccupation with babies and preoccupation with self.

The feminists, Rich (1977) and Mary O'Brien (1981), agree with Paige and Paige that menstruation is understood as a sign of fertility, but argue further that men are by nature threatened by women's childbearing ability and have organised a woman-hating culture to defend their egos from this threat.

BIOLOGY AND WOMEN'S OPPRESSION

It is a central feature of patriarchy that men explain and justify their power by reference to biology – patriarchal ideology revolves around representing female and male bodies as naturally expressing their different places as oppressed and oppressor. Nature is said to determine that a woman's place will be forever where men want her.

This is accepted as a commonplace among feminists, but it

is far less clear how we should attack it. For biology, at some level, is real. Some feminists, for example Shulamith Firestone (1971), have argued that women's oppression can only be overcome if biology itself can be changed, in this case by artificial reproduction. Others, like Adrienne Rich in *Of Woman Born* (1977), have accepted the common patriarchal view that women are oppressed because of their childbearing abilities, but seek to reinterpret that ability as a power rather than a weakness.

I find myself very reluctant to accept the notion that women's situation springs from the nature of human reproduction in this simple way. Perhaps this is because it does not fit with my own experience: I have not been forced into childbearing, and yet I am still oppressed as a woman. It makes little sense to me that the oppression of all women – including lesbians, old women, girl children, infertile women – should be seen as a side-effect of the attempt to control our reproductive capacity.

My view is that feminists need to look critically at this commonsense way of making links between biology and behaviour wherever it emerges.

Focusing on menstruation, then, how do we approach theorising about it? To me, any social theory has to develop from and be adequate to explain how the people it concerns understand their own actions and beliefs. This is not to say that people are always fully aware of why they do or think something, but that theories should at the very least take account of what they do think they are doing. A useful social theory, for me, is one which helps people to make sense of and therefore to gain power over their own lives. It follows that any theory which cannot be made sense of by those it is supposed to be about cannot be correct.

At the most obvious level, this means abandoning theories which offer universal cross-cultural explanations for social practices. Black feminists have pointed out many ways in which the attempt to generalise about sexual politics from specific, white, experience can lead to racist attempts to impose inappropriate theories upon women of other cultures, living in different conditions (Moraga and Anzaldua 1981; Combahee River Collective 1983).

From what is known about practices relating to menstruation in many cultures (which is severely limited) it is clear that these practices are very various, as are practices relating to all bodily matters. There may also be some common practices which are widely shared. However the first task is to understand the significance of such a practice in one culture, not to produce an overarching theory based on only superficial knowledge of many cultures. I was interested, therefore, to set the 'grand' theories beside some data on how some specific white British men regard menstruation, to get some comparison of how the two fit together.

MEN'S VIEW

I had originally intended to explore directly the question of the way in which men understood the relation between menstruation and reproduction in my interviews, but I was put off this idea at an early stage by the responses I got to this kind of questioning. My first respondent was emphatically negative on this question:

> Well . . . in a biological sense, of going back to why we're made the way we are . . . yes, but um, I suppose I tend to take those sort of things, not exactly for granted, but . . . I don't have a sort of intellectual yearning to know about questions like that. I mean I think the social understandings of biological facts are very interesting, but I don't think I need to know why women menstruate, in a biological sense. (A)

In the men's group, too, some of these ideas are emphatically rejected. This discussion gives a very interesting example of how theories feed back to the people they concern. In the men's group, following from a discussion about whether menstruation is painful for women because it is devalued or whether it is naturally problematic, one man asks:

> —Do men feel an envy, an envy? I don't mean of the pain particularly, but of women having that as being in some way symbolic of being able to have children. . . . Is there something that says that's an important thing that we haven't got? That they have? No?

[pause]
—not conscious of it
—[indistinct] are you?
—I don't know, when people were talking about it as
  something which happens every month, and that it
  represents something . . . a mysterious thing to which I
  can have no access, which is debarred for me, forever,
  because of my biological nature, then yes, I suppose I
  might be a bit. It's not a desire to have those experiences
  particularly, but it seems very other than . . . seems very
  different, something that's very inaccessible. I take it this
  is just me?
—[sigh] (Group)

As the speaker says, resenting the idea that something a
woman experiences is inaccessible to oneself and envying it
are two entirely different things.

When I was asking general questions about menstruation,
men rarely related it spontaneously to reproduction.
Although these men were on the whole well-informed about
the biological significance of menstruation, from school sex
education lessons and so forth, this was not high in their
consciousness on the subject.

When I questioned them specifically, three men spoke
about having anxiously awaited a period when they feared a
woman with whom they had a sexual relationship might be
pregnant. Two, one of them the only gay man in the group,
also mentioned having been aware of women friends being
in this situation. One man tells of a particular incident in the
past:

I don't specifically remember an occasion with my first
relationship, there must have been some . . . fairly sure
there were. With my present relationship, when we first
got together, which was a very romantic period, at the time
it seemed quite ordinary, looking back it was loony – we
didn't really discuss the question of using any contraception, and so that went on for a while . . . suddenly came
round and realised what was going on and so sweated . . .
sat and sweated for about two weeks, but fortunately . . . a
source of relief. Put it in those terms, yes I can remember
other relationships with women friends, certainly [. . .]
waiting on periods, see. (M)

Only one man had been aware of awaiting the time of a period hopefully, when his wife was trying to get pregnant. They had difficulty in conceiving and for a while they were extremely aware of her menstrual cycle, trying to time intercourse during her fertile phase. When I asked him whether he had been very conscious of the days she was due, he replied:

> I hadn't . . . Yes I suppose we were [. . .] Yes, I suppose we must have been, and there would therefore be a disappointment when and if the period came, yes and it would therefore signal that. I hadn't really thought of that, but it must have had that meaning, yes. I'm more aware of the pressure on timing that awareness of the cycle produced when we were trying to work out ovulation. And it's true, obviously, that a period meant lack of success that month, but I think this is more a male point of view, I was more worried about having to get the timing for having sex right in terms of ovulation. It's a real turn-off, let me tell you . . . no. I wasn't suited to that at all, I didn't find that fun a bit. (*C*)

Again the connection is recognised once it is suggested, but it is not spontaneously seen as important.

Another type of reproductive context for menstruation is as a time in the menstrual cycle when a woman is unlikely to conceive. Two of the men I interviewed spoke about menstruation as a good time for having sex since the risk of pregnancy would be minimal. One man raised this in response to my questions about his experience of waiting for an overdue period:

> I don't think I've had many relationships where there's been anxiety about being overdue. Only two or three occasions I think. I certainly remember times when someone either was or had just been menstruating and my trying to persuade them, sometimes successfully, sometimes not, that we can actually have intercourse, because she's pretty safe and she saying 'well, I'd rather not because it's not 100% safe' and me persisting and saying 'it's pretty well 100%'. (*H*)

Another said:

> I can remember vague references to the fact that it was,
> that there was a sense in which it was a good time to do it
> because you knew you were safe – I mean that was a bit of a
> common parlance, that I'd picked up somewhere, but it
> didn't really arise. . . . (N)

But awareness about fertility generally (for instance, recognition of their own ability to father children) varied enormously within my sample. Within the men's group, at one point one man is saying that he enjoys sex more during menstruation than at other times and he continues:

> —I think the extent to which that's true is partly that the
> fear of pregnancy is almost nil [. . .] I think you can be
> much more relaxed in that sense, so that you can actually
> enjoy sex. . . . That relates to contraception as well I
> think, specially if you're using contraception other than
> the Pill – you can be much more relaxed about things.
> —God, I never worry about that. . . . I never think about
> people getting pregnant when I'm making love. In any
> circumstances.
> —Yes, yes,
> —except if you're using durex . . . or sometimes the cap.
> . . . If you're conscious of it of course you are conscious
> of it . . . and I've never been conscious of the coil, or
> certainly the Pill.
> —Mmm.
> —I've never been able to forget coils.
> —No, I haven't, did you get . . . for what reason do you say
> that?
> —Just because they're so ever-present.
> —Did they pierce you?
> —Oh, god, yes! [. . .] I didn't know what it was the first time
> I came across one, I nearly died. (Group)

The group discussion, when it briefly focuses upon contraception, dwells solely on the inconvenience it may impose upon men. Indeed, for at least one man, being aware of the issue of contraception is confused with whether or not he can physically detect it. On the whole, these men seem extraordi-

narily unconcerned with the reproductive aspects of their sex
lives. Evidently even by this relatively pro-feminist group,
women continue to be awarded full responsibility for fertility
control.

It seems likely that such blithe indifference to these issues
is a particularly modern phenomenon. Recent years have
seen a tendency for men to be held less and less responsible
for pregnancies they had a part in creating. 'Shotgun'
weddings are far less common than they were. I cannot here
properly consider the question of why this should be – new
technology, changed social ideas about sexuality, the availability of safer abortions, must all be factors. Among my small
sample, in any case, it tends to be the older men who are
conscious of the reproductive importance of menstruation.

Looking at other ways in which men made connections
from menstruation to reproduction, there were three who
made an emotional, impressionistic connection of it with
aspects of childbirth. These ideas all came up in response to a
question I asked each man about how he saw menstrual
blood, whether he saw it as similar to other blood or as
something different. In each case the man seems to draw on
a connection to childbirth to explain his feelings, though the
feelings are different in each case:

> I don't think I do tend to associate menstrual blood which I
> would associate with an injury. ... I sort of see it as a
> non-violent association. And having seen natural child-
> birth take place, and things. ... Yeah, it's quite sacred for
> me, and the sort of, the smells, and the character of the
> actual blood is much less violent, much more primal. ...
> Perhaps primal is the wrong word? A sort of age old
> feeling, a sort of respect for one's body, or for another
> person's body, and what comes out of it. And what goes in.
> Yeah, I suppose that's it ... just sort of unifying body-
> mind, getting an impression of people's bodies and minds
> together in a relationship [. . .] I find that I still have to sort
> of battle quite a lot to even just sort of feel easy with the
> ideas and information that I'm getting about things like
> that. I think initially I was quite sort of tokenistic, saying
> ah, I'm very much into the women's movement, I'm
> interested in women, and feeling totally committed per-

sonally, but in reality I was just sort of being quite dogmatic and quite condescending. (*E*)

J: Well in a sense I feel the same about it. In another sense, when a woman I know is menstruating I feel quite protective towards her. . . . I've thought about this a lot and I've tried to work out why. . . . It's not just because of any pain she might be in, there is also another element, I'm not sure why, I just feel very protective.
SL: That she's vulnerable somehow?
J: Yeah I mean, the girl I'm having a relationship with at the moment, her periods aren't that much of a problem to her, she isn't particularly vulnerable, so it's not . . . I don't know what it is. It's got something to do . . . I've got some feelings about birth or something, I'm not really sure exactly why I feel it. But I just get to feel very soft, protective. . . .
SL: as if . . . that it makes you think of her as a person who could give birth? . . . or?
J: yes. Partly that it makes me think of her as someone who could give birth. Partly because I feel it's almost as if it is a small birth.

This last man has a woman friend who refers to her periods as 'giving birth'.

These speeches in themselves do support the idea that some men at least relate to menstruation as a reproductive event, or as somehow representing childbearing. However these men are a minority of the sample – others made quite different responses to my question.

I only managed to interview one man with grown-up daughters. I was particularly interested in whether or not he saw his daughters' menstruation as signifying their fertility. His response to my questioning about his thoughts about his daughters' first periods was most definite:

No, I didn't relate the two – yeah, I didn't relate the two events at all, in that sense, and still don't really. I don't think to look for telltale signs that they're not having them to find out whether they're pregnant. . . . I do see the two issues as not being connected really. (*N*)

Individual men, then do not seem readily to make the link between menstruation and the reproductive process. There are within our culture forms of discourse which do make this link more emphatically –. an important one being within medical discourse.

MEDICAL VIEWS

In contrast to the views of the laymen I interviewed, medical men do understand menstruation very much within the interpretive framework of their understanding of the reproductive process.

Gynaecologists would be expected to be especially focused upon the reproductive system, since this is the object of their work. The ideology they promote is one which defines woman primarily as a childbearing creature. One of the ways in which they interpret menstruation seems to be as a sign that the woman is not as she should be: pregnant or lactating. Menstruation is not felt to be entirely a natural event, and on the whole they are uninterested to the point of hostility in menstrual problems. One essay on the 'Control of Menstruation', published in 1977, sets out an alarmingly common line of thinking on menstruation:

> We have become conditioned to regard the menstrual cycle as the norm and pregnancy as an unnatural event. Contraceptive medication is designed to mimic this 'normal' cycle and menstruation is encouraged to occur once a month. But we tend to forget that in free-living communities of wild primates, menstruation is the exception rather than the rule. To undergo a repeated succession of sterile cycles is abnormal, and pathological changes may ensue. Is it not time that we re-examined our approach to contraception, to see whether this monthly turmoil would not be better abolished rather than encouraged? (Short 1977)

As has frequently been pointed out, this sort of reasoning from other species to establish the 'natural' state of human beings is always highly selective of the features it seeks to encourage. (See also Hubbard *et al* 1979; Brighton Women and Science Group 1980.)

But the medical view incorporates a number of aspects of the male perspective on menstruation, and contains its own contradictions – it cannot be summed up simply as seeing menstruation in reproductive terms. Menstruation itself and especially menstrual problems are also seen as evidence of women's physical inferiority, and as signs of a refusal of the female role. Women, accused of inventing menstrual pain, are suspected of trying to avoid housework or 'their responsibilities' as much as of refusing childbearing, though childbirth is often believed to be a solution. Medical men also share with other men the idea that menstruation is importantly a sexual event, signifying something about the woman's sexuality.

IS OUR CULTURE UNIQUE?

But is this tendency for modern men not to see menstruation as centrally a reproductive matter specific to our alienated modern culture? Might it not be a product of increased control over fertility, the drop in the birth rate? I think there is reason to believe that a strong consciousness of menstruation's role in reproduction could be the exception rather than the rule.

Clearly menstruation is something which happens to women and not to men – so is childbearing. Evidently it relates to the same areas of the body as does reproduction – but then this area could be seen as primarily a 'sexual' area rather than a 'reproductive' one. It is also observable that menstruation stops when a woman is pregnant. But the significance of all these facts is far from obvious.

Western medicine did not come up with an accurate account of ovulation and its relation to menstruation until this century. The ovum was only discovered in 1827. Seventeenth-century medicine operated with complex theories of the economy of the blood within the body and saw menstruation as the way in which women disposed of excess, potentially toxic, blood. Most diseases affecting women were thought to result from too much or too little menstrual flow (Hilda Smith 1976). Here is one explanation given for menstruation:

> Women were made to stay at home and to look after the
> Household employments, and because such business is
> accomplished with much ease, without any vehement stir-
> rings of the body, therefore hath provident Nature
> assigned to them their monthly courses, that by the benefit
> of those evacuations, the feculent and corrupt bloud,
> might be purified, which otherwise, as being the purst part
> of the bloud, would turne to ranke poyson; like the seed
> ejaculated out of its proper vessells. (Fontanus 1652:
> quoted in Smith 1976)

One writer who has looked seriously at similar problems of
interpretation is Gilbert Lewis (1980). He studied the Gnau,
whose men practise various rites involving making the penis
bleed, rites of a kind which are quite common in various
forms throughout New Guinea. Ethnographers of other
tribes have interpreted these rites as being evidence that the
men envy and seek to emulate women's menstruation and
hence their reproductive abilities. Bettelheim (1968), who
extended this case to make a general argument about human
nature, is the most commonly cited exponent of this line of
thinking.

Lewis found that the Gnau do not say that this kind of
bleeding has anything to do with menstruation, and did not
take up the parallel when he suggested it to them. He asks:

> Might not the anthropologist be revealing himself and his
> preoccupations rather than the Gnau's when he tells us
> that the Gnau penis-bleeding is a kind of male menstrua-
> tion when the Gnau do not see it so?

He reports further that the Gnau are 'undecided and uncer-
tain' when asked about the physical function of menstruation, though they regard it as very dangerous to adult men.
Their version of its place in the reproductive process is that if
a woman stops menstruating, she may then become pregnant
(p. 129).

I mention Lewis's very interesting work as a case where a
careful ethnographer has compared a people's own account
of their practices to an outsider's theoretical explanation and
has found the theory unconvincing. It is a distinctly deterministic viewpoint which reads biological explanations into the

practices of cultures which do not share with us even the same understanding of biology. Why should this view be so widespread?

COMPULSORY HETEROSEXUALITY

What I found in interviewing men about menstruation, along with a relative absence of consideration of its place in reproduction, has been a preoccupation with sexuality far beyond what I would have expected. Menstruation and even menstrual pain were seen as important and relevant most frequently in relation to how they affected men's sexual access to women. The jokes and the talk which go on in men-only groups, when they mention menstruation, focus on what men see as the sexual significance of periods, never on its reproductive meaning. It seems to me that menstruation is understood by men in the context of the enforcement of heterosexuality upon women, and that this meaning is in fact prior to any reproductive meaning.

Aspects of relations between the sexes, of the oppression of women, are very frequently explained by reference to some aspect of the process of reproduction. This presents women's situation as 'necessarily so' or even natural, for it places the cause of it in a process which is generally understood to be universal and necessary. It avoids consideration of sexuality (except as an assumed part of reproduction) and of men's general activity and motivation in relation to women.

Mary O'Brien has written a highly developed version of this account of women's oppression – *The Politics of Reproduction* (1981). She sees reproduction as a process in which the consciousnesses of all human beings are involved. However because the 'means of reproduction' are located within women's bodies, men and women have radically different reproductive consciousnesses. The labour of childbirth enables women to mediate their alienation from their seed, but for men there is no such process – they are in practice excluded from the work of reproduction. O'Brien sees men's appropriation of women and children as their attempts to deal with this alienation.

But she does see some hope for the future, for she regards contraception as having entirely changed the relations of reproduction. She believes that it will allow reproduction to be brought for the first time under 'rational control'.

What does it mean, though, to say that reproduction has not been under rational control all along, since people understood that coitus could cause conception? Surely it is simple enough, rationally, not to engage in heterosexual intercourse with penetration by the penis if one wished to avoid pregnancy. The point is, of course, that in practice women have not been free to make this choice, for women have not been allowed control over their own bodies. Men have demanded sexual access to women without regard to the consequences, and have had sufficient social power over women to have on the whole succeeded.

As Adrienne Rich argues in her essay 'Compulsory Heterosexuality and Lesbian Existence' (1980), where she develops her analysis beyond her earlier work, if heterosexuality were innate, why is it so easy to identify numerous ways in which women are coerced into it? The sexual division of labour in most societies makes living outside a marriage extremely difficult. Unmarried women are subjected to attacks which have ranged 'from aspersion and mockery to deliberate gynocide, including the burning and torturing of millions of widows and spinsters during the witch persecutions of the fifteenth, sixteenth and seventeenth centuries in Europe, and the practice of *suttee* on widows in India'. Rich continues that:

> Some of the forms by which male power manifests itself are more easily recognizable as enforcing heterosexuality on women than others. Yet each one I have listed adds to the cluster of forces within which women have been convinced that marriage, and sexual orientation toward men, are inevitable, even if unsatisfying or oppressive components of their lives. The chastity belt; child marriage; erasure of lesbian existence (except as exotic and perverse) in art, literature and film; idealization of heterosexual romance and marriage – these are some fairly obvious forms of compulsion, the first two exemplifying physical force, the second two control of consciousness. (p. 71)

Rich also discusses the practices of clitoridectomy, pornography, sexual harassment at work and female sexual slavery as parts of this network of coercive forces.

Indeed it is the way in which the institution of heterosexuality works which makes such abuses of women as sexual harassment, rape, especially rape in marriage, and what Kathleen Barry (1979) has called female sexual slavery – enforced prostitution – so difficult to define clearly and to struggle against. If women are not expected to be able to choose their sexuality, how can they be said to have been forced?

The naming of the institution of compulsory heterosexuality is very important for feminism, but also for understanding many aspects of human society. It breaks one of the connections in the set of linked social processes which together assure women's subjugation and which are so much taken for granted, and makes their social construction apparent.

None of this analysis denies the fact that women may desire heterosexual sex: this is irrelevant to the social *institution* of heterosexuality. The point is that though women may indeed choose heterosexuality, they cannot be said to have made a free choice, when the alternatives bring with them such costs.

What is presented to us by patriarchal ideology as the natural state of humankind is actually the result of the enforcement of heterosexuality upon women. It is only in a society where women have no right to refuse men access to their vaginas that women cannot be said to be in rational control of their reproductive power. Analytically, then, reproduction has in fact been under rational control for everyone who understood the basics of biology.

Once the compulsory nature of heterosexuality in patriarchy is made clear, one cannot continue to see reproduction as something which happens somehow by itself. It becomes necessary to examine in every society what actually motivates people, men and woman perhaps differently, to want children at all, as well as why people want the number and kind of children they want and why they raise them in the ways they do.

I have already presented data which shows that the men I interviewed were in fact preoccupied with a number of aspects of menstruation, but particularly with the way in which it affects their sexual access to women. The material in this chapter, those moments where some of the men did discuss the reproductive aspects of menstruation, do not appear to be of overwhelming importance.

Menstruation is understood by men within the context of the enforcement of heterosexuality upon women – their joking is crucially concerned with this. It is striking that so many explanations for the social marking of menstruation *also* take compulsory heterosexuality as given and prefer to focus attention upon unspecified social processes determined by dis-embodied reproductive necessities, than to attend to what men say they are concerned about.

It should only be necessary to look for invisible, or unconscious, causes of people's behaviour if such behaviour made no sense in other terms. This does not seem to be the case here, when men so clearly benefit from the ideology around, and the etiquette of, menstruation.

THE WOMAN'S POINT OF VIEW

Women in our culture are, I believe, well aware of menstruation's relationship to childbearing. Women generally know that a missed period is a sign of pregnancy, and at a very practical level this is important information. This practical knowledge does not, however, necessarily dominate women's consciousness about it. When a woman is in certain specific situations – engaging in heterosexual intercourse and either fearing or hoping to become pregnant – this significance of her periods will indeed probably be uppermost in her mind.

But how many women spend how much of their lives in this situation? Some women are celibate or lesbian, so that their usual sexual practice produces no anxiety about pregnancy – it would only be if, for instance, a lesbian was hoping to become pregnant by artificial insemination that she would see her periods as reproductive events. And among heterosexually active women, many women avoid the risk of pregnancy by using contraceptives or avoiding intercourse at certain times. Some women know themselves to be infertile and others have been sterilised. For all these women the knowledge of menstruation's connection to childbearing remains latent. A woman's thinking about menstruation could be dominated more by any or all of a variety of other aspects – the pain which may accompany it; menstruation as sign of health; as a stigmatised state; a sign of her womanhood; or her adulthood; or indeed as a sexual issue. These suggestions are drawn from Esther Merves's American study (1983). What her work most clearly indicates is that women's experience of menstruation is made up of a number of components, and that different women emphasise different aspects of it.

Interpretations of social meanings of menstruation need to be based in what people in society say and do, not in theoretical arguments drawn from reproductive biology. If we abandon the idea that social practices regarding menstruation can be explained away as part of the natural process of reproduction, it becomes necessary to find other explanations.

My view is that menstruation is used in our culture as the basis, the excuse, for a flexible and changing set of ideas and practices which reinforce men's power over women. Any theory which encourages us to see menstruation only in a reproductive context distracts us from most aspects of how menstruation is treated in British culture, and possibly in most other cultures. One instance of this is discussed in the next chapter: the way in which menstruation is understood to be linked to sexuality.

6 Menstruation and Sexuality: New Rules for Old

The avoidance of heterosexual intercourse during periods is often viewed as a crucial part of the playing out of women's oppression. Many theories of the origin of menstrual 'taboos' imply that all men are deeply repelled by the idea of sex with a menstruating woman. Men in 'primitive societies', supposedly closer to nature, are believed to be acting out what all men really feel if they avoid sex at this time.

How then are we to understand the finding that some men say they *like* sex during periods? How are we to see the jokes, which form part of male culture on the subject, which dwell upon the idea of sex with menstruating women? It is possible, within the framework of traditional ideas about male sexuality, to see this phenomenon as being the result of men's uncontrollable sex drive momentarily overcoming their underlying disgust at women's bodies. But this is not a very satisfactory explanation. Should we then see these men as not sexist, as having transcended their 'conditioning' in some way?

My suggestion is that what we are seeing is the development of a new ideology of sexuality and menstruation – one which expresses somewhat different, but equally oppressive, ideas about women. I will expand upon this idea after presenting some of the material from my interviews with men and from the men's group.

My material on this question demonstrates, above all, the extreme messiness of the social world. Each individual man I interviewed had different experiences, and each had interpreted them in his own way. However it is clear that individuals in this society are in no way simply 'free to choose' their sexual behaviour in relation to menstruation – each person must contend with a bewildering range of rules and ideas. That social rules about something are inconsistent and flexible does not mean that they have no impact.

What interests me about the way in which sexuality is related to menstruation within our society is in how this affects and is affected by women's oppression. For these purposes, what beliefs people hold about sexuality and menstruation is just as important as, if not more important than, what they actually do. The two things are not really separable, of course; what I would stress is that it is important not to make assumptions about what certain actions mean. When giving talks about menstruation I have often been told either that hardly anyone now avoids sex during periods, or that many people 'still' do, as if this automatically told us something about our society's general attitudes. But people may individually 'break' or comply with a social rule without this necessarily meaning that they reject or accept the basis upon which that rule rests.

WHAT MEN SAID ABOUT SEX

We have already seen something of how male culture deals with these issues. But men also talked a good deal at a more personal level about sex and periods, and it is some of this material that I will present here. This falls into several categories: some told me about their present practice, or their present feelings about it, others told me about how they had dealt with it in the past, and others still reported on ideas they had heard expressed by other people.

It would make little sense to try to summarise what the men told me in terms of such and such a percentage do have sex during menstruation, and such and such do not. Of those in heterosexual relationships, some do now and some do not. Some never had done, some had never not done so. What each of these things meant to them is equally various.

Many of the statements they made reflected changes in their consciousnesses about it: often the account is about how they learnt the rules and then how they learnt that they did not have to obey them:

G: when I was about 15, 16, 17 . . . I was going out with this girl . . . she'd only mention it if we couldn't have sex, she'd say, oh no, I'm having my period, so I thought 'oh, you can't have sex when you have a period'.

SL: So she taught you that, really?

G: Yeah, I didn't really question why. I didn't say was it because she'd feel bad? . . . I suppose I just associated it with the fact that . . . you just couldn't, because it was dirty, I think, the idea of blood and sex and all . . .

SL: Did you go on feeling that?

G: No, I don't feel like that any more. I live with two women in this house, and they're quite open about it, and they want us to know about it because they think it's important for men to know about women's bodies. (*G*)

SL: and with X was it that she wanted to talk about it?

I: Yes, because [. . .] I wouldn't want to have sex, not her actually, *I* definitely wouldn't want to have sex anywhere near the period, or before, when she knew that her period was about to start . . . I just thought it better not to.

SL: So did she mind that?

I: Well, sometimes it would be [an issue], and . . . she used to feel it was not to be discussed in any way . . . Because I suppose I was the controlling element in the relationship as well . . .

SL: Do you still feel the same about that?

I: No, not at all, it doesn't bother me now. My current girlfriend, you know, will have sex during a period as well . . . we don't have penetrative sex anyway, we gave that up years ago [laughs] so that makes a difference I suppose to what I felt about it being unclean and a bit, um, dirty.

D: It was a problem for me at first . . . I wasn't desperately keen on the idea . . . while X was having periods, um, but she talked me into it, not talked me into it but just kind of actually got me to realise that it wasn't any different. Although the actual idea, at first, wasn't very attractive . . .

SL: You'd always just assumed that one didn't, kind of thing?

D: Yes, that's what you're told, isn't it? I mean the sort of thing you are told. Looking back at school, that's the kind of jokes you would make, if you ever sort of managed to get off with some girl it would be just your luck if she'd be having her period, or whatever. So yeah, I mean, that idea was definitely there, not that it was physically impossible, but just that it was kind of ... almost a bit freaky, I suppose.

SL: Would it be dirty?

D: Mm, well, that's how I pictured it, but in fact ... you know, I got over that problem, and began to realise that actually it wasn't any different [...]

I suppose if I'm honest I'm still not terribly keen on it.

SL: So was it really because the woman you were involved with wanted it to be all right ...?

D: Well, I don't know if it's commonplace, but when she was having her period, she used to feel, quite randy, whatever the expression ... so ... I don't know if that's common?

K: Well when I was younger and they said that there was a lining on the womb, and that all this lining and a lot of blood came out as well, and I used to imagine all sorts of horrible things coming out ... Nothing specific, but something ... when they said the lining of the womb, came out, I thought, euch. Yeah, masses of blood, and they said there was a lot of blood as well, as I say, I used to be amazed that they could bleed that much and it not hurt them, not make them ill [...]

Until I was going out with this present girlfriend I still imagined what I'd thought when I had the biology lessons, but since I've been going out with my present girlfriend, I've just thought of it as just blood, just the same, because we've had sex when she's been on a period, and there has been, you know, some blood ... and it's just the same, it's not different, so now, it doesn't bother me at all. I must admit at first I was a bit worried, in case there was ... god knows what coming out [...]

But I'll tell you what changed my mind, I think, was back to the women's magazines, a woman writing in saying her husband wouldn't make love to her while she was on her period, because he said it was disgusting, and horrible. Now I was never quite sure what was there, with the period, but I always thought, because this woman sounded so upset and distraught, that I'd always try and make an effort, no matter what was happening, to be just the same,

and pretend it wasn't happening, and perhaps get over
things. So that changed my attitude a bit . . . and then when
it actually happened, it's no different, just the same.
   I couldn't imagine someone that supposedly loved her,
telling her that it was, basically that she was disgusting,
during that time of the month. (*K*)

SL: When you first started having sexual relationships with
women, did you just accept that there was a rule that you
didn't do it during their periods? [. . .]
H: I think to start with, yeah, and then I discovered that
you could actually do it. It depended on the woman as to
whether she could accept it psychologically and also
whether she could accept it physically and also that lovemaking doesn't necessarily have to include sexual intercourse so that you could have lovemaking while they were
menstruating without having intercourse without causing
pain or having to get over some psychological hangup
about it.
SL: Yes.
H: I can't remember how I found out that it was possible
[. . .] I tend to feel that it was through talking about it,
maybe in the context which we've discussed earlier [that is,
among male groups, see Chapter 4] that made me realise
that it was possible, or realise the possibilities of it. And
therefore try to persuade a woman that I was with, that
because she was menstruating it didn't mean we couldn't
have sex, or couldn't have intercourse. I think that's how it
arose. And then actually finding out, maybe both parties,
I'm sure both parties, that it was actually quite pleasurable,
often more pleasurable than at other times. (*H*)

Men, then, had got their ideas on this from a variety of
sources – individual women, male culture, even women's
magazines.
   Discussions in the men's group bring out some of the
issues:

   —It's true that when we discussed this very, very briefly at
     our Christmas party, I made the amazing interjection
     that I actually seemed to enjoy sex more these days when
     my partner was actually menstruating . . . which I partly

said as a provocative remark to get you thinking about
the issues, but is actually, on reflection is true. I find it
has an extra thrill about it, which is presumably something to do with breaking the taboo. I certainly am not
worried about having my prick covered in blood, I find
that, um, actually rather exciting, um, and certainly I
think my present partner seems to be very turned on,
into sex, at the point, when she's started menstruating,
and it seems to go well at that point.

—She actually feels randy at that time? [. . .]

—Gosh.

—I think the extent to which that's true is partly that the
fear of pregnancy is almost nil . . . I think you can be
much more relaxed in that sense, so that you can actually
enjoy sex . . . that relates to contraception as well, I think,
specially if you're using contraception other than the Pill
– you can be much more relaxed about things. [. . .]

—Does my experience . . . ?

—Yes, it rings bells, yes . . .

—It does for me . . . but like we talked about before, for me
at least is a part of it, is to do with the unacceptability of
periods, right from being little . . . I mean there was all
sorts of things. Like touching or looking at, well anybody's genitals, it wasn't on . . . and that makes the idea
of doing so quite interesting. And periods were really
sort of beyond the pale, you know, that's almost a last
barrier in not-allowed behaviour, which is now OK, and
I think that adds an extra . . . it's a forbidden fruit thing,
I think.

—I suppose that was what was obscenely attractive about
that Hells Angels thing . . .

—Mm, right.

—. . . that you're actually, they'd really done what was the
most taboo of things, and there's perhaps unfortunately
something slightly erotic about that.

—I don't think it's necessarily unfortunate . . . It's like a
range, you know, you're brought up with the idea, well I
was, that sex in itself is dirty, and that therefore in a way
that's part of its attractions, left over in there, to me [. . .]

—On the other hand the idea of oral sex [indistinct]

—I was going to say, yes . . .

—something that I haven't actually got down to yet, I still have a slight anxiety about . . . you know . . .

—Yes, right.

—Well, I must say, I don't know, I mean I feel in two minds about it, it would be very nice . . . but I haven't, I've resisted it.

—Mm, mm.

—I think it depends very much on people [. . .] it isn't . . . I don't mean to *do*, but for some people it's a possibility to do it with, and for some people it just isn't . . . for me. Because, I don't know, for some people almost menstruation as a whole is something that's unacceptable, perhaps for some people it's OK, and once the taboo's broken, it's broken in any way, but it only relates to particular people . . .

—I can't say I fancy the idea of the taste of blood particularly [. . .]

—. . . you know, in fact, in oral sex, I would imagine that it's quite unlikely that you would have to taste blood.

—Oh, yeah.

—You think?

—Oh yes, I mean . . .

—Well, taste and smell, it's bound to . . .

—Not much though.

—But smell certainly.

—Well, you can see it, so you're going to taste it, aren't you?

—but there's not much of it, at one moment.

—that's what I'm saying, that at any one moment, in the area that . . . where you're having oral sex [. . .] there's not going to be so much . . .

—when you make love, in that situation . . . well my prick's always surprisingly unbloody, I mean you don't really . . . it doesn't involve that much blood . . . which did I suppose surprise me. It reflects I suppose the sort of ideas that I'd had before, about pints of blood [. . .]

—A woman who had not taken on or had got rid of the basic taboo about menstruation . . . whether oral sex would? With a bloke, would perhaps be the ultimate in acceptance . . . I mean, that her lover would be so accepting of her as to be willing to have oral sex with her

when she was menstruating. . . .
—Mm.
—You know what I mean, the ultimate acceptance . . . of
her body and her body's functions . . .
[pause]
—that's a bit like . . . praying to a Greek goddess [laughs]
[pause]
—anyway the thought of having sex with people who are
having periods doesn't sort of turn me off or on, any
more than normal [laughs] . . . no particular thrill, or
particular rejection, to be quite honest . . . state my point
here . . . quite boring really [laughter]
(Group)

BREAKING A TABOO?

Here we have at least one man speaking with what sounds
like self-satisfaction about enjoying sex during menstruation.
Interestingly others in the group do not take that pleasure at
face value, but analyse it as a sense of power he gains from
rebelling against the standards set by the culture he grew up
in. One of the individual respondents puts it in similar terms:

I think that I thought that it was . . . no, not dirty . . . I think
I thought that it was exciting, you know, that we were sort
of breaking some rule . . . [pause] . . . that particular rule
was broken along with a whole lot of other rules at the
same time . . . it developed in terms of what I was thinking
about things in general. (A)

It is striking, too, that in the group discussion (the only place
where this is mentioned at all) men who are calm about
penetration with the penis, which they call 'making love',
during menstruation, express anxiety about 'oral sex'. They
see oral sex as involving them in extreme closeness to the
woman. The remark about the 'Greek goddess' would imply
that oral sex is seen almost as servitude – more than a mortal
woman could expect of a man! Surveys such as *The Hite
Report* on female sexuality (1977) find that women are more
likely to find oral sex to themselves sexually satisfying than
they are conventional intercourse. We can see, then, that if

men decide to engage in what they regard as 'real sex', the
sexual practice which they tend to prefer, during menstruation, it does not follow that they are ignoring the fact that the
woman is menstruating, acting as if her menstruation had no
effect on their relationship; they are merely adjusting the
boundaries of what may and may not take place.

For some men in my sample, then, their experience of
deciding to 'break the taboo' against sexual intercourse
during periods is closely linked to their feelings about the
culture which made such rules in the first place. So what
characterises the 'old' system they are reacting to?

In a few places in my interviews men referred to what they
thought older men's practice and ideas were, but in the main
they did not offer clear notions of systems of sexual relations.
Unfortunately, the oldest man I interviewed was only 40. It is
important, therefore, not to work with a stereotyped idea of
what 'would have' been so in the past. Although we know that
many 'traditional' social systems have supported ideologies in
which menstruating women have been regarded as polluting,
we should not therefore assume it is obvious what exactly
that means in any given situation. Some cultures have beliefs
that sexual intercourse during menstruation is dangerous to
the man's health, some that it is damaging to his sexual
energy, others that it is dangerous to the woman herself or to
other people, and others still that it is sinful rather than
dangerous. Each of these leads to quite different consequences.

I have found a few traces of danger beliefs about sex
during menstruation in this country. Several gynaecology
texts are anxious to allay fears that sex at that time is
physically harmful. I have heard one anecdote from a friend
about a young working class woman who was afraid she
would develop 'VD' as a result of having done this. But I do
not know how widespread or important this sort of belief is.
None of the men I interviewed reported ever having believed it to be dangerous to themselves or to women, though
some said they had assumed it to be 'physically impossible'
when they learnt that it was not done.

More often than this I have heard the idea that 'a decent
man leaves his wife alone then'. Behind this formulation we
can plainly see a familiar set of beliefs about male sexuality as

constant, energetic; female sexuality as nonexistent – sexual service as the wife's marital duty. Heather Clark (1983, unpublished) quotes in her dissertation a story her mother told her:

> During the 1940s, in one Birkenhead shipyard, it was common practice to 'send to Coventry' any man whose wife give birth to a baby with a 'strawberry mark', as this was believed to have resulted from intercourse during the wife's 'period'. 'You couldn't even stay away from her *then*' was apparently the derisive accusation.

A similar attitude comes through in some things men I interviewed said. In one story already quoted in Chapter 4, one man tells another about a third that 'he was a really dirty little fucker' because he had sex with his girlfriend during her period.

So the 'respectable' attitude is reported thus:

> that's certainly what I would have got if I'd ever asked my father, who would I think have believed ... Sort of thinks that women are frail creatures and, you know, there are certain times when we must, you know, stand back and let them be. (*C*)

Another describes a typical conversation among young male friends:

> gone out with a girl, picked her up at a party or something, and they'd gone off together, and you'd ask, sort of roundabout questions, you know, what happened, and they'd say, 'oh no, it was a problem, it was time of the month, *got to give her her due*, you know, and you'd shrug your shoulders. And when I was younger, you know, used to say 'oh hard luck, kind of thing, [laughs] picked the wrong one', that kind of thing [laughs]. (*I*) [my emphasis]

Some feminists have suggested that the 'social rule' against sex during menstruation was originated by women. As I have explained, I do not think there is good evidence for this as an original cause; women have not had the power to enforce such a rule, and it is unclear why, if they had such power, they would choose this rule. But these notions perhaps show something of what may be the present-day origin of such an idea. If women's sexuality is essentially under male control, then at least in the 'old' system the demands a man might make upon a woman are limited to some extent by social rules encoding ideas of 'decency' – which is an acting-out of 'respect for women'.

Further research into the ways in which menstruation was really understood and dealt with in the past would be extremely interesting. While I could not pursue this very far, my reading turned up some material within studies of the lives of working-class women earlier in this century and in the late nineteenth century. Both the report (prefaced by Bondfield 1943) *Our Towns*, and Elizabeth Roberts's work (1984) say that many working-class women did not expect or particularly want to wear sanitary protection. Jill Liddington's research (1984) discovered a belief among Lancashire cotton workers that the smell of menstrual blood on a woman's clothes would be sexually arousing to men.

It also seems possible that a careful study of women's writings from past eras might yield more reference to menstruation than one might expect. Many modern feminist writers refer to menstruation, especially to the experience of the first period (eg Alther 1977; Morrison 1970; Walker 1982). But it is also mentioned in novels of the early 1960s like Paule Marshall's *Brown Girl, Brownstones* (1960) and Doris Lessing's *The Golden Notebook* (1962). Perhaps a more informed view of the reality of the 'old-fashioned' approach to menstruation could be developed.

What Men Say Women Say

It is interesting to look further at what men said about women's part in this. These various reports of specific women's feelings about sex during periods must be seen in the context of the material in Chapter 4 about male culture, which maintains the idea that women 'use' periods to get out of sex.

Two men I interviewed said that women they had had sexual relationships with had a greater sexual desire during their periods. In one case that was what had persuaded him to try sex at that time, which he had not previously 'liked the

idea of much' (*D*). And we have already heard this idea from
the men's group.

Several men reported that women they were involved with
were more worried than they were about making a mess:

> She's actually more preoccupied than I am . . . I mean at a
> practical level, I think it's *reasonable* to stop things getting
> stained, I do actually, I appreciate in some ways her taking
> care of that, being careful in that sense, but I suspect it's
> also careful partly in the sense of kind of protecting herself
> and slightly hiding herself away. And I respect that, and I
> don't want to push her, in that way, so it may be that in one
> sense I feel less exposed to the existence of the blood and
> its flow than I might be. (*C*)

—I mean quite often, you find you've made love with
   someone and they start having a period [laughs] and no
   one's known anyway, so it leads to embarrassed faces and
   blood on the sheets job or something, er . . .
—Mm
—Quite often far more embarrassment in the woman, well,
   certainly than in me, because I've sort of lost that taboo
   quite some time ago.
—Yeah
—I think I actually, before, yes, before I started sleeping
   with anybody, I remember going along to some sort of
   Women and Anthropology classes or something, which
   was just discussing the menstrual taboo. Till then, it was
   obviously quite a big taboo, I guess . . . [. . .]
—Certainly some women that I've slept with have been
   totally embarrassed by having a period, and that's actually because of prior experience, and I've said, look, it
   doesn't bother me, if it bothers you, then, fair
   enough . . .
—Most people check it out, don't they?
—Yes, but . . . quite a lot of women have actually felt
   incredibly rejected, not just on the sexual basis but, you
   know, also how dare you come into the bed sort of thing,
   at all . . . been physically not usually cuddled or anything,
   actually feel incredibly worried about it, because of that
   sort of rejection.

—Well, I think X was telling me that in a previous relationship she'd had that sort of reaction from a bloke, and he had the taboo rather than her, he didn't like it, had a hangup about it . . . certainly wouldn't want to make love, and that upset her quite a bit. I mean I can understand how blood might be that, might have that feeling, that taboo, obviously, from that whole thing about impurity, dirty, you know (Group)

N: Yes, she was more squeamish about it than I was [. . .] I was with the woman I'm having a relationship with at the moment, and she's having a period, or coming towards the end of it, and she was in bed, and she was looking for something. I said 'what are you looking for?' she said 'it doesn't matter'. She was looking all over the place, so I said 'sit down' [unclear] and it was a bit of a joke, um, and it happened that she was looking for a sanitary towel, and we couldn't find it . . . anyway I thought, I know where it's gone, it's gone between the duvet and the duvet cover, that's the only place it could be [. . .] So anyway, there it was, and I handed it to her. But again *I* didn't feel any sort of problem with that, at all, but she did.
SL: Embarrassed?
N: Well, yes, embarrassed, . . . shy, I suppose, which is amazing in a sense – it's obviously a block that she's got, because I mean in every other respect she is not the least bit embarrassed.

When we analyse this series of statements using the idea of an etiquette which is quite different for women and for men, it is plain that the etiquette operates in much the same way in bed as it does elsewhere. The men I quote often use the notion of 'taboo' which implies that men and women stand in the same relationship to a general social belief. They can then interpret women's observance of menstrual etiquette as a kind of personal inadequacy, excessive conventionality, on the part of the woman.

Some men make it clear that they are aware of their own power in this situation, and use this awareness in their guesswork about what women might want: 'there was, I think, there was an initial resistance from her, and I think that was probably based on feeling that I would maybe react adversely to that . . .' (N) One man even observes that women cannot be free of the fear that a man will react badly to their being menstruating, whatever the man says:

> *F*: yeah . . . yes I feel that quite a few women, if I were, if a man were to say to them that he, that they were in favour of having sex when they thought that their partner was also in favour of having sex when they were menstruating, that the woman would feel that they were saying that in spite of their real feelings.
> *SL*: Yes, I can see that . . . they'd be so sure that it really was . . .
> *F*: repulsive . . . Yes, I'm sure there's one end of the spectrum of attitudes by men which that does hold true for, but I don't think it's as pervasive as a lot of women think. (*F*)

Who Decides?

The difficulties of interpretation presented by this material are well illustrated by the following sequence of questioning:

> *M*: that was a discussion about whether we could have a sexual relationship during the time when she was menstruating, and she had quite strong views about that, which was 'no', although she related the story of her friend who said you could do it in the bath, kind of thing [laughs] [. . .]
> *SL*: So [. . .] in your later relationships, . . . there's some point where you stop not having sex during menstruation, is there?
> *M*: Yes, that's right. But in the first relationship it continued the whole way through.
> *SL*: So for you that's always been something women have decided . . . or has that been negotiated?
> *M*: yes . . . it's difficult, isn't it? If I can, I feel I would go for the first. I don't feel it was a subject for negotiation. I sort of felt, if that was the position, then I would accept that. In the second situation, it isn't the same sort of issue or problem – in fact . . . sexual interest tends to be greater during that period, anyway, so it's a different order of thing. I don't really feel conscious of having negotiated it

... I felt, in my first relationship in that sense, it was far more unilateral – that was the decision. And I could take it or leave it if you see what I mean. [laughs]

SL: So you weren't feeling you were part of a general rule, but that this was *her* feeling about this ... it was that she said you couldn't rather than that you just couldn't?

M: Oh, no, I think the second. I think that was true, she said we couldn't, therefore I did actually assume that that was the normal practice. I had no other standards on which to ... I mean if ... certain circumstances that subsequently became reversed, at some stage ... if I was faced again with a woman who said you couldn't have sex during menstruation, I would now be in a different position, because I would now know about my own experiences that that isn't necessarily the case ... so therefore it becomes a different order of thing. . . .

Women may, then, be active in managing the sexual situation: evidently it is common for a woman to be the one who says 'we can't, I've got my period'. But this is hardly an exercise of autonomy when many women have been taught to believe, exactly, that they 'can't', without risking various serious consequences. However men do seem to see this as the woman exercising power. It may, of course, suit a woman, for her own reasons, not to have sex at that time. This last possibility forms a major part of male discourse on the subject.

This accusation against women, that women manipulate male ideology to gain advantage over individual men by denying them sexual access to themselves, is important in and of itself, whether or not it bears any relationship to what women actually do. The accusation in itself implies that it is illegitimate, in bad faith, for a woman to refuse sex at that time – she is held to be 'making excuses'.

I think it is clear from the data I have presented that neither of these ideological systems allows for women to have power over their own sexualities. Clearly the ideal situation for women is that each woman should herself be in a position to decide what her sexual practice will be – she should not be subject to rules which aim to control her as a member of the class 'women'. In this situation, she would decide what she preferred to do depending upon how her periods affected her and on how she felt about whatever sexual relationship she might be involved in at any given point. Obviously for this to happen the way in which heterosexual relationships generally work would have to be transformed, not just in relation to menstruation, for woman cannot be free as individuals in a relationship where the male-female sex-class relation is always present.

Although in a lesbian sexual relationship there is no pre-defined power difference between the two women so that no specific etiquette in relation to menstruation would necessarily exist, lesbian relationships cannot be seen as existing in isolation from patriarchal culture. Lesbian women have grown up and continue to live surrounded by many of the same constraints and influences as do heterosexual women and men. All women internalise some part of the male culture's opinion of women. Lesbian relationships can, however, have the potential for women to develop their views of themselves in the context of a relationship of equality.

Returning to men, then, we must consider the question of whether my data can be regarded as a valid indicator of anything about British society generally. I deliberately chose to work with an untypical sample of men. It is on this subject of sexual practice and ideas about sex (if only simply in their willingness to talk to me about it) that I think my sample is probably most unlike men in general, for many of them are part of a subculture very much imbued with 'sexual liberation' ideology. However I believe that members of this subculture are disproportionately influential on these matters, if only because of their articulacy.[1]

So how are we to see the phenomenon of some men wanting sex during menstruation? Are men freeing themselves and us with them from old-fashioned sexist restrictions? I suggest that we must look again at both the 'old' and the 'new' set of ideas to seek the solution to this puzzle.

The 'old' system (which I feel we know too little about) is indeed sexist – it is based upon rigid notions of women's and men's 'place'. However, the idea of 'respect' for women, even though it is a hypocritical kind of regard for one's inferiors, could suit women in certain situations. Rules do at least protect women to some degree from men making arbitrary sexual demands upon them. And, conversely, though the 'old' system serves the power of men as a group, this may be, perhaps, at some cost to the desires of individual men.

The joking recounted in Chapter 4 is very much about men negotiating the power structure of the 'old' system. Men repeatedly acknowledge that the 'old' system trained them to see women as set on trying to deny them sex. In the group discussion, one man stresses that what he saw as new about 1960s feminism was that *women* were advocating what the male culture had wanted all along. It is clear here that he is interpreting the feminist impulse in a narrowly sexual way, as like to what men had been talking about:

> —One thing that influenced me a lot was reading Germaine Greer [*The Female Eunuch*, 1970], it wasn't long after I'd had my first proper sexual relationship . . .
> She has something about how women should liberate themselves by being able to drink their menstrual blood, i.e. come to terms with the taboo, and it really . . . I can see that as a 'before' and 'after' . . . the fact that women were saying those things definitely broke the taboo for me . . . If *women* could say that sort of thing . . . and obviously there was a lot of talk about it at the time, then it seemed to me that the taboo was a taboo worth breaking. (Group)[2]

What is the new ideology then? Both the old and the new ideas define menstruation largely by reference to sex with men. Put in the simplest possible terms, the new ideology makes menstruation out to be a sexual thing, where before it was seen if anything as anti-sexual, inimical to sexuality. It is part of the 'sexual liberation' ideology, which emphasises the *sexual* nature of women. This sexualising can be degrading in a new way – it involves seeing women more as a herd than even as a class: 'all the same in the dark'. Women are seen as driven by needs which they may not be aware of – which male researchers may be able to discover by methods which entirely bypass the consciousness of the woman. For the characteristic mode of this discourse is sex research.

SEX RESEARCHERS INTERVENE

I have been looking at the problem rather as one negotiated between men in general and individual men, but of course this is far too simple – institutions intervene. Specifically this century the development of 'sex research' – the supposedly scientific investigation of human sexual behaviour – has given rise to a new set of experts who compete with the spokesmen of moral systems such as religion for a legitimate voice in determining the sexual mores of the society. They have built up an ideology of 'natural' sexuality, by using purportedly non-invasive natural-scientific methods to observe sexual behaviour. They then declared what they saw to be eternal truths about male and female sexuality.

This movement has been analysed by feminists as an attempt to control women's sexuality – and as a response to the beginnings of a mass feminist movement (Jackson 1983; Jeffreys 1982, 1983). It is characterised by the refusal to consider social factors as affecting sexual behaviour.

A classic example of this approach, relating to the topic we are considering, is an article by Udry and Morris in *Nature* (1968), entitled 'Distribution of coitus in the menstrual cycle'. It reports on two studies of women's reports of their sexual activities over the menstrual cycle. 'Orgasm' and 'coitus' are plotted against cycle-days. It is taken for granted that if any pattern can be found, there must be some sort of hormonal explanation for it. When variations in the patterns are found between two socially different groups the authors comment:

> Variations from one sample to another suggest that the influence of cyclic female hormones on sexual behaviour is more apparent in some groups than in others.

An absurdly self-serving line of argument.

The sex researchers have been very interested in the 'issue' of sex during periods, and have in general been in favour of it, as they are, also, in favour of sex of any sort men like at any time men please. Havelock Ellis, a very influential early writer, devotes considerable space to discussion of this issue (1913). He begins his work by summarising research that had been carried out which attempted to establish 'facts' about a cyclic pattern of desire in women. Evidently for every possible theory about at what point in the menstrual cycle women most want sex, there was even then a serious article written advocating it – usually with some sort of anecdotal evidence. Similar research continues (cf Dennerstein and Burrows 1983:207). I would see this preoccupation as part of the larger enterprise of producing evidence first that 'women really want it' and secondly of identifying *when* women really want it. This enterprise in itself reduces individual women to 'thing' status – it is an attempt to produce 'information' which could overrule women's dangerous tendency to make up their own minds about their sexual activities. The present-day consensus among the researchers, not surprisingly, seems to be that women really do want it when they have periods – this is 'proved' in a number of ways, not I think worth criticising here.

It is striking that these researchers, like the men I inter-viewed, while they are very concerned with the 'taboo' against sex during periods show no interest at all in changing the general etiquette of secrecy about menstruation. Why should they? There is nothing for men to gain from doing so.

In Sheila Jeffreys's work on the sex researchers (1982), she focuses on their creation of frigidity as a disease of women, and Ellis's advocacy of the 'erotic rights of women', as defined by himself. She sees this as a backlash against the early feminists' refusal of male-controlled sexuality. Perhaps there is a parallel here with male concern about menstrua-tion at present. Men's concern is that women should be 'free' to have sex with them – not that women should be free at all times to determine their own behaviour.

Jeffreys points to the two causes most commonly put forward for female frigidity or 'dyspareunia': ignorance, that is, lack of sex education, and trauma from their first sexual experience. There is here a remarkable echo of present-day discourse on menstruation, which is dominated by the idea that women's problems result from lack of 'information' or 'education' and/or from having gone through a trauma over their first period. In both cases, this account focuses attention upon the individual woman's mind, and away from her present-day conditions, back onto past experiences. If only women would take 'the right attitude' everything would be all right!

Another aspect of the sexual liberationist message is that

it emphasises the heterosexual couple as a social unit above other units such as the family or society generally. In relation to menstruation, when this is sexualised, it can be used to emphasise the specialness of the couple relationship. Men 'in general' are still not supposed to know if a woman is menstruating. She is required to hide it at work, in most social situations and indeed within the family, from her father, her sons, and any other male relatives. Paige and Paige cite three US studies of menarche which had found that 'a father is less likely to be told of the event than siblings, female friends, and relatives' (1981:273).

However, a woman's husband or sexual partner *is* expected to know when she is menstruating – this is part of the 'carnal knowledge' which marks off this relationship from all others. Liberal opinion in our culture seems to be rather shocked by the idea that a husband might not know of his wife's menstruation – and yet secrecy is taken for granted as part of all other female-male relationships.

Once this knowledge is made part of the sexual relationship, this may then have effects in itself, and the knowledge become seen as connected with sexual access. Perhaps this is some of the meaning involved in boys' teasing of girls about sanitary towels.

Mary Douglas made a similar point, relating menstrual rituals to the practice of couvade, in her article 'Couvade and menstruation: the relevance of tribal studies' (1975). She suggests that particular cultural emphasis may come to be put upon female reproductive events where the heterosexual bond is relatively weak, due, perhaps, to women having some degree of independence. In this way men seek to act out their connection with a particular woman, and perhaps their claim to rights over her reproductive capacity.

Several of the men I interviewed spoke about seeing their taking an interest in menstruation as part of the process of getting more closely involved with their wives or girlfriends: 'we'll understand each other better' (*C*). In the men's group they discuss their feelings about helping the women they have relationships with to deal with painful periods, by rubbing her back, or fetching a hot water bottle.

—Is that a form of, of self-flagellation, you know, I mean? [laughter]

—But no, in some ways, . . . it's a ritual, isn't it? It's a way of
saying 'I want to be part of this with you' . . .
—a sharing (Group)

FEMINIST CHALLENGE RE-DIRECTED

This new ideology of menstruation can be seen as in part a
reaction to feminism, an attempt to contain and redirect
feminist energy. Women who want to refuse the old order of
menstrual secrecy are offered a new system where menstruation may be openly acknowledged within a heterosexual
relationship, though not elsewhere. Women wanting freedom to determine their own sexuality find their demands
reinterpreted as a sexual desire for 'sex' during periods.
Indeed the issue of how society stigmatises menstruating
women, seen through this lens, reappears as a question of
whether or not one has sex during menstruation; a challenge
to the public world redefined as a private problem.
    The intellectual elaboration of this position is spelt out in
The Wise Wound, where menstruation is interpreted as in
itself a form of sexual energy, one aspect of women's
(inherently) heterosexual being. Shuttle and Redgrove write:

> What a strange coincidence that the very same time in the
> cycle of the 'paramenstrual plague' – the time when
> intercourse is almost universally tabooed – should also be
> the time of a rise in that very inconvenient commodity,
> female sexuality! (1978:86)

They represent the whole sexist etiquette of menstruation as
stemming from the suppression of a specifically sexual
energy – one which is dis-embodied and described as a
commodity. The solution, implicit throughout the book, is
more heterosexual sex during the menstrual period – this
will somehow free women to express their 'true' selves. How
it will inconvenience men is unclear. Again, the evidence
these authors draw upon comes from mythology on the one
hand and psychology and sexology, 'science', on the other:
anywhere but out of the mouths of living women. Women's
motives are reconstructed without reference to women themselves.

I have tried to discuss men's view of menstruation and sexuality. My difficulty is that I do not wish to engage with any of the debates which currently take place around questions like 'do women *really* want sex during periods?' or 'is the sex taboo good or bad for women?', but would aim to challenge all the terms of these questions. Women are not all the same. It is part of the patriarchal system of thought that we are so routinely discussed as part of a class rather than as persons. The very focus upon these questions is part of the sexualising of menstruation.

For women, menstruation is a phenomenon which is basically independent of sexuality. As we have seen, women see it in various ways: as relating to reproduction, in terms of health, perhaps as a nuisance or a source of pain, perhaps as part of being a woman. Women menstruate and are subject to menstrual etiquette in relation to men whether or not they engage in heterosexual intercourse.

It is men who experience menstruation as a sexual matter – principally because they see women as sexual beings above all else, and also because they define anything which comes from 'there' as sexual. The new ideology enshrines this male perspective at its core, and diminishes female experience to match.

Two women have told me stories of experiences they had as young girls which I think illustrate the imposition of a sexual atmosphere about menstruation upon women. Liz Kelly (1984) describing her experiences of sexual assault/harassment in adolescence, writes:

> After another incident I couldn't even explain why I had arrived home from town without the new school shirt I had been sent to buy. I had in fact been followed around the shop by a man who kept touching me up. Perhaps the reason I said nothing was that at the time I had my period and his interest was touching me where my sanitary towel was. I found this embarrassing and totally confusing.

Another woman told of visiting her father (who was separated from her mother) and sitting on his sofa, not realising that her period had come. It left a bad stain, and her father never cleaned it. She felt he left it there to humiliate her when she visited him.

Both these women felt some puzzlement over the men's behaviour, as I felt listening to the jokes men told me. They also felt a sense of menace, as I did. For when we say that men have sexualised menstruation, we must remember what sexuality means to men in patriarchal culture: that it is the key to the subordination of women. Modern Western culture increasingly uses explicit reference to sexuality as a way of representing the power relation between the sexes. It is through this sexual reference that the new ideology expresses the inferiority of women in relation to menstruation – the sexual reference to some extent replaces the simpler anti-sexual 'taboo'.

NOTES

1. Information from other sources indicates that what men said to me was not wholly atypical. Shere Hite's postal survey of US men asked the question 'Do you enjoy sex with a woman who is menstruating?' Of those who replied anonymously, 67 per cent said yes, and of those who replied non-anonymously, 81 per cent said yes. Two and three per cent of the remainder said they would try it, and the rest said no (1981). Sharon Golub's study (1981) of college students drew a similar response to the question 'Would you have sexual intercourse with a menstruating woman?' – 86 per cent said yes. However rather fewer, 79 per cent, said that they were 'as attracted to and aroused by a menstruating woman'. Asked about real life, 43 per cent of the male students agreed that they did 'make fewer sexual advances toward a menstruating woman'.

2. I was very interested to come across the following feminist criticism of Germaine Greer's work written in 1970 by Sheila Rowbotham, when it first appeared: 'There's a danger that you start to throw out alternative stereotypes of the liberated woman. These are just gags on other women. You reduce what is a unique dialogue for every woman, between her, the movement, and the world outside into simply new ways in which she ought to behave. Thus the liberated woman is ready to lick menstrual blood off his cock, she doesn't make up reading lists or sit on committees. There's a funny way in which people who are most concerned to resist all the rules individually start inventing a whole lot of new ones for other people. I mean, menstrual blood on his cock might just be a matter of taste, not liberation.'

7 Gynaecology: One Patriarchal Mode of Knowledge On Menstruation

As is so often remarked, menstruation is little discussed within British culture. It features in only a few contexts, a few modes of discourse: one of these is the medical. What, then, can be learnt about the social construction of menstruation from gynaecology texts? Where does the medical mode of knowledge fit into the more general picture of the patriarchal construction of menstruation?

Paula Weideger writes that the gynaecologist occupies a place of 'leadership as the enforcer of the menstrual taboo' (1978:144). I have already said why I find this usage of 'taboo' unhelpful; I would disagree further with the idea of doctors as leaders of opinion. Gynaecologists act primarily as men, and only secondarily as doctors – their work is a form of mediation between the male culture's view of women and the problems that women seek help with. Men's view of menstruation could not be said to be dominated or led by any single mode of discourse on the subject – certainly the medical mode does not dominate, but rather is entirely dependent upon other sets of ideas. For this reason I discuss much of the material I gathered from medical sources within my chapters on menstrual pain (Chapter 8) and on mood change (Chapter 9), set in the context of men's ideas on these subjects more generally.

However gynaecologists do occupy a special place within the larger struggle between women and men and this has been recognised by feminists in their critique of the male domination of the medical profession and of medical ideas about women (Frankfort 1972; Boston Women's Health Book Collective 1973; Howell 1974; Ehrenreich and English 1979; Scully 1980; Elston 1981). Gynaecologists are particularly involved in confrontations between female definitions

and male ones, and therefore will often be led to articulate
certain pieces of ideology in very explicit ways. They also
have the task of distinguishing normal phenomena from
abnormal (Scully and Bart 1978) – something which they
find particularly problematic in relation to menstruation.

My purpose in looking at gynaecology texts was to get a
picture of the 'modern' medical view of menstruation. I have
therefore only used texts of which editions had been published in the 1970s or 1980s.

First of all I wrote to the Royal College of Obstetricians
and Gynaecologists, to ask them which texts are the most
generally used and respected among gynaecologists. Their
librarian replied, pointing out that reading lists used in the
education of doctors vary a great deal from one institution to
another, but giving me a basic list of six books which she
thought were very widely used.

This list reads as follows:

Barnes, Josephine, *Lecture Notes on Gynaecology*, 4th edn 1980,
   1st edn 1966 (Oxford: Blackwell).
Clayton, Sir Stanley and J. R. Newton, *A Pocket Gynaecology*,
   9th edn 1979, 1st edn 1948 (Edinburgh: Churchill Living-
   stone).
Dewhurst, Sir C. J. (ed.), *Integrated Obstetrics and Gynaecology
   for Postgraduates*, 3rd edn 1981, 1st edn 1972 (Oxford:
   Blackwell).
Garrey, Matthew M., A. D. T. Govan, Colin Hodge, Robin
   Callander, *Gynaecology Illustrated*, 2nd edn 1978, 1st edn
   1972 (Edinburgh: Churchill Livingstone).
Jeffcoate, Sir Norman, *Principles of Gynaecology*, 4th edn
   1975, 1st edn 1957 (London: Butterworths).
Llewellyn-Jones, Derek, *Fundamentals of Obstetrics and
   Gynaecology*, Vol 2, *Gynaecology*, 3rd edn 1982, 1st edn 1970
   (London: Faber & Faber).

My other method was to look through the catalogue and the
borrowers' book at the library in the Lancaster Postgraduate
Medical Centre. I looked at the books in the library which
seemed to be used regularly by the doctors of the district.
Only Dewhurst and Jeffcoate, of the first list, were also
present in the Lancaster library.

Further work could very usefully be done on the history of these ideas – historical work on gynaecology in Britain has been developing gradually: Audrey Eccles on Tudor and Stuart England (1982); Hilda Smith (1976) and Patricia Crawford (1981) on the seventeenth century; and Ornella Moscucci (1982; 1984) on the more recent history, have added detailed information to the American sources, such as Barker-Benfield (1975) and Ehrenreich and English (1979). More material exists on the Victorian era, especially the uses made of menstruation by both sides in the argument over women's education: Showalter and Showalter (1972), Bullough and Voght (1973), Carroll Smith-Rosenburg (1974).

The medical mode is an especially important one to bring into question as ideology because it is presented as objective scientific truth, attempting to make women feel they have no basis on which to doubt its 'information'. One thing which struck me very strongly in my reading was how extremely unscientific medical discourse in fact is – only some of the texts I studied made any attempt at a scientific approach, most being more 'commonsensical' in their tone. Circularity of logic is rife, and the notion that a hypothesis might be disproved and then abandoned seems a very foreign one to most authors. Referencing to sources was extraordinarily rare in most texts.

One difficulty I found in interpreting these texts was in how to deal with those mentioning some theory or kind of treatment only to deny its usefulness. I came to feel that in a number of instances, the denial itself helped to perpetuate the idea it was supposed to be disposing of. I will return to this problem later. Another issue, in general, was the language of objectivity, the manner of writing by which the author avoids stating his or her own opinion. How is one to interpret a statement like 'Some doctors regard the menopause as an endocrine deficiency disease' (Clayton and Newton:22), when it is followed by no clear contradiction?

The image of medicine as 'science' may perhaps be a more common illusion among lay people than among doctors themselves. Medical sociology has often attempted to separate out the ideological parts of medical discourse from the 'purely' medical parts – something I found to be impossible and undesirable (cf. Armstrong, 1982).

Margarita Kay (1981) has identified a very interesting phenomenon in her study of the beliefs of Mexican American women. She found that many of what are now seen as 'folklore' notions held by the women she studied can be traced to origins in the 'scientific/medical' beliefs of an earlier era – for example the idea that menstruation performs a cleansing function, removes excess blood from the body. This process can also be seen in the way in which venereal disease is now sometimes held to be connected to menstruation, for instance as being a consequence of intercourse during a period – something which some doctors believed in the nineteenth century (see, for example, King 1875).

ATTITUDES TO MENSTRUATION IN GENERAL

It was not possible to identify distinct schools of thought among the doctors in their attitude to menstruation – they all express ambiguity towards it. There are numerous assertions about the normality of the process, and about the need to impress this upon women. However gynaecologists are very strongly oriented towards disease and disorder, and make few statements about 'normal menstruation'. Although they stress the normality of menstruation, they do not describe it at all clearly. For this reason we must deduce what they consider to be normal from what they discuss as abnormal.

The notion of normal menstruation is, for these gynaecologists, highly problematic. There is a line of rhetoric common to several of these texts, in which the author quotes, from the Bible or some other source, some negative attitudes to menstruation. Then they say:

The beliefs should be resisted and corrected. The menstrual function should be explained to girls truthfully, if simply, and they should be made to realise that they are not excreting something which is noxious but rather a manifestation of womanhood. (Jeffcoate:88)

Menstruation itself is surrounded by a veil of myth and nonsense. . . . These pejorative adjectives stress the abnormality of menstruation, but are happily being replaced by a realisation that menstruation is a normal function, not a manifestation of uncleanliness. (Llewellyn-Jones:72)

At the same time the language used in describing the physiology of menstruation is peculiar. Jeffcoate gives the memorable picture, already quoted, that 'menstruation is sometimes described as "the weeping of a disappointed uterus"' (p. 77). In three texts, McClure Brown, Llewellyn-Jones and Dewhurst, the process of the shedding of the endometrium (the lining of the womb) is described as necrosis, that is death, of cells. I had accepted this as technical language for a specific process, but was struck by the fact that Josephine Barnes gives a very full account of this process without using this term at all.

Several of the texts give some kind of general assessment of the significance of menstruation for women, in different contexts. Writing on dysfunctional uterine bleeding, Garrey states that 'since menstruation is central to women's existence, any departure from the normal is likely to produce some psychological disturbance (and vice versa)' (p. 86). Discussing the treatment of amenorrhoea, Dewhurst writes that the majority of women can be induced to accept their condition if they can be persuaded that lack of bleeding in itself is harmless, but that for some women, 'amenorrhoea appears to present a threat to their body image, menstrual bleeding being a visible red badge of femininity' (p. 70). He suggests that these women may 'cheaply and conveniently' be put on the Pill.

Llewellyn-Jones writes about hysterectomy, that the 'uterus, and menstruation, is to many women the core of their femininity, and the loss of the uterus has a considerable emotional response in susceptible women, particularly as it can no longer be the focus for the conversion symptoms' (p. 81).

The technique of reinforcing an idea by denying it seems to me to be operating in the tendency of gynaecologists to refer in passing to ideas about hysteria. Three texts do this, for example, under 'dysfunctional uterine bleeding':

The Greeks believed that a woman's emotions were controlled by the womb − *hysteros* in Greek − and that a disturbance of the womb led to an hysterical state. The opposite is more nearly true, and emotions acting through the hypothalamus affect menstrual function considerably. (Llewellyn-Jones:75)

The idea that women are dominated by their wombs has a very long history (Bart and Scully 1979). Hilda Smith (1976) describes the seventeenth-century medical view of women:

as beings whose health was determined, basically, by the fact that they were female. To be a woman meant that one was subject to fevers and ill vapors arising from a malfunctioning menstrual cycle, to hysteria resulting from a diseased womb, and to general bad health developing from a life of ease. (p. 97)

The most general diseases of women were held to 'proceed from the retention, or stoppage of their courses, as the most universall, and most usual caurse' (Fontanus 1652). Modern gynaecologists do not seem free from this thinking in their more rhetorical moods.

There is a double bind here – the womb can be seen as important to all women, when it is seen as influencing their minds in an uncontrolled way; or it can be seen as only important to neurotic women, when their concern with it disrupts medical treatment in some way. Are all menstruating women seen as neurotic, or only when they mention the fact that they menstruate? This is unclear. However this ambiguity is very important since these attitudes have a real influence on decisions about hysterectomy and on the treatment of post-hysterectomy patients.

The value of the womb to women is seen in almost mystical terms: it symbolises 'femininity', not the most exact of terms. Garrey's idea that it is 'central to women's existence' is particularly chilling. Somehow one feels it to be unlikely that a doctor would write, like this, that the penis is central to men's existence. Men's sexual parts are not discussed in the same way – and when the context of this statement is the knowledge that this 'central' organ is frequently removed by medical men, such a remark about men could not have equivalent impact.

What is entirely absent is any recognition that menstruation may act as a practical indicator to women of health and of non-pregnancy, clear findings of surveys like those of Merves (1983) and of Snowden and Christian (1983).

Another interesting index of the doctors' attitudes towards menstruation can be found in their comments on sexual intercourse during menstruation. Two doctors comment on this. Llewellyn-Jones writes:

> Coitus during menstruation may be unaesthetic, but it is not medically dangerous, and patients who seek advice can be reassured that there is no medical reason to avoid coitus at this time. (p. 72)

And Jeffcoate has a good deal to say:

> Although most married couples are so fastidious that they naturally shun coitus during menstruation, its practice at such time is probably more frequent than is generally realised. Medical arguments against coitus during menstruation are that sexual excitement may cause uterine congestion and increase the menstrual flow, that the more vascular and friable vaginal walls may be injured, and that the associated orgasm may encourage retrograde menstruation and the development of endometriosis.

But these are 'theoretical' considerations, he says, and in the 'healthy couple' there is no reason why not:

> The only real objection is the obvious aesthetic one, and even this can be overcome if the woman first douches the vagina and then temporarily contains the uterine discharge by inserting a Dutch Cap. (p. 88)

I should perhaps explain that Jeffcoate is alone in worrying about retrograde menstruation, his idea being that in some circumstances menstrual blood may flow the wrong way, and that this could be the cause of various problems.

These references to aesthetics rather than to any danger support my view of the sexual etiquette of the present day, that the mild sense that menstrual blood is dirty leaves men reasonably free to determine their own sexual practice, while women in general are still viewed as producing unpleasant substances. Jeffcoate's instructions for cleansing to avoid any contact between penis and menstrual blood are rather in contradiction with the threats to health that he suggests may arise from sex during periods. All that activity could surely only affect 'friable' vaginal walls more, and if blood might flow backwards, surely douching would be one of the more likely ways of encouraging it to do so? His concern is clearly for the man rather than for the woman.

Normal Menstrual Cycles?

One of the issues, for the gynaecologist, is to determine the normal limits of menstruation. However the figures given vary considerably:

Normal limits for cycle length:

Barnes	21–35 days
Clayton and Newton	25–32 days
Garrey *et al*	21–30 days
Jeffcoate	28 days
Llewellyn-Jones	24–34 days

Number of days of flow:

Barnes	2–7
Clayton and Newton	5
Garrey *et al*	3–9
Jeffcoate	4
Llewellyn-Jones	1–8

In among this muddle we get statements like this:

The normal menstrual cycle lasts 28 days, including 5 days of bleeding. . . . No woman is absolutely regular, and cycles of 25 to 32 days may be accepted as normal. (Clayton and Newton:15)

Only Barnes produces such a liberal statement as this: 'The menstrual cycle itself also varies in different women, each having her own normal pattern' (p. 36) and even she does not resist the temptation to spell out normal limits. One wonders what is to be done about women whose cycles do not fall into these narrow patterns?

And how are we to deal with the flow, each month? All these authors recommend either towels or tampons. (These books were published before the naming of the toxic shock syndrome associated with tampons and it is not mentioned.) But there are hazards, it seems. Tampons may be left inside, 'even by intelligent women' (Llewellyn-Jones:72), and Jeffcoate suggests that 'In young girls they may arouse unfavourable reactions such as a morbid interest in the genital organs, masturbation and revulsion.' They are however, 'harmless in the normal woman' (p. 88).

And how are we to think of the end of the reproductive period? Can women pass through this in good health?

> Emotional instability, depression, fatigue, loss of libido are often met with and psychotic traits and personality disturbances tend to be aggravated. (Garrey:64)

Jeffcoate suggests that 'In well adjusted women' the psychological changes of the menopause amount to 'no more than a period of slight emotional instability', but that a woman's reaction will depend upon 'whether she is childless and grandchildless or surrounded by a happy family' (Jeffcoate:90). Apparently there can be no such things as a happy childless woman, or an unhappy family.

As usual, Jeffcoate regards a woman's social situation as the cause of her problems. This sort of attitude towards menopausal women has been much criticised by feminists (Reitz 1979; Weideger 1978; Seaman and Seaman 1977).

The practice of offering an idea of the proper length for menstrual cycles, and for the bleeding itself, appears to be part of the attempt to gain control of the process through understanding. The variations in their estimates only shows up how absurd this project is – but the only alternative is to acknowledge that a woman must learn what is normal for her through experience, a recognition which undermines the doctors' claims to authority. There is an element of self-fulfilling prophesy, when medical men are giving out oral contraceptives which tidily produce 28 day cycles, so that a population survey carried out now would have a very strong tendency towards 28 day cycles!

PROBLEMS OF COMMUNICATING WITH WOMEN

It seems to me to be crucial to see the doctors' descriptive and prescriptive statements in the context of an understanding of the *process* of a gynaecological consultation. What can be said, and what can be heard, are to a large extent determined by the context of any given piece of communication. These doctors' advice to their readers (other doctors) reveals a consciousness of struggle with their patients which is not so apparent in other parts of the text.

Doctors express great frustration with women's ways of describing their menstrual experiences. Each doctor in each book patiently explains that the cycle must be counted from the first day of one period to the first day of the next. We can deduce that women tend to count bleeding days and non-bleeding days, and that the translation is beyond the patience of busy doctors. One text, Garrey *et al*, suggests that by-passing speaking with the woman at all is a good plan, since she is unlikely to know what has already been done to her:

> Previous gynaecological history is best learnt about from clinical records if obtainable. Gynaecological pathology and terminology are mysterious to most women. (Garrey:66)

Even with simple information like the date of the last period, doctors are advised not to accept the woman's word. Women are expected to be unable to report on their cycle length, and Jeffcoate suggests that when investigating symptoms related to the menstrual cycle 'if reliable information on menstruation is needed, ask the husband!' (p. 4).

Various studies (for example Stimson and Webb 1975; Graham and Oakley 1981) have identified the methods by which the passivity of patients within medical consultations is achieved. Richman and Goldthorp (1977) have looked specifically at gynaecological consultations, and found in their 1974 study that only two-thirds of the patients gave recognisable reasons for their treatment. Over one third did not know which organs were being treated or removed. They suggest that 'the patient's ignorance of her anatomy facilitates the gynaecologist's sequencing techniques' – that is, his reorganisation of the information given him into some kind of explanation.

One striking finding was that 'the word most frequently used by all gynaecological patients is "yes" and its equivalents' – the patient is not allowed to take the initiative in defining her own troubles. Thus it is interesting that the texts I studied start their discussions with such definite assertions that women are likely to be unable to discuss menstruation in an appropriate way.

I found, further, that women were expected to attempt to mislead the doctor. This appears very clearly in relation to menstrual pain. Jeffcoate thinks that dysmenorrhoea 'may ... be an excuse to avoid doing something which is disliked' and that 'a description of intense pain dating from the menarche should raise doubts about its reality' (p. 538). Since individual men, too, expressed doubt about the reality of menstrual pain I will discuss this lack of empathy with women's pain as a general phenomenon in my chapter on pain. However a woman's word is doubted in a much more general way. Garrey, for instance, suggests that complaints of pain generally cannot be taken at face value, for 'A neurotic patient will employ colourful imagery like "red-hot" drill' (p. 69).

Jeffcoate introduces his textbook with a section discussing psychosomatics in gynaecology where he sets out his view of his patients:

> A woman faced with unwanted responsibilities, or with any distasteful situation, often tries to escape by blaming genital organs about which there remains an air of mystery which secures for her the sympathy of other women or of the over-solicitous husband. ... The majority of women are unconscious of these factors in their illness and, when made aware of them, ... can adjust themselves to ensure a cure. There are a few, however, who deliberately set out to deceive. (p. 2)

Women are also believed to lie about how much they are bleeding: 'Sometimes patients give dramatic accounts of heavy loss which direct observation in hospital does not confirm' (Clayton and Newton:104).

Because of this problem, some of the texts give estimates of the proper number of towels or tampons women should use per period.

About a dozen internal tampons might be used for one menstruation; but the patient's estimate of loss may be unreliable, especially if she uses phrases like 'torrential' or 'welling up'. (Garrey:67)

The previously normal pattern should be ascertained and an attempt made to estimate the blood loss from the increase in the number of towels used. In this respect some patients will use words like 'flooding' and 'coming up like a well', giving an impression of haemorrhage not supported by appearances or by the haemoglobin level. (Garrey:86)

Jeffcoate reckons that women should use three 'diapers' (an unusual term, surely) or tampons in 24 hours, two by day and one at night, and should use up to 12 to 15 for one period (Jeffcoate:87).

It is difficult to see what interest a woman would have in persuading a doctor that she was bleeding very heavily, if there was no real problem behind it. Heavy bleeding appears to be difficult to treat successfully, short of hysterectomy, and one cannot help wondering if this explains the hostility expressed towards women complaining of it.

Gynaecologists seem to regard their patients as persons without honour. Scully and Bart (1978) summarise the doctors' attitude to women as follows: 'She is considered a cranky child with a uterus'. But the British texts discussed here seem to see women as positively calculating; not so much irresponsible as actively using their bodies in an attempt to avoid work, or some other 'distasteful situation': sexual intercourse perhaps? One of the tasks of gynaecologists appears to be to prevent women from 'using it to get out of things' – the accusation from male culture.

Beard *et al*'s (1977) study of pelvic pain in women shows this motivation. They conclude that 'the basic psychological defect of these women appears to be difficulty in externalising their feelings when subjected to emotional stress'. They focus their problems in the pelvis because 'a number of our patients undoubtedly used the symptom, whether consciously or unconsciously, as a reason for avoiding close physical involvement with their partners' (p. 570).

I find this prophecy particularly alarming:

If psychosexual disturbance can be one of the causes of pelvic pain, then it seems likely that with the greater sexual freedom of our society this symptom may become a more common complaint in gynaecological and surgical clinics.

Why would sexual 'freedom' make women sicker? Unclear though the doctors' image of society is, it is plain that they see themselves as maintenance engineers working to ease heterosexual relations.

There is an element of distrust of the patient within much medical discourse. However I think that *women's* honour presents special problems. In patriarchy, what makes a woman honourable is that she has some satisfactory relationship to a man. A woman's honour refers to her success as a virginal daughter or as a faithful wife (Rich 1980). It is very clear that gynaecologists regard the majority of their patients as suffering from social or psychological problems stemming from failure properly to fulfil the feminine role. Thus they are by definition under suspicion of being dishonourable in this specific sexual sense – how can they be expected to act with honour in their interaction with the doctor?

One way that patients can escape from this suspicion is to get better quickly and as a result of the treatment the doctor deems suitable for her condition – the sicker a woman is, the more she is suspected of neurosis, or of some kind of evasion. 'Intractible' comes to refer equally to her personality as to her medical condition.

There is perhaps also a kind of double standard operating within this system, for a wife should be accorded some respect. Doctors may, like men generally, see women in general in one way, while maintaining a different view of particular women – their own wives, or women like their wives in some way. Thus a woman who behaves in a feminine fashion may draw out kindness and concern, a protective attitude, for she will be seen as likely to be striving to have honour as a male-defined woman.

Manner

Another aspect of the interview situation which came to my

notice in the course of studying these texts is the issue of
how, in a very general sense, gynaecologists should speak to
women. This is not always regarded as a problem. I was very
struck, on reading a text published in 1948, by Wilfred Shaw,
that he devoted considerable space to a discussion of how the
doctor could investigate very personal aspects of a woman's
life without giving offence. 'First endeavours should ... be
directed towards gaining the patient's confidence; details in
the history can conveniently be left for later' (Shaw
1948:100). Of the more recent texts, only Barnes includes a
statement equivalent to this concern: 'Many women find it
difficult to discuss the intimate details of their lives and tact
and discretion are needed' (p. 26).

Garrey's section on these issues, in which he does recommend that the patient needs privacy, time and sympathy,
begins with these statements:

> The ancient Greeks believed that the behaviour pattern of
> hysteria was related to disease of the womb (Gk: hystera,
> womb). A woman discussing some condition related to her
> genital tract will often show signs of stress – embarrass-
> ment, fear, shame. (p. 66)

Given what we have learnt about the etiquette of menstruation, it is plain that this etiquette must be negotiated in some
way for a gynaecological consultation between a woman and
a male doctor to take place. Indeed even with a woman
doctor, the doctor's office will be seen as a public place, and
the doctor is certainly initially a stranger. Most women do not
ordinarily discuss menstruation or refer to their sexual and
reproductive organs in any way except in the most private of
interactions: it is hardly to be wondered at that it can present
problems. Garrey's implication that women may appear
embarrassed by discussing what he calls the 'genital tract' as a
result of some direct relationship of the womb to the mind is
a startling example of a mode of thought which ignores what
must be obvious social phenomena to place blame on the
individual patient.

Jeffcoate, interestingly, advises that doctors should adopt a
'coldly scientific attitude', rather than being excessively familiar and addressing women as 'my dear' or 'mother'
(Jeffcoate:3). That this advice should be thought necessary is

interesting. Perhaps we are seeing a shift in the personal style of doctors, from the purely paternalistic-authoritarian to a more removed, godlike stance? Perhaps this is found to be a more successful method of bracketing-out the medical consultation from other male-female interactions. It is notable too that Richman and Goldthorp observed that ordinary everyday politeness, a greeting like 'Good day', is not normal in gynaecology, while, they say, it is routine in ante-natal clinics.

There seems also to be considerable variation among the texts as to what kinds of questioning women should be put through. I have an impression of a trend towards more questions aimed specifically at finding out about the patient's sex life. Some texts (Llewellyn-Jones 1982; Styles 1982) also express an assumption that women with menstrual pain are likely to be sexually maladjusted in one way or another without spelling out a method of investigation.

Jeffcoate, whose first edition came out in 1957, and is therefore the second oldest text, suggests quite other types of questioning as appropriate to the gynaecological interview:

> Why does she go out to work and who looks after the children while she does? [. . .] Why is she worrying about a trivial symptom or is it her mother worrying on her behalf?

These are two from a long list (p. 3). The change we see here is only that the prescription for healthy femininity now goes beyond a concern for a woman's performance as a mother to a focus on her attitude to sex.

The idea seems to be that confession may have some therapeutic value in itself. Like religious confession, this process gives the confessor, the doctor, a great measure of power over the patient – it contains the potential to be a very humiliating experience for the woman.

While on the subject of the generally invasive nature of the gynaecological examination, I was startled to find two of my six texts suggesting examination under anaesthesia as a useful procedure. Llewellyn-Jones recommends it for cases of irregular menstruation in adolescence which do not respond to treatment (p. 249). It is not explained what is being looked for in this way. Dewhurst suggests that when investigating secondary amenorrhoea, 'In many unmarried women it is better to perform [the vaginal examination] under anaesthesia' (p. 64). Better for whom, one wonders, given that general anaesthetics are by no means without risk?

I was interested to find that, in a 1969 article on pelvic pain, Jeffcoate cautioned against the use of examination under anaesthetic by the gynaecologist 'in doubt or too hurried to "listen" to and analyse the patient's story'. He cited two cases he had known of women who died after a doctor ruptured an ectopic pregnancy in this way, and notes that a cyst could also be ruptured. This seems an extreme case where medical technique is used in an attempt to avoid problems created by the etiquette of the power relations between women and men.

MENSTRUAL PROBLEMS

These texts appear to have difficulties in the definition of every kind of menstrual problem. Both menstrual pain and 'premenstrual tension' are areas where there is a basic conflict over whether they are to be seen as normal parts of life, as illnesses, or perhaps as some intermediate phenomenon. Pain and PMT are discussed in Chapters 8 and 9. The next most common menstrual disorders are amenorrhoea (no periods) and excessive menstrual bleeding (also called menorrhagia or dysfunctional menstrual bleeding).

With both these conditions, the doctors' first concern is to eliminate the possibility that they are a sign of some underlying disease. Amenorrhoea can be produced by a very wide range of systemic diseases, while excessive menstrual bleeding can be a symptom of uterine cancer, among other illnesses. Both polyps and fibroids (myomata) can produce heavy bleeding, but these should be possible for the gynaecologist to feel during the standard pelvic examination, so present fewer problems of diagnosis.

Patients with amenorrhoea may undergo a number of tests to seek out any underlying causes; with excessive bleeding, after a simple pelvic examination, a 'D and C' (dilation and curettage) is the usual next step. This can diagnose cancer of the endometrium, but is also held to be curative in some cases. Richman and Goldthorp write that 'The often prescribed D and C has much the same medical curative status as ECT (electro convulsive therapy) has in psychiatry'. There is much disagreement about its effectiveness, and it undoubtedly holds some ritual meaning beyond this.

If no 'cause' can be found, the doctors acknowledge that treating either problem is quite unlikely to be effective. In many cases the conditions will resolve themselves spontaneously, and the doctors therefore cannot know whether any treatment has in fact made a difference (Clayton and Newton:104). Both conditions are said to be frequently psychologically caused. Which comes first, inability to treat, or the psychological label, I do not know. Garrey writes:

> The root cause of dysfunctional bleeding is often psychological and no treatment aimed to the uterus will cure the patient. Also, there is a tendency especially in the younger woman towards a spontaneous return to a normal cycle. (Garrey:87)

Of amenorrhoea, Llewellyn-Jones writes in different language:

> once chromosomal and congenital abnormalities are excluded as causes of amenorrhoea, over 60 per cent of cases are due to hypothalamic malfunction. These are mainly due to environmental and psychosomatic (emotional) factors. ... (p. 84)

There are a number of psychological mechanisms which are said to cause amenorrhoea, among them stress, loss of weight, pseudo-pregnancy. Amenorrhoea is only to be treated if the woman wishes to become pregnant.

It is not clear to me what the psychology of 'dysfunctional uterine bleeding' is supposed to be – no author goes into any detail. Whatever it is, it must be very common. Dewhurst says that this category covers 10 per cent of new gynaecological patients (p. 606).

Llewellyn-Jones states rather generally that 'Anxiety states, marital disharmony, submerged fears, separation, over-work and sexual frustration may lead either to amenorrhoea or to abnormal uterine bleeding' (p. 75). It is remarkable how lightly some doctors assume some undisclosed psychological cause. Introducing a recent book on psychology and gynaecological problems, R. W. Beard refers in passing to 'conditions with a primary psychological aetiology such as menorrhagia' (1984:x).

Again there is thought to be a problem of definition. Four authors estimate the volume of blood which is lost in normal menstruation, presumably in the hope of these estimates acting as some sort of control.

Quantity of blood normally lost:
Barnes: 6 to 170 cc, average 50 cc
Clayton and Newton: 30 to 90 ml fluid, of which half is blood
Garrey: 1 to 7 oz, 30 to 200 ml
Llewellyn-Jones: 10 to 120 ml, average 50 ml

The treatment of women with dysfunctional uterine bleeding is determined by the fact that the emphasis is on investigation for other underlying disease. Once this has been concluded (a lengthy process), a woman is given various hormones to suppress the bleeding, and if that does not work (and there is every indication that it will not), she may be offered a hysterectomy.

It is not at all clear to me whether or not the doctors believe that excessive bleeding is in itself at all damaging to women's health. There is some discussion of the problems of anaemia, but apparently not all women with this problem become anaemic. Perhaps doctors do not concern themselves with this question because women themselves regard excessive bleeding as a problem. Thus we get a strangely flat statement like this from Clayton and Newton: 'In exceptional cases hysterectomy is required' (p. 105). There is no way of telling in what way these cases are exceptional, or by whom the operation is 'required'. Garrey is more enthusiastic – under the heading 'Total hysterectomy' he writes:

This is the best treatment for the woman over 45 and is a last resort for the young patient who has not responded to drug treatment. It puts a stop to the constant blood loss and gets rid of an organ which is a common site of cancer. (Garrey:88)

Radiotherapy (that is, the use of radium to induce an early menopause), seems to be a treatment which is going out of fashion. It is only mentioned in Dewhurst, and is said to have a small place in the treatment of women over 40, though he acknowledges that it tends to cause cancer.

Llewellyn-Jones includes an argument against the use of hysterectomy, which he says has been excessive, criticising this practice mainly on the basis that the problems for which it is used are often psychological (p. 81).

There is certainly a contradiction in the gynaecologists' practice, for they are forever advocating the treatment of problems they see as psychogenic with surgery or with hormones. They hardly ever suggest any form of psychotherapy, unless you count pep talks from themselves: for example Jeffcoate suggests that

> The best hope of limiting the intensity of spasmodic dysmenorrhoea, or the incapacitation it causes, lies in teaching young girls a proper outlook on menstruation, sex and health in general. . . . (p. 529)

Psychotherapy, though, or any deep exploration of the woman's feelings, is never mentioned.

This seems to have been a special feature of gynaecology for a long time – Barker-Benfield (1975) notes that in the 1860s and early 1870s doctors 'began to practise the surgical treatment of the psychologic disorders of women'. Barker-Benfield analyses this practice in late nineteenth-century America as an attempt to re-establish control over women. Of course this was before any 'talking therapy' was widely practised or accepted. In modern gynaecologists this attitude is more surprising in its illogicality.

Angela Coulter's work on hysterectomy (1984) brings out the problems here. Feminists have tended to focus on attitudes like that of Garrey quoted above, where doctors see the womb as an unnecessary cancer-prone organ. In the US especially, there has seemed to be an alarming enthusiasm for hysterectomy (see also Morgan 1978; Daly 1978). But at the same time, Coulter found that many British women who suffer from heavy bleeding find that doctors are unsympathetic and uninterested in giving treatment. Hormonal treatments are a possibility, but not especially safe or effective, and women often want a hysterectomy as the only solution to a debilitating problem.

The texts I looked at spell out exactly the attitude such women report — that excessive bleeding is unimportant unless it produces some 'objective' measureable effect like a low blood iron level, and that women who worry about it have probably produced it themselves by their own neurosis. No account is taken of the discomfort and inconvenience of this condition, whether or not it also has other physical effects. These problems are of course exacerbated by the etiquette of secrecy which men require of women in this society.

My overriding impression of the material in gynaecology texts on menstrual problems is that very little is known about them, and that little more is likely to be learnt unless some major change of attitudes comes about for the texts are full of 'let-out clauses' providing excuses for their lack of attention to these problems.

DON'T LISTEN TO YOUR MOTHER

One special aspect of the gynaecologist's attitude to menstrual problems, as opposed to the general male attitude, is that the doctors seem particularly concerned to blame the mother for a woman's problems. Perhaps this arises from the doctors' need to establish their own authority in this area — they must therefore attack alternative sources of information. The attack on mothers is most prominent in relation to menstrual pain.

The Lennanes wrote in their excellent early article, criticising medical attitudes to women (1973), that given the evidence it is remarkable that the medical fraternity do not declare dysmenorrhoea an inherited disorder.

But they do not. The first place I came across the line of thinking they favour was in Margaret Mead's *Male and Female* (1950). She writes that:

> Careful studies of dysmenorrhoea in America have failed to reveal any consistent factors among women who manifest pain except exposure during childhood to another female who reported menstrual pain. (p. 208)

Mead gives no references for these 'careful studies' nor do

the doctors whom I suppose to be the originators of this theory. Jeffcoate states:

A dysmenorrhoeic mother usually has a dysmenorrhoeic daughter. A girl who is an only child is more likely than most to suffer from dysmenorrhoea. (p. 538)

McClure Brown agrees. On the psychological factors relevant to the aetiology of period pain he writes:

Often the patient is an only child, the 'apple of her mother's eye' who has been coddled and protected from childhood, and whose every minor upset has been a cause for maternal concern. (p. 91)

So the mother's relationship to her daughter in itself can create pain in the daughter. And a girl whose mother is especially concerned for her welfare is particularly likely to suffer!

To be more specific, mothers may give their daughters a 'bad attitude'. An article in *Update* (Styles 1982) states that '. . . factors that undoubtedly contribute to the severity of the pain are the patient's attitude to menstruation and in particular the preparation she received for it from her mother' (p. 1694).

There is, the gynaecologists say, no pain in cycles where ovulation does not take place; and they claim that girls never ovulate during their first few menstrual cycles. Therefore:

Dysmenorrhoea during the first few cycles may suggest it is due more to the incorrect attitude of the girl and her parents than to painful contractions of the uterine muscle. In such cases it may be manifest when interviewing the parents that the girl has been influenced by hearing graphic accounts of her mother's suffering, which not surprisingly may affect her own. It may not be easy to undo the harm done in this kind of case, but a simple explanation of the physiology of menstruation given sympathetically should help. (p. 31)

This passage is part of one third of a page devoted to period pain in a book of over 600 pages, a respected gynaecology text.

Llewellyn-Jones' book follows the same line of thought.

Dysmenorrhoea comes in a chapter on adolescence:

> The severity of the pain is influenced by cultural attitudes,
> particularly those of the child's mother and older sisters.
> (p. 249)

So, some doctors think that mothers actually *create* their
daughters' pains, others that they merely make them worse;
they are unanimous that mothers are a crucial problem.
Jeffcoate, who seems to be more openly engaged in sexual
politics than most, remarks in a general way about psychosomatics in gynaecology that:

> The mother who does not wish to lose her daughter by
> marriage, and the elderly husband who is afraid of losing
> the affections of his young wife, are particularly prone to
> encourage illness in the object of their affection. (p. 2)

Gynaecological problems are suspected of being a form of
indirect marriage-resistance. And in the case of period pains,
this resistance cannot be in the interests of the daughter – for
nothing but marriage could cure her:

> It is important that the girl should realise that her com-
> plaint is likely to be shortlived and that immediate pros-
> pects of marriage and child-bearing justify the deferment
> of drastic measures. (p. 539)

How is this mother-induced condition to be treated, if it can
be treated? As we have seen, the 'girl' will be encouraged to
confess, and then the doctor will attempt to inculcate a 'better
attitude' in her. There is great emphasis upon this notion
that a good attitude can be produced, and that pain-free
menstruation will follow.

I want to suggest that the crux of this practice is the denial
to women of information about other women's experiences.
Women who suffer pain with menstruation are presumably
expected to lie to their daughters about it. And what exactly
is this healthy attitude? The problems are firstly, the fact that
for many women it hurts, and secondly, the cultural require-
ment, the etiquette, that it should be kept secret from men.
What women must be taught is, quite literally, to suffer in
silence. They must be persuaded that their pain is their fault
and that it is evidence of weakness or rebellion for women to

refer publicly to menstruation at all. Women have to be persuaded to participate in the loud silence which surrounds menstruation. Mothers and daughters must learn that it is bad for them to communicate with one another about their similar bodies.

The content of a 'healthy attitude' in a discussion which precludes any challenge to patriarchal culture is silence. What is interesting and worth discussing about menstruation is the way in which it is used against women by men, and that is not on the agenda. Those gynaecologists who mention the cultural restrictions which surround menstruation brush them aside as if to say that only neurotic women would perpetuate these practices. Men, as usual, are absent from the picture.

This kind of mother-blaming is not confined to gynaecologists, but can be found running through much of what is written about menstruation. A pamphlet put out by Tampax Ltd, designed to help mothers explain periods to their daughters, nicely sums up the way in which the mother is trapped by the etiquette of menstruation:

> Happily we now live in more enlightened times. Menstruation has now come to be recognised for what it is – a completely natural bodily function. No woman need feel 'unclean' or restricted during her period. . . . Your daughter should be assured of this – no one else need ever know that she has a period.

The mother is required to teach her daughter concealment without conveying a sense of shame – surely an impossibility.

Another twist to this tale of enforced betrayal of daughters by mothers can be found in Shuttle and Redgroves' *The Wise Wound*. In a long book, all about menstruation, they only mention the mother–daughter relationship twice, to quote other writers' negative remarks about it. Their hope appears to be for women to be cured by a new kind of heterosexual relationship. What they do focus on is the effect on children of both sexes of their mother's suffering. They feel that children are constantly being traumatised by their mothers' failures to acknowledge that they are menstruating.

It is striking, though, that interest is actually focused on the experience of the boy child (p. 74). C. D. Daly, it seems, has created an entire system of psychoanalysis revolving around the trauma the mother's menstruation causes in boy children (p. 55). And Shuttle and Redgrove devote several pages to a reanalysis of dreams by which they attempt to demonstrate that the infant Jung was traumatised by his mother's menstruation (pp. 105–9).

What Shuttle and Redgrove seem to be concerned with is warning civilisation that it must take account of the experience of menstruation or be in danger from menstruating women. As followers of psychoanalytic theory, they believe that human personalities are crucially formed in early childhood. They see women during their paramenstruum ('around menstruation' – a term they take from Dalton which covers half one's menstruating life) as out of control, emanating dangerous influences, *correctly* perceived by men as threatening. The unfortunate infant is of course especially vulnerable to this monster, being in close contact with her. The obvious implication from what they say, admittedly not spelt out, is that women as mothers, having menstrual cycles, have driven men mad, and that is why men do not wish to know about menstruation.

This kind of theorising is particularly pernicious when it sets up the mother–daughter nexus as in some way explanatory of other social relationships. In fact the reverse is likely to be more nearly true – women's relationships to their daughters are very much determined by the requirements of patriarchal society.

Mary Daly (1978) has drawn attention to this phenomenon, where women, often mothers, are used as 'token torturers' within patriarchal institutions. She discusses genital mutilation, also called female circumcision, in Africa, and footbinding in China – both ritually carried out by women. In both these cases, a girl who had not undergone these mutilations would not be regarded as eligible to marry: certainly she could not make a 'good' marriage. When women must marry to survive, how many mothers will refuse to inflict such practices on their daughter? In the same way, everywhere, a woman who failed to train her daughter to survive in patriarchy, for instance who neglected to teach her the etiquette of menstruation, would merely expose her to ridicule or worse at the hands of men.

THE MEDICAL POINT OF VIEW

How are we to regard the medical mode of discourse on menstruation? Paula Weideger titles her chapter on this subject 'Witch Doctors: The Gynaecologist as Shaman'. The image of a shaman fits in certain ways – gynaecologists do attempt to fulfil the function of reintegrating the deviant woman into her correct place in society, of producing words to reinterpret her experiences to her in such a way that they make sense. But the image of the shaman is that they are very successful healers, well-integrated themselves into their culture, well-accepted. Even within their own textbooks there is evidence that gynaecology does not work in quite this way: successful cures are rare. Beyond the textbooks there is a great deal of evidence that women are not satisfied with gynaecology – the movement for better women's health care is at the heart of the women's liberation movement, and has had great influence (Marieskind 1975a; Ruzek 1979).

Nor is this struggle anything new. Medical arguments were used in the nineteenth century against women's rights, particularly women's right to education. When the achievements of a few women began to make the view that women were simply too stupid for higher education untenable, Edward H. Clarke at Harvard (1873) and Henry Maudsley (1874) in London produced theories about the development of the reproductive system which asserted that intellectual effort would permanently damage women's health (Burstyn 1980). A number of the earliest women doctors did research specifically to refute these arguments – they were also concerned in general to establish the normality of menstruation. Clelia Duel Mosher (1923; 1980) and Mary Putnam Jacobi (Walsh 1977; The Women's Medical Association of New York 1925) carried out surveys of women's menstrual experiences.

Feminist historians (Rugen 1979; Blake personal communication) suggest that this may have been one of the reasons for the male resistance to women becoming doctors – that for the first time women would be able to refute their misogynist arguments as professionals. This long history of resistance within medicine does not, however, seem to have

had a great deal of impact on the ideas expressed in the texts
I studied.

It is not, however, an entirely straightforward matter to say
what it is that feminists want of gynaecologists. There is a
tension between two directions of analysis: firstly that men
tend to focus on women's sexual organs as the cause of their
problems and to engage in invasive, often surgical treatment,
which attacks the integrity of women's bodies (Raymond
1980; Daly 1978). Secondly it is also true that many women
feel that doctors *ignore* everyday and indeed sometimes very
serious health problems when they happen to women. But
this contradiction may not be at all deep.

An interesting perspective on gynaecology emerges when
one looks by contrast at the way in which medicine attends to
the male reproductive system. Naomi Pfeffer (1983, 1985),
has recently drawn attention to the other side of the issue –
that men's sexual and reproductive systems are represented
as flawless. Researching infertility, she found that medical
knowledge about men's problems, for example with the
prostate gland, is at a very primitive level – even though such
problems are extremely common. Men are evidently suffering physically from propaganda which benefits them socially.

Diseases of the male reproductive system are frequently
categorised as belonging to other systems – there is no
equivalent medical specialism to gynaecology, only 'urology'.
Once we focus upon this refusal to acknowledge any possible
weaknesses or malfunctions in the male reproductive system,
it becomes clear that an image of the female system as
especially prone to problems depends upon an implicit
comparison with the supposedly superior male. And that the
widespread belief that women's reproductive systems are
particularly elaborate and finely-tuned is a function of the
fact that they have been studied extensively. Complexities
appear when one looks at a thing in detail. Pfeffer's comparative approach produces extremely useful insights for the
sociology of gender and of medicine.

The very existence of gynaecology sets up a group of
people, surgeons in fact, for whom the female body is the
field of their work – as Barker-Benfield found in the
nineteenth century, their gaze has not been confined to the
body, but has attempted to 'cure' 'the very soul of woman'

(Dr Charles Meigs 1851). Thus while the two analyses, of invasion and of neglect, may conflict in certain cases, both are generally true, for the essential motivation of the profession of gynaecology is towards control, control over women.

Gynaecologists struggle with women for a monopoly on the right to distinguish the normal from the abnormal – to control the boundaries of normal femininity. Their writings are not always theoretically consistent, for what they are engaged in is very much a practice: texts do not explain so much as impart a tradition. They tell what 'it is usual' to do. This is one reason why it seems to be such a very closed, unchanging, system of thought.

In a sense, gynaecologists do the dirty work of the patriarchy, dealing in areas which are on the whole hidden from the male view. The speciality is not highly respected within the medical profession, perhaps exactly because it is only women over whom the gynaecologist can exercise medical power.

Perhaps menstrual disorders are the dirtiest of the dirty work they must do, unredeemed as they are by direct connection to childbearing, unredeemed too by any potentiality for saving lives. Certainly menstrual problems are seen as evidence that the woman is in rebellion against, or failing at, her job of being female.

8 Men's Views of Menstrual Pain: A Failure of Empathy

Menstrual pain seems to be a crucial example of the way in which men's and women's versions of the meaning of menstruation conflict. Women in Esther Merves's study said that pain or discomfort was one of the most common reasons why they would mention their menstrual periods to someone else. Surveys show that over half of all menstruating women experience some sort of discomfort with menstruation. And yet pain is very rarely referred to in the academic literature on menstruation.

The etiquette of menstruation generally appears to apply equally to menstrual pain. The majority of the men I interviewed had never heard mention of menstrual pain at their workplaces. As I questioned them, they often realised for the first time the concealment by women that this must signify.

Reference to menstruation is most often implicit, silent, but women may be explicitly told not to mention it. A friend rang in to the personnel department of the large firm she was working for and reported that she was taking the day off because of period pains. The woman in the office said 'You can't say that. You must say you've got a cold'. When pressed, she agreed to put the truth on the form, but she clearly expected some terrible consequence to follow from this.

Similarly, in social situations, women are unlikely to mention menstrual pain to male friends and acquaintances. Only a few of the men I interviewed, those who had feminist friends who believed in speaking openly about such things, had heard women friends mention it. As one man put it:

> even close friends are not likely to come up and say to me, 'I've got a really bad period' – I mean it might come out in a discussion of . . . sexual feelings, or whatever, gradually [. . .] in conversations about contraception or relationships or – in that way . . . (M)

160

However it appears that a woman does generally tell a man she is in a heterosexual relationship with when she has pain. Not always, certainly, but among the young men I interviewed, this would be the norm. The existence of pain appears to make little difference to the rules of etiquette for menstruation generally.

In this chapter I will set side by side data from individual male interviewees and from gynaecologists, as representing some elements of the complex and contradictory perceptions of menstrual pain among men in this society. One can describe a spectrum of views, from a straightforward disbelief in the existence of menstrual pain, through rationalisations of this disbelief such as the idea that such pain is psychological, through also an acceptance that the pain exists, but is caused by failure to conform to sex role or to some other prescription for healthy living, to an acceptance of it as physical pain. After discussing these views, I will look briefly at how individual men relate to menstrual pain when it features in their personal lives. Finally I shall return to the issue of psychosomatic pain, to suggest that the notion of psychosomatics is a particularly important one to analyse in attempting to understand the sociology of gender and health and illness.

EXPLANATIONS OF MENSTRUAL PAIN

Basic Disbelief

Discussing pain generally, Ivan Illich (1976) identifies the problem of pain's 'exceptional epistemological status' – that one cannot *know* another person's pain:

> I am certain about the existence of their pain only in the sense that I am certain of my compassion for them. (p. 141)

Thomas Szasz, too, has attempted to analyse the meaning of pain (1957). He sees one of the symbolic meanings of pain as a method of asking for help. It follows then that:

> If the expression of pain is so fundamentally associated with asking for and getting help, it follows that pain

suffered in silence, or persistently unrelieved, may readily be interpreted as punishment [. . .] In order to secure this help (with getting relief from pain and with dealing with the danger signalled by the pain) it is essential that the meaning of the dangerous state be conveyed to another person. Whether this is easy or difficult depends upon how well the persons who are interacting understand each other. The distinction between physical and mental pain presupposes a two-body frame of reference. Physical pain denotes agreement, and mental pain denotes disagreement between sufferer and observer. (p. 86)

He therefore calls the notion of psychogenic pain a 'pseudo-explanation' which hides a real failure to respond to the person's problem.

Hear now how men described male culture's attitude towards menstrual pain:

I can remember that that was often a male reaction to period pains, that it was something that was not completely understandable, that it was something that was, that shouldn't happen, so therefore, men tended to think that it didn't happen, that it was something that women made up, to get out of things, or to sort of say, you know . . . I think a lot of men, I think I thought about it to an extent, and a lot of men probably still do, that it's something women do deliberately to cut themselves off from men to sort of make absolutely clear their difference, and their power in that sort of situation, and that they can sort of use it as a way of exerting control of the situations. I mean I certainly thought that when I was very much younger, in my teens. I can remember feeling irritated, feeling annoyed, feeling that there was nothing . . . that I didn't have any control over the situation, and that it was something that women used to exert control. (A)

I asked whether this related to sex in particular, or whether women were suspected of using it to get out of other things as well.

Mm, it's difficult because, I mean, when I was, I suppose, in my mid-teens, when I started to go out with girls, it *was* something that girls did, or used, to have some sort of control over men in general. But I suppose that became much more personal in terms of the first sort of proper sexual relationships that I had in my late teens and early twenties, that it was something that meant I wasn't in control of the situation, or that . . . not even that, that the person I was involved with had actually more control of the situation than I did. (*A*)

This is backed up by another man:

There's also a thing about men being very unsympathetic about it and . . . um . . . like if someone's got pains, backache or whatever because they're menstruating . . . and men being very unsympathetic. Bloody hell, it happens every month, you know [. . .] But also just that it's, it's a bit of a . . . it's as inconvenient, well, not *as* inconvenient, it's also inconvenient for the male who's having to deal with being sympathetic when he, when it's very difficult for him to do so, it becomes uncomfortable for him as well, I won't say *as* uncomfortable as for the woman who's experiencing the pain . . . and also, um, the impression is a lot that . . . that men tend to think that women play on it, that they're menstruating and therefore they've got a bit of pain and they can accentuate that pain to gain certain benefits, to get time off work, to get . . . whatever. (*H*)

In the men's group discussion, men strive to empathise with women by producing analogies – one explains his idea that men should not be angry but should make allowances for pre-menstrual women by saying that if you've got a hangover, you need people to be a bit more tolerant of you. Another man complains that 'you can't identify with it in the same way as if someone's got a cold, or the flu, or had a tooth out, or whatever it is'.

Gynaecology textbooks, as I have shown, display the extreme lack of trust with which the doctor regards his female patients. Several texts suggest that there is a general problem about assessing women's claims to be in pain – Garrey (1978) has a full page entitled 'complaints of pain'.

The section of this book which deals with dysmenorrhoea contains this interesting statement:

A moralistic attitude should be avoided. 'Pain' comes from

the Latin word poena, (punishment) [. . .] and the doctor should never imply that he believes the pain to be 'all in the mind'. (Garrey:117)

Jeffcoate writes as follows on 'congestive dysmenorrhoea':

> In most cases [. . .] the congestion is 'functional' (even hypothetical) and is due to over-anxiety, emotional insta- bility, inability to cope with domestic responsibilities, a sedentary life, mental and sexual upsets [. . .] Daily cold baths or showers in the inter-menstrual phase may tone up both circulation and mental processes. (p. 543)

There are, as we have seen, some special cases where the doctors are particularly suspicious – when their theory denies a woman's experience:

> A description of intense pain dating from the menarche should raise doubts about its reality. True dysmenorrhoea reaches a maximum between 18 and 24 and thereafter diminishes. (Jeffcoate:538)

In an otherwise quite practical article on pelvic pain, Jeffco- ate writes that 'the commonest form of alleged dysmenor- rhoea encountered in practice is a unilateral pain in one or other iliac fossa' (1969). Since he had just been lamenting the degree of medical ignorance which existed about the ana- tomy of the nervous system to the pelvis, that 'alleged' seems particularly uncalled for.

Most of these texts also refer to low pain threshold as a possible 'cause' of menstrual pain. Barnes writes that women with primary dysmenorrhoea (that is, pain starting with their first period) 'have a lowered threshold for pain and this may be caused by emotional disturbance or boredom with mono- tonous work' (1980:44).

The notion of low pain threshold is rather difficult to pin down. Certainly, with an individual, it is possible to say that their experience of pain may vary as a result of factors outside of the level of stimulus. But how can anyone judge the level of pain one person feels against that felt by another? When low pain threshold refers to a group of people (for example, young women) or to a category of illness (for example, dysmenorrhoea), I can only understand it as a judgement of prejudice. The doctors somehow *know* that the pain cannot be that bad, therefore the women must be oversensitive.

Gynaecologists' ideas about menstrual pain cannot simply be summed up as disbelief, though plain disbelief does seem to be the position from which they start. If the pain is real in any sense, it is seen as the creation of the woman, either individually, or as part of the category 'modern women'. Women with menstrual pain are faced with a network of interlocking ideas – all present both in everyday male discourse and in medical 'knowledge'.

Psychosomatic

The notion that menstrual pain is in the mind is expressed in a number of ways. The men's group discussion produced two of them:

> —the other thing is how much outside factors actually affect someone's periods. If they're feeling fit and happy and healthy, and life is generally wonderful, or, then, do periods fly by without anything, without anyone really noticing? On the other hand . . .
> —stress relating to periods . . .
> —right. And does stress ultimately reflect itself in periods whereas in men it reflects itself in other ways . . . ? Certainly periods do become heavier, or they don't have their periods, or they just go on for longer and longer . . . more or less any possible variation seems to occur if a woman's having particular problems [. . .]
> —I would suspect that for women if having a period is seen as a problem by society in general, and if you treat it as a problem as an individual, that could definitely cause problems itself, a sort of cyclical thing . . . I mean there's no way of really finding out how that operates . . . (Group)

The following speech from one of the men I interviewed shows how he feels he should offer me the psychosomatic theory as well as the one he had evidently been operating with himself:

I've put it down to bodily, I suppose, physical aspects –
hormonal balance and so on, and to some extent maybe
possibly genetic things. I've got children and they, three
daughters, who are menstruating and they've had a rough
deal ... hereditary, coming from X, probably. A couple of
them have got heart murmurs, for instance, nothing
serious, like X ... that was my thinking ... obviously I now
don't accept the concept that there is anything that is
purely physical, obviously the attitude that you approach
something in will influence how you personally perceive
something, how you perceive pain, in that sense. Whether
there are circumstances in which X was living with me,
were such that, the stress around her was particularly
accentuated at a time when maybe her body was dealing
with its natural function ... whether that was exaggerating
other tensions I don't know. You have to investigate that
proposition ... (N)

It is striking that heredity never seems to be investigated in
relation to menstrual pain, although mothers are frequently
blamed for teaching 'bad attitudes'. The possibility that some
kind of predisposition to menstrual pain might be passed on
genetically (through the father as well as the mother,
obviously) does not seem to have been considered. A large
US study (Chern *et al* 1980) has looked at inheritance in
relation to age at menarche, length of menstrual bleeding
and age at menopause, and found significant correlations
from mother to daughter. But these researchers did not look
at menstrual pain. The Lennanes point out this gap in the
research in their important article (1973) in which they
argued – for the first time in a medical journal – that doctors'
insistence that dysmenorrhoea, along with nausea in pregnancy, pain in labour and behavioural disturbances in
infants, is psychogenic, might be a 'manifestation of sexual
prejudice'.

Jeffcoate (1975) sets out his view that this is a problem of
personality as follows:

Menstruation is frequently accompanied by minor physical
and nervous disturbances ... The degree of disturbance,
however, depends to a large extent on the individual's
outlook on this physiological process, and on her deter-

mination not to allow it to interfere with her normal life. Highly strung and emotional women exaggerate the significance of menstruation while well-balanced individuals disregard it. In Britain and the USA 50% of women of less than 30 years of age experience aching or pain in the lower abdomen, pelvis or back before or during menstruation. (p. 87)

And this kind of attitude has a great deal of influence. Whisnant, Brett and Zegans quote the following passage from a Kimberley-Clark Corporation leaflet designed to educate young girls about menstruation:

A goodly share of that discomfort is in the mind. For modern doctors know that fretting can cause sickness, even pain, when there's no physical cause for either. (1975:817)

Whisnant *et al*'s analysis shows how young girls are urged to manage physical symptoms through what is essentially 'mind over matter', in just the same way as they are encouraged to manage the practical etiquette.

Linda Gannon (1981) has written a very interesting survey of the evidence for a psychological aetiology of menstrual disorders, looking at the studies doctors refer to and testing the adequacy of their methodology. She notes several ways in which studies comparing levels of 'neuroticism' with menstrual symptoms tend to produce self-fulfilling prophecies. Often researchers test out a great many correlations, for example Gruba and Rohrburgh tested 160, and found only 16 to be significant. They then reported these positive correlations and not those found not to occur. This is bad practice when actually the assumption the researchers begin with is that the correlations *do* exist.

Gannon also found three important cases where researchers had reported results which fitted their hypotheses regardless of the lack of actual findings to back them up from their experiments. There is a tendency to ascribe causation where only correlation can be shown. Levitt and Lubin (1967), for example, found a correlation between negative attitudes towards menstruation and reports of worse menstrual symptoms. They conclude that 'This appears to support the gynaecologists' contention that an unwholesome attitude towards menstruation may be involved in the etiology of menstrual complaints.' As Gannon points out, 'such conclusions are particularly unwarranted when common logic supports causality in both directions'.

The terminology used is interesting: the term 'psychosomatic', which at least acknowledges that the body is involved, only appears a few times in the texts I studied. Far more frequently, the term used is simply 'psychological'. Collins English Dictionary says that this means: 1. of or relating to psychology; 2. of or relating to the mind or mental processes; 3. having no real or objective basis; 4. affecting the mind. So the doctors' ideas have not strayed far from the commonsense male belief that women put it on.

Gynaecologists never recommend that women suffering from these complaints be sent for psychiatric treatment beyond 'reassurance' from themselves. Interestingly, some women psychologists in the USA have recently taken up the gynaecologists' theories and have tried to develop treatments from them – involving women in discussions about menstruation, and teaching them 'autogenic' relaxation methods (Heczey 1980). This sort of training teaches people to bear pain better – it does not prevent them from feeling it (Weisenberg 1977:1032).

If the doctors treat women at all, it is usually with surgery or with hormones. One operation which used to be used to treat severe menstrual pain is called presacral neurectomy – the relevant nerves are cut near the spinal column. Four of the texts I studied mentioned it as a last resort, though two argued against its use. Jeffcoate writes that because it is only used after simpler measures have failed 'it is usually reserved for the hopelessly neurotic type of patient' (p. 540). This kind of cheerfulness about the use of major surgery to placate women seen as actually mentally ill is most frightening.

Stereotyping the Sufferer

This is the gynaecologists' speciality. The very narrow image gynaecologists have of the kind of woman who has 'true dysmenorrhoea' is not one many people outside of medicine share. Women understand its consequences – that most women cannot get gynaecologists to take their pains seriously – but often do not know the cause.

The texts I looked at see menstrual pain primarily as a complaint of adolescence. Dewhurst only discusses dysmenorrhoea under the heading of 'Puberty and its disorders'. Other writers have various estimates as to the age group of women who suffer dysmenorrhoea: Llewellyn-Jones, 15–25; Jeffcoate, 18–24; Garrey, 16–26. Barnes says it 'tends to lessen after 25 and disappear after 30'. It is not entirely clear to me where this belief comes from. Perhaps gynaecologists never see older women with dysmenorrhoea because such women will already have learnt that they will get no help from them. This may be connected to their other belief that childbirth, at least 'usually', cures the pain.

But the descriptions of the dysmenorrhoea patient are more detailed than this. Barnes writes that 'it is commonest in single women and in infertile married women', and that 'Women with dysmenorrhoea often lead a sedentary life with lack of fresh air and physical exercise' (p. 44). Garrey considers that:

> There is no characteristic personality or physique but the hysterical patient will make the most of her dysmenorrhoea as she will of any other gynaecological complaint. (p. 117)

In this he is in a minority. As we saw in the last chapter, attention is focused upon the 'girl's' relationship with her mother, and the mother is held to teach her daughter to feel pain, either by example or by excessive concern for her well-being.

In a recent (1981) article on the subject, M. W. P. Carney asserts that 'This syndrome seems to be particularly common in introverted intellectualised neurotic women of obsessive personality' (p. 107).

I found that most of the men I interviewed had not considered why one woman suffers from pain when another does not – they took it more or less as given. Perhaps the gynaecologists' particular position encourages them to produce general theories of this kind.

Failure to Conform to Sex Role

The most blatant and widespread example of this thinking is
the doctors' insistence that having a baby – as they see it,
letting your body do what it is intended for – cures menstrual
pain. The explanations offered for this idea, where explanations are thought necessary, are at odds with one another.
Barnes suggests that this may be so 'possibly because the
parous uterus is more vascular and does not become
ischaemic' (p. 44). Garrey, on the other hand, looks for an
explanation in 'the psychological changes of motherhood'
(p. 117).

   It seems that in the past it was claimed that marriage alone
would cure period pain. Shaw (1948) writes that 'almost all
married women will say that they have not suffered so much
from dysmenorrhoea since marriage' (p. 346). None of my
later authors go so far, though Jeffcoate thinks marriage may
have an effect:

> Marriage may cure by removing the tension of a long
> engagement and by providing happy security; on the other
> hand, if it proves disharmonious, it can cause dysmenor-
> rhoea. (p. 538)

So although childbirth is not listed among the cures to be
offered to women, it would be logical if it was and in practice
doctors do recommend it. Jeffcoate even provides, under the
heading 'You need a baby!', a polemic against doctors
advising women to have babies. He suggests that:

> The nervous and physical reserves of some women àre
> limited and they can only tolerate a relatively easy and
> sheltered life . . . The woman who cannot adjust herself to
> being without a baby may be the very one who fails to
> adjust herself to having one. (p. 2)

There is strong evidence (Snowden and Christian 1983) that
this theory is simply not true as a general rule, although of
course some women's menstrual pain may disappear or
lessen after childbirth. I was most interested to read that
Indian doctors nearly always advise marriage and childbirth
as a cure for dysmenorrhoea. Mira Sadgopal (1983) notes the
fact that few women in India seem to be told their pain is

psychosomatic, as is so common in the West. She analyses this as follows:

> The expectation that women will of course want to get married and have children is so much a part of social tradition that this is accepted as the single most universal solution for dysmenorrhoea. Doctors have no second thoughts in recommending it . . .
>
> Can the universal advice that dysmenorrhoea is cured by marriage and giving birth be seen in isolation from women's position in society, and her nearly inevitable imprisonment in the home?

A complaint closely related to dysmenorrhoea, intestinal pain associated with menstruation, produces statements which show other ways in which doctors expect women to conform to their sex role. This is only dealt with in two texts, although Llewellyn-Jones writes that it is 'especially common in women aged 20 to 60, who often have a background of marital stress or sexual frustration'. However:

> Treatment is unsatisfactory and many patients have to learn to live with their disorder, until their domestic problems are resolved. Unfortunately the condition may persist even then, and since many patients have had a variety of surgical procedures, may become fixed in the patient's personality. Recently, amitriptyline (an antidepressant) has been used . . . (Llewellyn-Jones:74)

Jeffcoate also describes the patient with this complaint:

> The subject is nearly always the over-anxious type, finds it difficult to face up to her responsibilities, gives a history of several operations (including appendicectomy) and probably has an oversympathetic husband or mother.

Women will suffer if they fail to have happy marriages, enjoy sex, enjoy housework, or if they forget never to listen to their mothers.

The notion that specifically sexual maladjustment is at the root of menstrual pain seems to be a new one and to be growing in influence. Llewellyn-Jones, first edition 1970, advises that the investigation of dysmenorrhoea should feature centrally 'an assessment of the child's and her mother's attitude to sexual matters' (p. 250). A summary article in *Update*, published in May 1982, recommends that women complaining of dysmenorrhoea should be asked to take part in an 'exploration of attitudes to menstruation, sexual development and sexual activity' (Styles:1694).

'The right attitude', which gynaecologists regard as essential to painfree menstruation, also appears frequently in their chapters on sexuality. Women's sexual problems apparently generally derive from wrong thinking on their part, or, again, from an unfortunate upbringing.

Penelope Shuttle and Peter Redgrove, the authors of *The Wise Wound*, have different theories about how women's sexuality ought to be organised. They think that women should 'naturally' experience active heterosexual desire throughout the menstrual cycle, and that sex during menstruation is what is needed to cure period pain:

> In the human, or so it appears, the womb has become an organ particularly open to stimulation through the genital organs, and this is why if there is intercourse during menstruation it can be exceptionally deep. Without practice, the rawly-open womb may react with pain and irritation; as it is immensely alive to all that goes on in the individual, if she is told she is disgusting at that time, it writhes and cramps in anger and disgust. If the truth is told, however, and sexual stimulation is gentle and gradual, sex at menstruation can build up to an experience with completely different dimensions from that of sex at other times of the cycle, as for instance at the child-offering time, the ovulation, a fortnight earlier.
>
> If the sexual experience is not offered, the desire is there still, and the womb seems to cramp in unsuccessful attempts at orgasmic experience, and the result is spasmodic dysmenorrhoea. The orgasm cures. (pp. 147–8)

Given how much male ideology sexualises menstruation, and relates it to heterosexual intercourse specifically, it is not surprising that this conclusion could be arrived at. Some women may find that the muscle relaxation after orgasm relieves menstrual cramping, for a little while afterwards. It takes a masculine logic to conclude from this that what women need is more sex.

While in the modern period these ideas present themselves as new and 'progressive', one finds interesting echoes elsewhere. Both Hilda Smith and Patricia Crawford report that seventeenth-century doctors 'recommended sexual intercourse as a cure for menstrual disorders – matrimony for maids, vigorous sex for wives' (Crawford 1981). Margarita A. Kay (1981) found, too, that Mexican American women hold this belief. Sex, in these cases, is of course to take place at 'appropriate' times, not during the period.

Associated with these ideas are others which relate in a less straightforward way to women's sexual role.

Bad Living

Particularly in the older texts, gynaecologists recommend fresh air and exercise as solutions to menstrual pain. This is part of a general enthusiasm for outdoor exercise and a belief that it would cure all ills. But in the present day, when most people are able to take a reasonable amount of exercise, the constant recitation that it relieves pain participates in the myth that women spend their days in idleness. This notion comes up in the men's group:

—I often wonder how the Western lifestyle affects us, the pain it causes on women, I mean I know that certain remedies for women that do suffer a lot of pain is actually to take loads of exercise ... before the period starts ... Because the pain is ... really coming away from the wall, that's what's actually causing the pain, that's the cramps, the contractions, and often apparently taking a lot of exercise is one remedy that's been pushed around certainly ... by feminists ... whether it works ...
—develops the muscles so they don't get cramped?
—possibly, I don't really. . . .

Women athletes doing intensive training are often said to have fewer and lighter periods and less pain than other women – whether or not this is so, and also whether it is the result of training, I do not know. A woman with debilitating menstrual pain could find it very difficult to keep up a strict training programme. Shangold (1983) found that most women athletes report no change in their menstrual symptoms.

But I have found no evidence that an ordinary amount of general exercise, or the specific exercises which are prescribed from all sides for alleviating menstrual pain, have any effect. The ideological basis of this notion can be seen in that the possibility that menstrual pain may be made worse by the heavy lifting and carrying which most women do as part of housework, or by the endless standing and limitation of mobility which women who work in shops, factories and offices must endure, is never considered.

Another kind of bad living which one man I interviewed held to be responsible for women's problems is an impure diet. He was interested in 'natural' medicine:

H: could be useful in preventing and helping all sorts of complaints, which include women's complaints and menstruation, menstruation problems.
SL: Yes, and was it diet you thought was particularly successful?
H: Diet, to a large extent, to a great extent . . . exercise, also to a large extent . . . massage can be used both as a preventative and as an analgesic . . .
SL: so as a preventative, would that be about generally relaxing the person?
H: yeah, the person, and particular regions, the small of the back and the kidneys . . . and exercises, yoga exercises, for example, which act as a massage as well, which keeps your body in general good trim, so that any changes in the body can happen without too much . . . pain or whatever.
SL: And the diet you'd use, would that be a general purifying diet?
H: Yeah, sort of, vegetarian, wholefoods, cutting out processed, refined foods, chemical foods, additives, all that sort of thing. Because that ties in with what I'd heard about the purifying of the body through menstruation, that if someone is eating a lot of chemical stuff, they're likely to have more impurities in their blood which . . . they'll probably have a heavier menstrual flow and more difficulty menstruating . . . and certainly animal products tend to create menstrual difficulties . . . In fact women's complaints

in general ... probably a lot of men's complaints in the
same region, although men seem to have less complaints in
the reproductive system ...
SL: You think eating meat really affects that?
H: Meat and cheese, and stuff?
SL: Well, I don't know ...
H: There are a lot of women who've actually reverted to a
diet in the lines that I've said have cured, if you like,
menstrual problems ... have cured menstruation. The
problems which come with menstruation, they've managed
to alleviate ... and actually make more regular, that's
another thing which happens, the more balanced the diet
is, the more sure they can be about when they're going to
be, and they often go very much in line with the lunar
phases, they either come at the new moon or the full moon,
and fertility in conjunction [. . .]
   ... I don't know many women that don't have menstrual
problems, or I haven't met many women that don't have
... the ones that don't have, tend to be the people who are
very careful about their diet, and the other things I
mentioned, massaging and exercise ...

The logic of this line of thinking is revealed in this man's
response to a question about whether he saw menstrual
blood as similar to other blood:

No, I don't because I, it doesn't bother me so much but I
think there are certain impurities which are ... it's almost
used as a ... what, an excretory mechanism to get rid of
certain impurities from within the body. And I believe that
some women have heavier periods because they're trying
to get rid of more impurities ...

I know people who're on what I call a pure diet, a balanced
diet, er, they tend to have very little menstrual bleeding ...
I know people that have actually controlled their menstrual bleeding by using diet, virtual control. So I tend to
believe that theory of using the menstrual process because
you are getting rid of something that is not needed, that's
to say the lining of the uterus and in the fact I mean that,
physically that is different to the blood when you cut your
finger ...

... there's a lot of waste material mixed up with the blood
... I mean, the, the lining of the uterus, the unfertilised
eggs, are discarded because they're not needed and in a
way they are foreign bodies, they are impurities. On that
level certainly. But also as a sort of cleansing process of the
blood. I don't know whether menstrual blood has been
analysed to see if it contains ... (*H*)

The slippage between curing pain and 'curing menstruation',
and between an 'impure' diet and an impure female body, is
particularly evident in this man's thinking.

'Primitive' women don't have it

A further sophistication of this line of thought runs that
menstrual pain results from some aspect of civilised living,
and that 'primitive' women, living in a supposedly more
natural way, do not suffer from it. The men's group refers to
a mythologised primitive society:

You take other primitive in inverted commas societies, and
you know, pregnancy, isn't a problem, and quite often
that's because the women are, like, a lot fitter and stronger,
and I mean it would be actually quite interesting to find
out, you know, how much menstruation actually affected
those sort of women in societies where they were very
active, I mean in the physical sense, rather than the actual
taboos, I mean I've no idea how it actually affects them.
But I mean you never, in the sporting pages, see women
whingeing about 'oh I had my period, therefore I didn't
run 2/10 of a second faster', it's not a problem that comes
up on 'Sportsnight', or in the Olympics and yet all these
women have periods ... Olympic games, do you cut
somebody out if they're going to have their period?
[laughs] Is this what coaches and trainers do? I mean,
presumably not ... And [laughs]
—No, three gold medals, in *Our Bodies Ourselves* it quotes
three gold medals won in the Olympics by women who
were having periods ...
—mine of information, thank you ... (Group)

The gynaecologists, too, hold this belief. Llewellyn-Jones asserts:

> Thus adolescents in 'primitive races' are said to suffer less severe pain than those in more sophisticated Western societies. Within a single community the incidence of dysmenorrhoea is higher in the higher social classes. (p. 249)

An older text claims that there is 'reason to believe that its incidence has increased with the degree of civilisation of the community' (Shaw:342). The thinking behind this, for the doctors, seems to be that women were designed for constant childbearing, and that a 'natural woman' would therefore be cured by the time she was an adult by early marriage and childbirth:

> Presumably, if women married shortly after puberty and had a succession of pregnancies through the childbearing period of life spasmodic dysmenorrhoea would be extremely rare. (Shaw:346)

Are these statements entirely mythological – relating only to men's fantasies about what women's 'natural state' would be? Or when they say 'primitive societies' do they really mean that they believe women in underdeveloped countries do not suffer pain?

If it is the latter, the WHO's survey (Snowden and Christian 1983) gives no support to these ideas. It is true, however, that women on a very poor diet, and women living in very difficult conditions, for instance in a war zone, are likely to have scanty and irregular periods or none at all. Regular menstruation is a sign of health and women in underdeveloped countries are likely to suffer from malnutrition and the diseases of poverty which result from poor housing, bad water supply and so forth. Westerners are often happy to mythologise about 'primitive' societies regardless of the realities of life in the poor countries. What these myths are certainly about is victim-blaming. Robert Crawford (1977) has written about modern 'health education' that it distracts attention from the social causes of ill health by focusing on the notion that people are responsible for their own health. He sees a growing general tendency to link disease with

affluence, and regards this as a politically-motivated procedure which diverts people from the perception that, actually,
poverty causes most illness.

We can see this process in operation in relation to menstrual pain – we are being told that our own failure to
exercise, eat properly and think about sex in the right way
are the causes, and, further, that this is the price we pay for
not being peasants giving birth once a year in the corner of a
field.

Physical Causes

We should perhaps beware of attending only to the *explanations* given for menstrual pain in the gynaecology texts I
studied, for the treatments recommended may in fact point
to another logic altogether. A successful treatment may
undermine old theories of causation and this is to some
extent occurring at present in relation to menstrual pain and
the anti-prostaglandins. If this treatment is widely found to
be a success, this will give support to the idea that the cause of
menstrual pain is an excess of certain prostaglandins creating
overly intense cramping of the uterus (Shangold 1983).
Some writers (Budoff 1980; Haynes 1982) are highly opti-
mistic that this theory will replace the sexist explanations I
have discussed. Perhaps they are right. Only three of my
texts explain this theory and all give several alternative
theories as well; but time will tell for it is a relatively recent
theory.

All of these texts, however, were enthusiastic about oral
contraceptives as therapy for menstrual pain. The fact that
these are very often effective would seem to undermine the
claim that menstrual pain is a neurotic reaction, for surely
such neurosis could not be remedied by hormones? One can
only hope that such contradictions will in time come to have
their effect.

INDIVIDUAL RELATIONSHIPS

As well as giving me information about male culture on

menstrual pain, the men I interviewed also spoke more personally about how they themselves related to menstrual pain in women they knew. Whether or not men have anything to do with period pain varies greatly from one man to another. Partly it depends upon how much they are involved with women, and the particular experience of the women they are involved with. One man in the men's group said:

> [Painful menstruation] has been the experience all the time of the person I've been closest to, so that's very dominant in my mind.

However one of the younger men said that 'most of the women [he'd] known would tend to keep it very quiet' (K).

But the man himself has some control over this, as we saw when a man in the men's group described how he would in the past prevent a woman from telling him about it (see Chapter 3).

The men I spoke to reacted to menstrual pain in various ways. Several men spoke with straightforward sympathy about the women they knew and the pain they had seen them going through. However men also spoke of feeling resentful.

One man spoke about his feelings about his first girl-friend's menstrual pain:

> Initially I'd talk ... what's the problem? You've got a stomach upset? Take an Alka-Seltzer or something – I mean I would have been fairly ... fairly unsupportive, with something I was ignorant of. I wouldn't have been very understanding of it – it was gradually having to educate me to understand what was happening, to take a more suppor-tive role [. . .] It doesn't – I didn't experience that it got rid of my feelings of resentment – I still felt, slightly ... [inaudible].
>
> And maybe in that way I resent menstruation in itself, I don't know, maybe in that kind of way that it is something that seemed to interfere with ... our relationship and our enjoyment, and so on ... (M)

The men's group discussion brings out these issues:

> —And I'm not sure, other than verbally reacting different-

ly, and being more conscious of the problem it created,
I'm not sure in practical terms whether I actually have
progressed much from that.
—I remember having . . . being . . . what do you say?
extended stomach stroking periods, when I was . . . that
was my role [laughter]
—gosh, yes, memories coming back! bloody hell, yes,
[laughter] . . . yes, with the girl who found it very
painful, yes . . .
—But what's strange about it is that when I say it, getting
quite resentful about that . . . isn't that? I was just saying,
that was my job, you know [laughs]
—yes,
—I'm glad it's not just me [. . .]

—whether anybody else feels a bit sort of . . .
—guilt, guilt
—No, not so much guilt, but lacking in ability to be able to
respond properly, or to be sympathetic.
—Feel that the need to compensate is there . . .
—Yes, yes.
—You were mentioning the stomach rubbing, and one of
the interesting things is it's almost like an automatic
response to me, because it's been knocked into me for so
many years that this is how you respond to period pain,
that if somebody complains of it, I almost, I mean my
hand goes to . . . [laughter] I mean it's absolutely ridicu-
lous, and what's strange is that I mean I suppose I'd
learnt a response that was supposed to be to do with
providing a compensation for someone who was complaining of pain, but that response . . . was what that one
person wanted, and so different people . . .
—you've got a role there, haven't you?
—. . . and so different people, I suddenly think, oh god,
what's my job? I don't know, because they actually
mightn't want that . . .
—My response is to put the kettle on, fill two hot water
bottles, . . . one in front of the stomach, one at the
back . . .
—you had a whole routine as well then?
—. . . and then a back-scratching job. Well, more stroking,

rather than scratching . . .

—rubbing of hot water bottles, definitely!!

—Is that a form of, of self-flagellation, you know, I mean? [laughter]

—But no, in some ways . . . it's a ritual, isn't it? It's a way of saying 'I want to be part of this with you' . . .

—a sharing . . .

—well, I didn't create that, X created that, X created the hot water bottles, it's just occasionally I would notice that it was actually rather . . . she preferred to be lying down in bed rather than be pouring water into two hot water bottles. Sure, I would feel I was doing something useful by doing it for her.

—In some ways it's helpful, if someone's complaining of something, if there is a task to perform . . . If there isn't, I think you feel rather useless.

—I didn't feel bad or guilty . . . I didn't feel compensating . . . just that there was a need I could respond to. (Group)

One man in the group had recently undergone circumcision, and a speech he makes again reflects this ambiguous attitude:

This is wonderful. This is the first time in my life I've ever been able to turn to women and say 'you don't know what it feels like!' [laughter] I mean the number of times that I've had something like this guilt laid on me about sort of having babies, menstruating, being the . . .

—You've got a men's problem at last!

—[. . .] I'm actually for the first time in my life able to turn to women and say 'you don't know what it feels like' and you know it's true, it's wonderful. I've got some self-respect back . . .

[laughter] (Group)

Along with resentment, as I have already suggested, some men seem to use the women's pain in a ritual of togetherness. Thus they seek to reinforce the connection between them by entering into the experience with her, in a way analogous to the practice of couvade (cf. Douglas 1975). So her pain is made acceptable by relating it to himself in an intense way.

The feelings these men are discussing, then, in part produce and in part are produced by the larger context of how a male-dominated culture deals with menstrual pain.

NEW QUESTIONS

I have set out in this chapter some of the elements of men's view of menstrual pain. The basis from which men's attitudes seem to develop appears to be a refusal to accept women's description of their experiences. Women stand accused of inventing the pain so as to gain some advantage in their dealings with men. Medical theories further elaborate this denial with notions about psychosomatic pain, and with a whole range of theories which attempt to restrict the description of 'true' dysmenorrhoea to some limited section of the menstruating female population.

The logic of the male culture, that it shouldn't happen, therefore it doesn't happen, is very pervasive. Summing up the highly political and highly ambiguous way in which menstrual pain is understood in our culture, here is the reply given by one 15-year-old boy to Prendergast *et al*'s questionnaire (1982), when asked whether he thought menstruation had any effect upon women's lives:

It doesn't necessarily make any difference, it's all part of molly-coddling girls. They are equal now.

My own experience of contradictions around the subject of menstrual pain was one of the problems which led me to want to study the sociology of menstruation. My investigations of men's attitudes clarified for me why I felt such a weight of oppression in relation to this specific subject. It was still not easy, however, to work out a satisfactory way of understanding my own experiences for myself.

Many questions are raised in a new way if we wish to reconsider these androcentric beliefs. How widespread is menstrual pain? Is it confined to certain types of women? Is it a modern phenomenon, or a feature of certain kinds of society?

I have not been able to investigate these questions fully, but I did find evidence (Snowden and Christian 1983: Consensus Research Pty, 1978; Wood 1983) to convince me that menstrual pain is very widespread among menstruating women, and that it is not confined to young childless women. Nor does it appear to exist only in Western industrialised nations. Historical evidence is not plentiful. Samuel Pepys discusses his wife's pains in his diaries, from 1661 to 1669, with considerable sympathy. The medical sources from the sixteenth century and later (Eccles 1982; Crawford 1981; Smith 1976) mention menstrual pain, but this information remains scattered and inadequate. Menstrual pain entered into politics in the nineteenth century, when it became an issue in relation to the education of women (Showalter and Showalter 1972; Mosher 1923).

To accept that it can be so that menstrual pain really does exist as it seems to, requires one to rethink the conventional medical view of pain, that it signals some disorder, some danger to the body. It may perhaps be only within this modern mind-set, where we expect our lives to be free of pain, that menstrual pain appears as in any way anomalous. The notion of psychosomatic pain seems to be a peculiarly twentieth-century way of dealing with the existence of such an inconvenient phenomenon. I want, finally, to look more closely at this set of ideas about psychosomatic pain, because I think that the material on menstrual pain specifically raises important broader questions about attitudes towards female pain.

WOMEN, MEN AND PSYCHOSOMATIC PAIN

The notion that some kinds of disorders are psychogenic is very much part of the mechanical medical model – not a departure from it. It is something quite other than a recognition that *all* physical problems have a mental element – that the mind and the body are not separate entities.

The concept of psychosomatic pain seems to have developed during this century as a consequence of the failure of the medical model to account for all forms of disease. Doctors use it to stop the gaps in their knowledge – while claiming that their recognition of this sort of illness just shows how sensitive and subtle their approach is.

As I read generally about how notions of psychosomatics arose (importantly influenced by psychoanalysis), it gradually became clear that women and 'female troubles' were from the start one of the main problems that doctors concerned with psychosomatics aimed to deal with. Merskey and Spear's

book *Pain, Psychological and Psychiatric Aspects* (1967) is at once
a history and an advocacy of the psychological approach to
pain. It is striking that they write that in the early days of its
development: 'For a medical view that pain might be psychological in origin it seems that one must go to physicians and
surgeons' (p. 6). Psychiatrists were not interested, apparently, though their ideas were borrowed.

The first concept they identify as the seed of the idea of
psychosomatic pain is that of hysteria. Bart and Scully (1979)
have written an interesting historical account of the politics
of hysteria. They write that:

> while hysteria shows remarkable instability over time and
> lacks an objective or even uniform clinical picture . . .
> certain notable consistencies do emerge. Throughout the
> history of the concept . . . it is almost exclusively seen as a
> female problem.

The great majority of cases cited as evidence throughout
Merskey and Spear's book relate to female patients – though
their complaints are not necessarily specifically female ones.
Starting as they mean to go on, Merskey and Spear appro-
vingly quote 'a famous surgeon', Brodie, writing in 1837,
asserting that he 'estimated that in "upper class" women,
four-fifths of joint-pains were hysterical' (p. 7).

Evidently the 'cases' which worried the doctors, then as
now, which set them thinking about psychological causes for
illness, were most frequently women. This can be understood
as the result of a failure of sympathy from men to women –
men basically doubted the reality of what women said was
happening to them.

I would see this as part of the process of oppression. It is
interesting that doctors also hold a belief that men of the
manual working class 'use' pain (Weisenberg 1977; Spear
1967 quoted in Merskey and Spear). Spear identifies a group
of men of 'social class 5' who complain of lower back pain as
'routine-minded, obsessional types' (and see also Sternbeck *et
al* 1973). In a section titled 'personality attributes', Weisenberg says that using pain is a 'labouring class' attribute. The
contrast between this description of back pain patients and
the popular image of the coronary patient is striking. I would
see this as an analogous failure of sympathy: upper- and

middle-class doctors labelling the problems of working-class men psychological in the same way that they do those of women. In both cases the class interests of the doctors are closer to those who benefit from the labour of their patients than they are to the patients themselves. If they cannot be swiftly fixed up, their pain must be denied and disregarded – it is seen as a potential 'excuse'.

Around the turn of the century, Merskey and Spear identify another influence upon medicine – that of the sexologists. Just as evolutionary theories were promoting the idea that pain is a useful tool for survival, discussions began to develop about sadism and masochism. Writers like Kraft-Ebbing and Havelock Ellis drew attention to the existence of sexual sadism and masochism and, following their usual methods of thought, held them to be normal and natural. That women enjoy pain was for the first time presented as scientific fact. Ellis argued (1898), in 'Love and Pain', that pain was essential to women's sexual pleasure. Freud agreed with him.

This development justifies and carries to its conclusion men's tendency not to see women's pain as real. Women's psyches are presented as 'naturally' entirely different from men's, and conveniently designed to enjoy whatever abuse men want to subject them to. Merskey and Spear themselves regard masochism in women as normal and desirable:

> If, too, it is the case as Charles Kingsley puts it that 'Men must work whilst women must weep' then the value to women of some degree of all four types of masochism can be affirmed on biological, psychological and social grounds. (p. 123)

Merskey and Spear cite a great number of articles to support their thesis – mainly they are simply statements by doctors that they believe this or that group of patients with this or that complaint to be suffering from some psychiatric problem. The authors themselves have carried out some research which at least attempts to investigate these opinions in a systematic way. But the way they use dysmenorrhoea demonstrates how deeply prejudiced they are in their approach. They take it entirely for granted that dysmenorrhoea is a psychological problem, and try to use it as a kind of measure of a woman's tendency towards psychological pain generally.

But when they actually carry out comparisons between groups of women with other kinds of pain and control groups, they are obliged to report: 'A surprising finding, by both Spear and Merskey was that dysmenorrhoea was not reported significantly more often in the index groups with pain' (p. 82). Not to worry! They conclude that 'if the evidence on dysmenorrhoea was negative in these studies it nevertheless seems likely that there is a relationship between it and other types of psychological symptom' (p. 84). And again, discussing the notion of the 'pain-prone' person. 'It could be argued that in women dysmenorrhoea would occur more commonly in those who were pain-prone' (p. 175). They do not seem to even consider allowing their experimental findings to interfere with their theories.

Joan Busfield (1983) has argued in relation to the categories of psychiatric illness that it is not so much the case simply that women and men suffer to different degrees from different categories of mental illness, as that the categories themselves are constructed with reference to the different life experiences of women and men. In a similar way, the category 'psychosomatic pain' contains within it a connection to the gender division. This implicit reference to notions of women's proneness to imaginary complaints also carries with it a further reference to women's sexuality: a vague suggestion that women are not entirely averse to pain, that women may not only 'use' pain, but also even enjoy pain in certain ways.

This ideology encourages men to regard women as 'other', not to extend to them the fullest human sympathy. Women are not given the respect involved in an acceptance that a person gives a true account of their physical sensations.

The old Christian way of thinking allowed men to see women as fulfilling different functions from themselves within God's scheme and as therefore subject to different conditions of life. Modern ideas about women's tendency to suffer from psychosomatic pain carry with them reference to female masochism as well as to female weakness. Combined with an etiquette which cautions women against drawing attention to their own pain, especially to pains relating to the 'female parts', they successfully ensure that most women will opt to suffer in silence rather than to risk the discredit attached to complaining of menstrual pain.

9 Mood Change and the Menstrual Cycle: The Meaning of 'Premenstrual Tension'

In contrast to the silence surrounding menstrual pain and many other menstrual problems, recent years have seen an increase in public discussion about premenstrual tension. Premenstrual tension (PMT), or premenstrual syndrome, has definitely 'caught on' as a subject for features in newspapers, magazines, and on radio and TV.

So what are the sexual politics surrounding all this public talk about something related to menstruation? Is this a positive change for women? My study here is not of the media: I will concentrate in this chapter on the micro-level of sexual politics which reflects and is reflected by the same processes on the larger scale.

As we have seen, Esther Merves's study found that US women said that mood change was one of the most likely subjects for interactions between women and men in relation to menstruation.

I have written elsewhere (1983; 1985) more generally about the development of a new medical ideology of 'premenstrual tension' as a treatable disease. My argument is that premenstrual tension cannot be seen as a naturally occurring disease entity only recently 'discovered' by scientists.

It is undoubtedly true that the menstrual cycle produces a whole range of little-understood effects, physical and mental, which may vary greatly in their impact from one woman to another and from one cycle, or time of life, to another within an individual. But using a disease model isolates the premenstrual phase from the rest of the cycle, concentrates on negative effects rather than positive ones, and attempts to construct an illness out of this picture of a subtle continuum of change (see Parlee 1973).

Women are encouraged to see themselves as 'not themselves' during the premenstrual time, to bracket out the feelings and experiences they have during that time and to attribute them to the menstrual cycle rather than to other factors (Koeske and Koeske 1975; Koeske 1980).

While women certainly want the effects of the menstrual cycle to be acknowledged, want it to be possible to speak about them, it is necessary to ask in whose interest this new discourse about 'PMT' operates. Doctors like Katharina Dalton, who are active in promoting the notion of PMT as an illness, will argue that they are acting to relieve women's sufferings – but are they? Barker-Benfield (1975) reports how in nineteenth-century America Dr W. P. Menton justified the 'castration' (removal of the ovaries) of 'demented' women in terms of 'their right to relief from bodily suffering'. Like the PMT doctors of the present day, the early surgeons who carried out such operations on women assumed the existence of what Barker-Benfield aptly calls a 'modest self', the self which these diseases of femininity are held to suppress. This argument can be used to justify any form of treatment, any analysis of 'women's problems'.

It is notable that interest in premenstrual tension should emerge in the years following the development of a powerful and energetic women's liberation movement. It can in part be seen as an alternative explanation for women's unhappiness – an explanation which places the cause of women's problems within our own bodies instead of outside, in social power relations.

'Premenstrual tension' is very much an area of change, a focus of debate, at present – no simple description of its meaning can be found. This chapter will look at the ways in which 'premenstrual tension' appears in some men's lives, how and where men and women may speak of it, and at the significance of medical ideology in this area.

MALE VIEWS OF MENSTRUAL CYCLE MOOD CHANGE

There was a great deal of publicity around PMT in Britain in late 1981, when two cases reached the courts within a couple of days of each other in which women offered pleas of diminished responsibility due to PMT as a defence against murder charges (Hey 1985). A *Guardian* headline to an article reporting on these court cases and the issues they raised read: 'Killing puts an end to the PMT taboo', and several other newspaper articles followed the same line of thought. But *does* public talk about PMT mean the end of the 'taboo' on talk about menstruation? We must attend to who may say what to whom if we are to observe whether or not the etiquette has changed in any profound ways.

So what information could be gathered from the interviews with men about individual men's attitudes to premenstrual tension? One striking finding is a negative one: no man reported any conversation initiated by a woman with a man in a public setting in which she referred to her own mood changes.

Men, however, do seem to feel free to speak about menstrual cycle-related mood change in public settings, to other men and to certain women. Particularly at work, men may put bad temper in a woman down to menstruation. Note that what the men refer to in this context is the notion that women are bad tempered or moody *during* menstruation, not before it.

> Especially when I was working in a factory, one of the supervisors was a woman and once she got really annoyed over something that was stupid, and that was when I first ... I was only 17 when I was working there, and I remember the bloke said 'oh, it's just the monthlies, you know, she'll get over it' ... 'don't worry about it' (*K*)

> *SL*: And would the women ever have said if they had periods, or anything about it [in the place you worked]?
> *H*: No, but it usually became evident ... er, well, whether it was actually evident or whether it was imagined that it was, like they were in a bad mood and I think you imagined that it was because it was their period [. . .] if there were a lot of women there'd obviously be someone who was in a bad mood because they were menstruating, at least that's what we put it down to.
> *SL*: Is that all of you, or you men put it down to, do you think? I mean, what would the women say to each other?

H: No, I mean it was not discussed with the women. Um, maybe sometimes we'd overhear women saying 'oh, she's in a bad mood, but it's that time of the month' so they'd sort of forgive her . . . But I think it was mainly to do with the men. And even, maybe because I'd worked with other men and we'd talked around that, you know, 'oh, she's in a bad mood, she's bloody menstruating again' [laughs] you know, when I worked on my own with women I still had that mentality, 'Jesus Christ who's menstruating again' [laughs]

It was remarkable to me that while the men had among them only heard menstrual *pain* mentioned as a reason for being off work a very few times, these ideas about mood change seemed quite widespread. One man says that he might ask a woman about it directly:

when I come to think of it, when I worked in [an office] where you could get on with people quite well, I suppose that we would refer to it there actually. If people were feeling quite fed up, especially people I knew a little bit, then I would say, I might well say, 'oh, is it the time of the month?' And they'd usually say yes. Sometimes no, but . . . But not where I've been working the last three years, it's just not . . . you just wouldn't bring it up . . . (Group)

I do not know how much this sort of thing goes on in this country. In Esther Merves's (1983) study when asked if anyone ever spoke to them about menstruation, 52 per cent said that at least once they'd been asked if they were menstruating by someone who didn't know. Among the women under 34, the figure is more like 75 per cent. They said that what they would be asked was 'Are you on the rag?' and that they would be asked this if they were 'depressed for no apparent reason' or 'bitchy'. Often the women said that they felt insulted by this, though some of them also said that it might be asked jokingly.

In some of my interviews, I found that when I asked about period pain, I was answered about PMT:

SL: Were you aware then that women had pain with periods, or any of those . . . how it affected them?
A: No, no, I wasn't, no, I don't think I actually became aware that it was painful, that there were physical side-

effects, until I was in my early twenties, actually. I think I thought that there were psychological side-effects, that there was sort of, ah, vague depressions and irritability, and things, but I worked that out more or less from my experience of it rather than being told about it.

SL: So did any of the women you've known have period pains?
K: It's difficult. Most of the women I've know would tend to keep very quiet, I mean they don't make it obvious if they're having a period, they don't say, 'oh, forgive me, it's the time of the month' or something. It's usually, say if they have a fit of pique or something, one of their friends would say [whispers] 'it's that time of the month, you know'. That's the sort of thing that happens more, that's when you find out about it. [. . .]
     The first proper girlfriend I had, she used to say something, 'such and such time of the month'. And when she'd say that I was always really curious, and I used to ask her about things. That's when things like premenstrual tension used to become more obvious because I used to try and notice when it was happening and notice the difference between before and after, and things like that . . .
SL: do you think you could, at the time?
K: with that particular girl, no. Not at all, I couldn't tell at all.

It is notable that what most of the men talk about is 'that time of the month' or something of the kind, not 'PMT'. But the content of their ideas fits in well with the image put over by the PMT doctors. In practice, for the man in the office who wants a put-down for a woman who's just spoken to him without a sweet smile, it doesn't matter whether he's accusing her of being on her period or just before. He can make a vague reference to 'the monthlies' in the secure belief that a woman can be belittled by calling attention to this aspect of her femaleness.
     This sliding between male beliefs about the mental effects of menstruation itself and the notion of 'premenstrual tension' is noted, in a slightly confused way, in the men's group

discussion. Why is cyclic mood change always linked to menstruation?

> —when you speak of *pre* menstrual tension, I mean, we're talking about several days before a period comes on?
> —the week before
> —which is crazy really, to talk about something that's happening now in terms of something that's about to happen . . . I mean you might just as well say that it's a few days, a week, after the sort of most pregnant part of the cycle.
> —What, ovulation?
> —Yeah.
> —Post-ovulation?
> —It's to do with the hormonal changes, basically.
> —The hormonal changes which are going to lead to evacuation rather than . . .
> —It would probably be after ovulation, bound to be after ovulation, but no, it is the hormonal changes.
> —Premenstrual tension, it's just a funny way of putting it really . . .
> —easier than post-ovulation tension . . . (Group)

From my interviews I had the impression that many men had held for a long time that periods made a woman a bit odd, cross, unpredictable, and that PMT was to them just a new name for something they knew about all along.

> *G*: Like I never really considered premenstrual tension or something like that, until I was 18 or 19, until I went to university. Although at home, I suppose, my mother was saying, like when my sister would cry, she would say 'It's the wrong time of the month', for my sister, and that sort of got my mind associating crying with periods.
> *SL*: Although she may have meant that she was having her period, mayn't she?
> *G*: Yeah . . . just really sort of . . . it's got a stigma attached to it, I suppose, in families. Well, it was in our family. Families are often like that.

Dealing with Premenstrual Women

For most of the men I interviewed who had much to say
about PMT, it was in relation to their intimate, sexual
relationships with women that they felt it to be important to
them. A number of them associated it with arguments; some
attributed difficulties in their relationships to it:

> D: I mean only one relationship which has actually in-
> volved kind of actually really talking about it [menstrua-
> tion], and that was actually talking about it quite a lot at
> times . . .
> SL: Was that because it was a problem for her, or between
> you?
> D: Not because it was a problem really, just because, um,
> you know, if she was feeling really kind of on edge, I mean
> quite often it would actually sort of be about having an
> argument, and then, maybe a couple of days later her
> saying, you know, explaining why, why she'd been so, . . . I
> mean I still can't actually begin to understand what hap-
> pens when women are having a period, in terms of, you
> know, premenstrual tension or whatever, or the rest of it
> . . . But yeah, um, I have spoken about it quite a lot.

> L: Well, she gets the tension . . . like you can always tell
> when she's got them because she gets really uptight, and
> anything you say is just wrong, and she snaps . . . whether
> it's right or wrong, if she's said, beforehand, such and such
> is right, you can try saying that, even, she just ignores it, it's
> wrong. It's just illogical.
> SL: And does she say that's PMT?
> L: Yes. Well, I didn't realise to start with, but after she said,
> it was fairly obvious . . . So you could see when she's coming
> up to it . . . and you've just got to adjust to it . . . stuff like
> that . . . It can be a bit difficult to cope with when one time
> she's being bad tempered, and she's in a really bad mood,
> and it's putting you in a bad mood, makes her difficult to
> get on with, but when you realise it is because of that, then
> you've got to adjust to it, otherwise, just, nothing will work.

> G: like I know that X gets really uptight, can get really in a

bad state, like the other day, we just had a really bad argument, and like she was really shouting at me and crying and stuff. And I suppose I didn't think about it then, but like that was the right time for her to be feeling that, feeling premenstrual tension. I suppose she was attacking me, and . . . oh, I don't know.

SL: Do you remember talking about it?
M: Yes. I don't think there was a vast amount of discussion, not initially anyway, about menstruation as such, but about the effects of menstruation . . .
SL: About the sex thing, or the pain?
M: Oh yes, both – yes, that's right. The first main relationship I had [. . .] the woman I was with had quite severe problems with her menstrual cycle, in fact when she had a period, she was completely, she couldn't do things, she'd literally drop things, she'd be a lunatic driving the car for about 2 or 3 days, she wouldn't go near driving the car in that time [. . .] in fact it became quite a major feature of our relationship, in a sense, that it was something, because of the way it affected her, the way it changed her, it became fantastically . . . bad tempered . . . I don't know whether that's related to other things, I don't know, but it, certainly she felt it was related to that, and that was how I experienced it particularly, so before [. . .]
SL: Did you find that upsetting?
M: Yes, I found it very difficult to take, because I wasn't used to that kind of response [. . .] 'It's down to this, I'm always like this', you know, and I think it's very difficult to get used to – I'm not sure I ever entirely got used to it, felt easy about it. It was difficult, but far more difficult for her than for me, see what I mean? [. . .]

I don't remember being resentful about her being menstrual, as such. Far more the effects of it that concerned me. In that sense, the fact that she was very difficult to be with for a couple of days, or the fact that . . . certain things she couldn't do . . . it was just . . . you couldn't look around for a minute, otherwise there'd be something broken on the floor, or something . . . It must have been a really awful experience for her – but I mean that was the sort of pressure. And I certainly did get to the point of dreading it for that reason. . . . (*M*)

He contrasts this with his present relationship:

it's the opposite way round, in a sense . . . menstruation, the period and everything, didn't seem to exist – it was totally the opposite, it made absolutely no difference and was tremendously played down. It didn't make any difference to her character or her behaviour or anything at all. And that was a tremendous relief, I must say that. It was really nice! [laughs] You know, it's a bit heartless to say that, because it's obviously worse or better from the woman's experience in it, but I have to say . . . it's much easier to live with. I think that made an important difference in terms of the relationship as a whole, in contrast, if you're right to view it in those terms . . . (*M*)

Other men, too, remarked on how different women's menstrual cycles affected them differently, though no others were so emphatic.

But not all the men regarded cyclic mood change as entirely a negative disruption – the image which is always put over in the 'PMT' literature:

I started having a very close relationship with a woman when I was 19, and then I first got to know about it on a personal level, from her personal experiences. She used to get very bad premenstrual tension, and . . . she was brought up as a Protestant [in Ireland], and she didn't seem to have the same taboos about it [. . .]

It was very obvious to me after a while, once she'd explained to me what it was, because I never knew about premenstrual tension before I went out with her. She explained to me exactly how she felt . . . the way she explained it to me was that she just got very, she was very, very sensitive, and it was obvious, she could get very, very angry sometimes, but sometimes she could be very soft, she was just very sensitive . . . (*J*)

C: So I kind of decided to get interested and get involved because it's something that, well, we'll understand each other better if I understand more about what goes on, how she feels, you know, during that regular cycle [. . .]

SL: So the book [*The Wise Wound*] helped you to think about it?

C: Yes, and I'm sure, her attitude has definitely shifted to being much more aware of how mood and other aspects of her body and her feelings change in that period, and that, things that she'd never noticed before but must have been there, about how her body feels different, and how she feels, and I think she's infinitely more comfortable with the situation, and in some ways I think so am I, just simply knowing and understanding a bit more, and being a bit more sensitive, to the process, if you like. And realising that it isn't just a nuisance, and that there might actually be rather good things, in terms of insights or particular activities which it's really appropriate to do, as well as some things that it's definitely appropriate not to do, during that particular 2 or 3, 4, 5 day period, and, you know, it can only help both of us to be aware of that and to see what one can do with it, how best to respond to it, and so I think we've been thinking somewhat about that, and beginning to talk . . . (*C*)

Although mention of PMT came up most in relation to men's intimate relationships, it did occur in other contexts as well. Several men mentioned in passing that they might on occasion be aware of mood changes in women friends of theirs, though only one had had women friends who would themselves tell him about it:

B: as we became much closer friends, and X said oh, if she's maybe snapped, or something, she'd say 'sorry, I'm on this week', or something, and that was just it, and left it at that . . . that wasn't until much later on [. . .]

SL: Have you any other friendships with women where you've been aware of them having periods?

B: Yes [. . .] Y and Z . . . I got to know them in my first year [at university] . . . and at the time they were writing the Women and Health leaflet for the university, and I remember, like, Y, talking about it, and it was always like, you know, 'I'm on this week', or 'I'm due on Friday' or whatever, and you know, 'I'm a bit tensed up' and things.

And I remember them telling me things they were writing for the Women and Health group, like decrease the amount of salt in your diet the week before your period, to increase the potassium level . . . if it's just before or during, I can't remember now . . . she used to eat a lot of bananas at that time . . .

Only one man spoke about being aware of mood changes in relation to his mother's menstrual cycle:

as I began to become aware, of her cycles, and my own cycles I suppose, to develop a feel of a rhythm, I began to feel that there were particular times of the month and year when I'd be most, either alienated from her, or close to her, when we'd both be able to communicate more easily. Initially I just thought they were good times and bad times, but after a few years I began to notice rhythms . . . starting to form. And in retrospect, it wasn't till I saw things in retrospect that I really began to notice what had been going on. I didn't sort of feel, until I was about 15 or 16, any sort of solid rhythm that I could almost say, my mother's got a period at the moment because of the way she's, she is, she's nervous and she's dropping a lot of things, and my father's giving her stick all the time for sort of doing things wrong . . . (E)

As I have said, several of the men I interviewed had never thought about menstruation in relation to their mothers at all: this man's intense involvement with his mother, and his active thought about reasons for her emotional states seem quite unusual. It is unclear what evidence he had for connecting the behaviours he could observe with the menstrual cycle.

Self-Criticism

Some of the men I have quoted seem to use the notion of PMT quite unproblematically, but a few of them had a critical consciousness that behaviours could be wrongly attributed to it:

what I've found is, specially, well, only with girls is, they're irritable, you immediately think, 'oh PMTs, can make allowances', that sort of thing. . . . Even when it's not, I mean, it doesn't matter, it could be anything could be irritating them, you tend to think 'PMTs, make allowances for that sort of thing' (K)

well the problem with X was, they were so irregular, then it was very difficult to gauge when it was, so we never got into a situation where we could immediately say 'ah, it's that time of the month', whereas I've known other women who more or less could tell the time they were due on the basis of how they start feeling . . . what used to happen, almost invariably was that we'd have a pretty tense time, and maybe arguments or what have you, and then she'd have a period, and we'd both say 'aren't we stupid' you know . . . Now to some extent, I think we may even have used [. . .] that as an excuse, as we were having rows fairly regularly, and things could have been quite tense regardless of that, but certainly it was a regular enough pattern, repeated, for us to say quite clearly that there was a certain tension and depression associated with that time of the month. She used to be really quite down, and when she started her psychological condition would improve, regardless . . . (N)

A discussion in the men's group brings out some of the issues more, as one man tries to challenge another about an attitude he finds patronising:

—I'm very aware that X gets extremely clumsy [laughs] and I get very annoyed [laughter] in about the week before her period. And we both recognise it now as a phenomenon, that she drops plates, crashes cars [laughter] . . . etc, etc, do you know what I mean? And it's just a kind of syndrome that we now both recognise. I don't know that *she* recognised it until recently, but we both laugh about it now, and when you're aware of that it is, it's kind of actually . . . [laughs] I mean when she was like that before I used to go spare [laughter], I used to be sort of ridiculously controlling, and I used to get very angry with her, and now I can usually realise that . . . and then I try to make her not do anything . . . 'look just sit down, and I'll do everything' . . .

—[interrupts] 'Does she take sugar?' [Reference to the title of a radio programme for and about people with disabilities] It's very close to sort of mistreating a woman to take that position I think. [laughs]

—Certainly is.

—I'm very, incredibly, cautious of actually having that sort of reductionist theory of explaining phenomena . . . [laughter]

 . . . I'll explain that: Whenever a baby starts crying, right, I've found a lot of parents have this sort of reductionist theory that, reduce the causes to – it's hungry or it's tired. Right? It can't possibly *but* be because the child is experiencing something in its environment that is nasty or unpleasant at that point in time. It's reduced to an explanation that covers everything. And I'm worried that the same sort of reductionism can occur when talking about the things that happen around the time when a woman's about to start menstruating . . . It's easy and I wonder if it's dangerous to start interpreting everything that happens as though it's part of, thereby dismissing the woman's actual identity.

—Oh, sure.

—Like if you have an argument before, to reduce that argument to a 'all right dear, it's because of . . .' is awful . . . and I'm very conscious that that is potentially a very, very bad thing to do . . . [laughter]

—Obviously premenstrual tension has varying effects, and it can be an extremely disruptive experience for the woman . . .

—clumsiness . . . [laughter]

—Well, that's not as bad as saying 'I won't take any notice of what you say when you're in this condition, because you're somehow not up to scratch'.

—Yes, yes.

—'We'll talk about it after your period' . . . (Group)

So we can see that there is a range of ways in which the men in my sample may mobilise ideas about cyclic mood change in their relations with women – and also a range of levels of sophistication in their self-consciousness about this. How does this everyday use of ideas relate to the medical discourse on the subject?

GYNAECOLOGISTS ON PMT

Interestingly, the 'information' about PMT in the gynaecology texts I studied was as patchy and incomplete as was the knowledge of individual men. None of them give much space to discussion of premenstrual tension: Dewhurst does not mention it at all, and Clayton and Newton only give it a short paragraph, a listing of possible treatments. Given what we have seen in relation to other menstrual problems, and the extent to which their reality is doubted, it is notable that despite a certain lack of interest, the reality of premenstrual changes seems not to be in question. In fact for Clayton and Newton (p. 19), discomfort before the period may be the only real symptom of the cycle, for it alone is accompanied by 'objective evidence of metabolic changes' of a measureable kind.

Proceeding in their usual way, the doctors do try to characterise the PMT patient. Unlike women with menstrual pain, who are held to be very young, women with PMT are felt to be: over 30 (Barnes:46); of average age 35 (Garrey:120); 30–45 years old (Jeffcoate:547). Garrey adds to this the notion that PMT is class-linked:

> Marriage and childbirth do not affect PMT but there is usually a preponderance of the more articulate patients, especially professional women who must appear before the public and cannot easily stay off work. (p. 120)

Jeffcoate would look to something within the woman's personality rather than to her conditions of life. He writes that 'there is nearly always a fundamental constitutional, and sometimes inherited, weakness which makes the individual "fail to cope" with the ordinary day to day stresses of life'.

He *also* suggests that PMT is a feature of modern conditions of life in Western 'civilised' countries and is rarely encountered in women of 'Eastern countries' (p. 547). The popular literature on PMT (for example, Lever 1980) contains various claims of this sort, about the relation between PMT and 'civilisation', its existence in other cultures, and so on. Sometimes all social practices relating to menstruation are attributed to the underlying threat constituted by out-of-control premenstrual women. At other times Western women are seen as particularly subject to stress, a notion which I think is linked to the idea that Western society is particularly unnatural, and that this especially affects women's bodies. People in other cultures, 'Eastern countries' in Jeffcoate's case, are seen in classic racist style as less sophisticated, less developed than Westerners.

Jeffcoate also discusses premenstrual mastalgia (breast pain before periods), something which is often described by doctors as a feature of PMT. This condition, he writes, is:

> Mostly seen in frustrated and unhappy nulliparae (women without children) of late middle age, and a background of nervous tension is important. Cancero-phobia is frequently present. (p. 550)

This last statement presumably refers to the likelihood that women going to a gynaecologist with lumpy swollen painful breasts might wish for reassurance that they do not have breast cancer. Considering how common this cancer is, it seems unfair and insulting to call such women phobic.

The causes of premenstrual tension are little discussed. Jeffcoate, as we might expect, suggests that the woman is just overdoing it:

> a reorganisation of her life or her outlook on life is often necessary . . . A sleep for two hours in the middle of every day is particularly helpful. (p. 547)

Garrey's text (1978) offers a list of four theories, which I think is worth quoting in full for its thoroughly patronising attitude.

Aetiology
There are several theories:
1. *Simple fluid retention* due to cyclic increase in steroid hormones. Fluid retention is certainly the commonest symptom (and about the only one that can be measured) but it is difficult to accept it as the cause of the more extravagant mood changes.
2. *Endocrine changes* Progesterone deficiency: oestrogen/progesterone imbalance: raised aldosterone levels during luteal phase: raised prolactin levels. None of these is constantly present (about one third of patients will show

progesterone deficiency) and in many cases the endocrine profile is normal.

3. *An evolutionary phenomenon* PMT represents post-ovulation sexual hostility to the male, thus increasing the frequency of coitus during the fertile phase of the cycle (and increasing the chance of survival of the species).

4. *Reaction of a neurotic personality* to normal cyclical variations in hormone levels. Hysterical women will certainly exaggerate, but many severely neurotic women are not sufferers, and no correlation has been found between PMT and psychiatric ill-health.

(Theories 3 and 4 should not be offered to the patient during an acute attack.)

In terms of treatments recommended, talk 'a simple explanation' (Llewellyn-Jones:74) is thought to be very helpful by half of these doctors. It is not so clear, as with the explanation which is held to cure period pain in adolescents, what exactly such talk would consist of.

Otherwise various drugs are suggested. Top of this list, recommended by four doctors each, are tranquillisers and diuretics (which reduce fluid in the body by increasing the excretion of urine). Three doctors suggest progestogens, and one each offer phenobarbitone (a barbiturate), bromocriptine and pyridoxine (vitamin B6). These last two are among the drugs presently being promoted as specifics for PMT, along with progestogens. Only Garrey mentions them.

PMT AS ILLNESS: NOT A NEW DEPARTURE

There is a large gap between the scattered material on PMT in these texts and the picture one can gain from the work of doctors like Dalton (1977) and Brush (1981) and from popularising books like those of Lever (1980) and Kingston (1980). What is most obvious is that the dismissive and patronising attitude which comes across in these more traditional texts is exactly what has driven many women to see the PMT promoters as a pro-woman force. Faced with doctors who regard a consciousness of emotional and physical changes with the menstrual cycle as a neurotic trait, women who have such consciousness are likely to prefer an account which at least takes their experience seriously. But while they affirm the reality of cyclic change, doctors like Dalton participate in a distinctly anti-feminist rhetoric which has encouraged a public scare about the threat of unpredictable, out-of-control, violent premenstrual women.

There is often little clarity about what defines the difference between 'all women' and 'PMT sufferers'. There is also often an insistence that women should take treatment, as a duty to their husbands and children (whom they are accused of battering and otherwise abusing while premenstrual) (Dalton 1982).

There is debate at present within the British medical establishment about the correct view of PMT. While the promoters of PMT as a disease have gained a good deal of ground, their greatest influence appears to be outside of medical circles. Dalton herself recognised this in setting up the Association for the Premenstrual Syndrome in 1984, which explicitly encourages patients to pressurise doctors for progesterone treatment. One suspects that medical resistance to the new wave of thought on PMT comes from several sources: the underlying resistance to change which is found in any profession; sexist belief that it is right for women to suffer; sexist belief that women invent ailments to 'get out of things'; proper scientific scepticism about the extreme claims often made by PMT promoters; and anxiety about the long-term effects of particular new treatments suggested, especially of hormone treatments. Two editorials in the *Lancet* in recent years (1981 and 1983) expressed reasoned doubts about the claims of Dalton and others.

But since these ideas are only recently gaining in influence, it is not yet clear how important they may become. That struggle is currently taking place at many levels, in public and in private, between 'lay' women and men, doctors and patients, as well as among doctors. One can see from the rather incoherent and disparate ideas brought up by the men in my sample how complex these issues are. Different ways of looking at menstrual cycle mood change bring with them different advantages and disadvantages for men individually and as a group, just as they do for women.

While the men I interviewed had absorbed only a small amount of the newer medical ideas about premenstrual tension, many of them held the same general view of women and mood changes as doctors like Katharina Dalton. A number of them had a long standing belief that at the 'time of the month' (possibly meaning during bleeding), women are bad-tempered and unreliable. Many of them readily offered accounts of occasions when they had had arguments with women they were close to, which they had attributed to some hormonal influence upon the woman. However others demonstrated an awareness that notions like 'premenstrual tension' are very flexible, and that there is a danger of attributing behaviours to hormones which are not in fact caused in this way. The individual men in my sample, and the discussions in the men's group, more explicitly reflect the debate which is taking place at the larger, societal level.

In contrast to the campaign against VAT on sanitary wear, the promotion of the idea of PMT as a disease has gained very wide publicity. Valerie Hey (1985) discussed the press coverage of the trial of Christine English in 1981 – a case which reached the front pages of several daily papers. She identifies two themes within the discourse: 'An Excuse for Anything' (which she draws in the particular from the wife of the man Ms English killed) and 'not responsible for herself' (the defence barrister's argument).

These two themes can also be identified in male culture's version of menstruation generally – that women 'use it as an excuse' (a view discussed in Chapter 4) and that it is over-whelmingly important to women's lives, that it sums up the extent to which women are more biological beings than men (Birke and Best 1980). These two in this case operate in contradiction to each other – but their simultaneous presence accounts for the fascination the subject appears to hold for the press. Within the supposedly scientific discourse on PMT, men see the potentiality for proof to emerge of the truth of the view of women which is enshrined in male culture.

At the same time, women are demanding to be allowed to speak about menstruation, about their bodies: PMT provides a kind of trade-off. 'Yes, let's *talk* about how your menstrual cycle affects you, but it'll be your own fault if it only turns out to discredit you further'. Women's efforts to define their own experiences for themselves are pre-empted by medical ideas imposed upon them.

10 Conclusion

Over the years, while I have been working on menstruation, I have increasingly asked myself how it came about that I have written such a nasty book. No-one wants to know about menstruation: why fight it? What men say about it is hateful; why not just ignore them? Why make women angrier than they already are, by showing them things they are not meant to see? Why should I myself have to feel so angry, again and again, just reading over the words of these perfectly ordinary well-meaning men? Don't I have enough trouble in my life without publicly identifying myself with this highly stigmatised subject?

And then yet another person responds to the mention of menstruation with a diatribe about how uptight some women are about it, how older women (mothers or school teachers) bully young ones about it. Always the women are blamed. If only we tried hard enough, if only women were good enough, all would be well.

Menstruation may not be important in itself, but it is highly symbolic of femaleness, and the ways in which people deal with it show us a lot about how women are viewed. This same scrutiny of women while men are let off the hook occurs, with a vengeance, for example, in relation to child abuse. Silence surrounds the man who actually abused a child, while the woman who failed to protect her child from him is endlessly discussed, inspected and finally blamed.

It is uncomfortable to focus directly on how men act in oppressive ways, partly because it brings up the question of why they do it, partly simply because it is frightening to look at these things face on. But women have been turning their heads aside, pretending not to see, for too long. If we do not hold men responsible for their actions, and continue to treat them as a given, just part of the environment in which we survive, we blame ourselves and each other for things which are not our doing. We also fail to challenge men and demand change.

Self-hatred is one of the saddest symptoms of oppression. Menstruation has been one focus for my own self-hatred, and this is why I wanted to look into its social meanings. I needed to thoroughly disrupt the stupid, but powerful, line of thought which both denies my pain and inconvenience and at the same time regards them as justifications for my social inferiority. Shame blocks self-expression. Mistrust of one's body creates a very weak basis from which to attempt to gain greater power over one's own life. I hope that my work will be of some use to other women seeking to construct a better understanding of their own experience of menstruation.

Learning to be a woman in any patriarchal culture has many painful aspects. Small insults pile up beside major restrictions and violations. Women have to be trained to behave as women are expected to, to maintain the *status quo*, and managing menstruation within the culture's rules is one compulsory part of attaining adult womanhood for nearly all women.

Feminists have worked in many areas of life to affirm women as women, our basic, natural right to exist, the normality of our femaleness. Constructing a positive attitude to menstruation has been somewhat problematic. Many women suffer pain and inconvenience with menstruation, and are not helped by attempts to assert that these are entirely created by patriarchy, especially when the implication is that one should by mental effort be able to overcome the effects of these attitudes.

Why do we have such difficulty in living with ourselves in this way? Why have women not more enthusiastically made public their feelings and views on menstruation? My view now is that the answer lies in half-heard threatening talk from men, which enforces the rule of silence which is the essence of the etiquette of menstruation for women.

My impulse to study menstruation came from a real confusion about how to think about it. The culture I grew up in links menstruation with women's inferiority, but in quite a complicated way. Women who draw attention to menstruation, who complain of pain or inconvenience, perhaps, are seen as 'letting the side down', as if polite avoidance of topics like this was the crucial basis for a pretence that women are seen as equal to men.

It was suffering physical pain during periods which compelled my attention to the subject, and I did not like the explanations I had access to: that it was a 'curse' symbolising punishment to women for being women; or that those of us with pain were maladjusted to being women or girls; or that we were putting it on.

I have tried to draw out, from what I could learn about menstruation, some of the processes through which women are oppressed by men. I have pointed to male-only groupings which men described to me as sources of a particularly crude form of anti-woman ideology. More frequently recognised institutions like medicine and the media have also featured. I have tried to consider changes over time especially in relation to attitudes towards sexuality, and have drawn attention to a new ideology of male-oriented 'sexual liberation' as well as the older more conventional 'home and family' one.

Relations between the sexes are patterned by etiquette and pollution beliefs in such a way that women are constantly reminded of our powerlessness, and men may be regularly reassured that their masculine privileges remain unchallenged. The interview material shows clearly, too, how individual men manipulate the range of ideas available to them in their relationships with individual women. There are also some interesting congruences between individual men's descriptions of their personal reactions and medical men's considered opinions on menstrual problems. Male power can be seen expressed through a number of different institutions and through individuals.

Much of what has been written about cultural attitudes to menstruation has looked much harder at 'other' cultures than at the researcher's own culture. White Europeans and Americans have inspected a range of cultures of indigenous peoples of other continents (seen as primitive) and of ethnic minority people in Western countries (seen as exotic). The tone has been 'isn't it interesting that they have such weird ideas about menstruation?'. These writers' complacency about how menstruation is dealt with in modern British culture offends me. Women's experience is missing from these accounts, both the experience of the women within the cultures studied from outside by anthropologists, and the experience of the women of the writers' own culture, who could point out the weirdnesses of their own culture, if only they were listened to.

Attempting to correct this bias, I have concentrated on an extremely narrow range of experience within contemporary British society – narrow in time-span and narrow culturally. I hope that what I have done may serve as a basis of comparison, and that more research will uncover more about other cultural traditions within Britain and beyond, and about the past. Attitudes to menstruation depend upon so many other social factors: gender relationships, beliefs about sexuality, pollution beliefs, religious beliefs, material conditions of various kinds, class attitudes, systems of medical knowledge – to name only a few. I have not attempted to 'cover' everyone's experiences, but to work on tools with which women may better understand their experiences.

One of the assumptions of many studies which take a cross-cultural approach is that human behaviour towards menstruation springs more or less directly from the characteristics of the physical process of menstruation itself. We need to consider to what extent biological factors determine social relations around menstruation: how flexible are people's responses to menstruation? The majority of existing theories about the origins of social reactions to menstruation seek their cause within some essential truth about the phenomenon itself.

Although there are feminist versions of the essentialist approach, for instance that which regards men's discomfort in relation to menstruation as evidence of their fear of women's power, symbolised by the womb, its logic can only be deterministic: it does not allow for the possibility of change.

My framework has been a social constructionist radical feminism – that is, an analysis of male political power over women which regards such domination as socially rather than biologically created. Throughout my work I have argued against explanations for present-day beliefs and practices which are based upon unproveable assumptions about either prehistory or 'universal' male reactions to female bodies. Many existing theories which claim to explain behaviour around menstruation depend upon a taken-for-granted understanding of its relationship to the process of reproduction. It is crucial to feminist thinking that 'sex', the biological base, be distinguished from 'gender', the social interpretations which are placed upon it. Too many of the justifications for women's oppression derive from ideologically embroidered notions about biology.

I have also found that essentialist explanations cannot be supported by the evidence. Cross-cultural research throws up an amazingly wide range of meaning and interpretations which women and men have given to menstruation. Even within one society it is not possible to make simple statements about the meaning of menstruation. It is not a unitary phenomenon, not a single thing, socially; menstruation means all manner of things to all manner of people. It is used as part of several kinds of discourse, both publicly and privately. Which of these an individual will be aware of or focus on will depend upon a large number of factors relating to their particular social location.

One of the forms in which the essentialist approach is expressed is in the idea of a pan-cultural 'menstrual taboo', an idea which features in both feminist and anti-feminist writing on the subject.

I have argued that the notion of a 'taboo' puts the phenomenon within the area of supernatural belief, when such beliefs are largely absent from present-day British culture. It implies also that menstruation may never be spoken of, which further misrepresents the situation. In fact, I suggest, what we have is a menstrual etiquette, part of a larger etiquette of behaviour between the sexes, which governs who may say what to whom, and in what context. Women are discredited by any behaviour which draws attention to menstruation, while men may more freely refer to it if they choose to. Thus the etiquette expresses and reinforces status distinctions.

Another problem with the idea of a taboo is that it is insensitive to gender – it erases power differences to present an image of 'society' or 'culture' on the one hand, which makes the rules, and 'people' on the other, who are bound by them. Closer examination shows that the social rules around menstruation are very much about gender.

In imagining how social life is organised it is necessary to balance the individual's ability to construct her or his own social world with the influence and constraints of the power structures of the society: importantly those of gender, class, and race. Understandings of menstruation are very various: each piece of research I did threw up rich, complex material. But these understandings are not chaotic.

Because I do not see attitudes towards menstruation as determined in a strong way by the physical facts of menstruation, it makes sense to study a single culture, to map out the specific connections made in different contexts by different individuals within that culture. Such findings, though, will not be transferable: only further close study of other cultures could discover whether or not patterns are similar elsewhere.

Menstruation is an absurdly difficult area to research, since the etiquette which is a large part of the subject of research forbids the investigation itself. I have therefore attempted to study the subject from several angles at once by looking for evidence from a number of sources – individual men; 'the literature', including data from research on women; and gynaecology texts and related writings. I found this to be an extremely valuable approach, for each new piece of work shed light on what I had learnt previously.

I chose to concentrate mainly upon men's point of view, because men's attitudes seemed to me to be an amazingly silent area in much work on gender relations, as if men were passers-by while 'society' produced problems for women. Considering their influence on society as a whole, it seemed to me likely that studying their attitudes would be highly revealing. This attention to men's views has been the most unexpected aspect of my research, for other people and for myself. I discovered a tremendously strong expectation that research on 'women's issues' should involve interviewing women, and found it something of a struggle to resist it. Was my choice correct?

By focusing on men I did indeed discover things I had not already known about. The effort to take an initiative, to act upon men in the powerful way that sociological investigation involves, produced both positive and negative results. It turned up some fascinating information, and turned out to be a very interesting exercise in methodology. However it had its costs. I found much of what I learnt was most unpleasant knowledge – it was extremely disturbing to feel personally attacked by one's own data. Further, I found that this created problems of interpretation.

I became acutely conscious of the extent to which doing sociology depends upon the sociologist's empathy with her subjects, her pre-existing ideas about how their minds work. I could and did attempt to empathise with my interviewees, to an extent, but because of my own simultaneous location as researcher and as woman, the object of male talk, I often did not wish to take the effort very far. It was a slightly insane position to be in, and an interesting anomaly as an example of the power structure of a research project.

It became clear, from comparing material from women to my interviews with men, that women's consciousness of menstruation is radically different from men's – not only do the sexes speak of it in different language, but their consciousnesses on the subject have quite different constituent parts. For example I discovered in my interviews a whole discourse on menstruation which exists among men only, a 'sick joking' which forms part of sexist male culture. Much men's talk about menstruation sees it as sexual, in a way which women may not. Information about menstruation is often shared between women and men only in heterosexual relationships, and not in any other kind of relationship, which further ties it to sexuality in men's eyes.

The women interviewed in Esther Merves's (1983) study said that it was in relation to menstrual pain and to mood change that they were most likely to discuss menstruation with another person. Therefore I have examined these areas of men's talk particularly closely. Looking at male attitudes to menstrual pain one can see very plainly the range of social practices involved: an etiquette which dictates silence to women; an elaborate denial of the reality of the pain, resulting from men's failure to empathise with women.

Gynaecology can be analysed as one form of male discourse on menstruation, and the notion of psychosomatic pain must be seen in this sexual-political context. I have shown how medical views of menstruation seem to echo those of men generally, rather than springing from any other dynamic, such as scientific logic or observation.

The public denial of menstrual pain stands in interesting contrast to 'premenstrual tension', for it seems that PMT *is* possible to discuss in public. In recent years it has featured regularly in the national press. I have looked at the way in which the idea of premenstrual tension has been constructed, creating a medical disease-like category with very negative connotations for women out of the continuum of physical and mental change which the menstrual cycle produces. Avoiding reference to menstrual blood, the object of male disgust, talk about PMT focuses on those intangible forces, hormones, and their control over women.

While women have wanted to be able to speak in public about mood change related to the menstrual cycle, 'premenstrual tension' as it has emerged is an idea which has many benefits for men. It can be used publicly to discredit women generally, and privately to undermine a particular woman at particular moments. 'Taboo-breaking' is not necessarily liberatory in this case, as women found also with what was called the 'sexual revolution' of the 1960s.

In deciding to focus my work on men's attitudes, I have essentially given the responsibility to women who read this book to think about their own experiences and to find out about other women's. Women have a very wide range of physical and social experiences around menstruation, and much more remains to be said about how these differences affect us.

My hope is that the anger induced by listening to men on the subject of menstruation will transform itself into an increased confidence that women can and must change these attitudes. The search for the individual 'healthy attitude' comes to seem absurd when we grasp the scale of the problem in the social attitudes surrounding us. Women need to talk about menstruation as friends, lovers, sisters, mothers and daughters, but *on our terms* this time. The question is not what is wrong with us. If we refuse to let patriarchal ideas set us against one another, we could come up with entirely new ways of seeing our bodies, and a new set of problems worth discussing.

Appendix: A Note on Studying Men – Ethics, Empathy and Power

This note is written mainly for those involved in research and in teaching research methods. As I have explained in Chapter 2, my methods of research are unusual within British sociology, and I found that this created some interesting problems. It seems important to use the experience of doing the work to raise wider questions about how we discuss research methods generally.

INTERVIEWING MEN

It took me a very long time to get around to the idea of interviewing men as a way of learning about social attitudes towards this 'women's' subject. It was actually a seminar on patriarchal relations and the research process given by Sue Scott which made me consider it as a real possibility. She reflected there on the ways in which the social relations involved in the actual doing of research affect what research gets done, particularly the way that qualitative methods 'fit' with femininity, and raised questions about the assumption that such methods also unproblematically fit with feminism. She pointed out how little feminist research is done involving interviewing men.

So I had to think about how this idea had come to my mind before and been dismissed as absurd, unthinkable. I realised that I had not taken the idea seriously, not because it was an uninteresting research idea, but because of my assumptions about the social situation I would be creating for myself. I wrote at the time that:

> I would actually feel quite threatened, afraid, sitting in a room with a man asking questions about his views on my body. There's also an element of not wanting the truth

spelt out to me . . . But it is surely illuminating that I myself am so willing to speak with women about it but can barely contemplate speaking to men. (Journal 16.2.82)

A Lack of Models

My final decision to focus my study on men has on the whole seemed to me to be successful. However there are real problems with this, which I would not wish to minimise. The first of these is the personal cost to the researcher. I have often found my research a painful process, for I have had to make myself pay attention to men's sexist views of myself in a way which I would 'naturally' avoid in any other situation.

Another problem was the lack of a literature to refer to in evaluating my own experiences with the work. A few studies have been done by feminists on men in recent years. One which springs to mind as comparable to mine is that by Stanley and Wise, on obscene phone calls (1979). But they did not go into this study by choice – they began studying the calls in self-defence, as a way of dealing with the experience of receiving them as a result of their work for a lesbian support phoneline.

Even the special issue of the *Women's Studies International Forum* edited by Sue Wise and Liz Stanley devoted to 'Men and Sex: a case study in sexual politics' (1984) contains only one account of research involving interviewing men, and that was of men as part of heterosexual couples.

O'Brien and McKee (1982) have written about interviewing men, drawing on their work in studies of fatherhood. They raise many important issues: the way in which men manipulated the interview situation; their sense that men at times spoke more easily to them when they had put them in a wife-like role; the ways in which the issue of sex arose in certain interviews. They tell of a number of occasions when they felt threatened by an interviewee, or felt that he was using masculine behaviours to assert dominance. A number of the 'lone fathers' (one of the samples) used the interview to rail against their wives and women in general, which made the interviewers very uneasy.

From their account, O'Brien and McKee suffered much

more abuse during their research than I did doing mine, but while their writing describes their own behaviour, it does not directly address issues of power, and does not fully let us under their skin to learn about what it made them feel.

I found that there was a related problem about my ability to understand what the men were saying. There are two kinds of understanding involved here, an understanding as a woman, what you might call 'getting the message' which often led me into a reaction of anger or despair, and also an understanding *with* the men, of what their words meant to them. The difficulty was that I had in a sense to overcome my hearing of 'the message' in order to understand in any other way – to 'make sense' of what they said.

Certainly I found that I understood and indeed heard very little of what was said in the interviews and the group discussion the first time I heard it. It was absolutely essential to have them on tape so that I could read and reread the transcripts, and so that I could benefit from other people's comments on them.

Interpretation was often difficult. One of my problems was I think that having interviewed men, I was perversely reluctant to let them set the agenda. I found it difficult, in any case, to free myself sufficiently from my own preconceptions to produce a coherent description of the men's point of view.

This experience has made me very aware of how much sociologists generally depend upon empathy with their research subjects in making their interpretations. A great many studies are done on groups of people the researcher initially feels some empathy with, and in other cases, researchers describe the speedy development of such empathy (for example, Geer 1964, quoted in Denzin 1970). 'Going native' is a recognised research problem, but what is rarely noted is the utter dependency of all research upon some kind of fellow-feeling. If social reality is indeed a matter of shared meaning, what happens when the researcher does not and cannot afford to share meaning with the researched? I am not here talking about the interview situation: it is relatively easy for a person with average social skills to simulate rapport with a wide range of other people for the duration of an interview. The problem is one of interpreting the words of someone whose social location is in some way alien to one's own.

The fact that in this case I was in the less powerful social group made me clearly aware of this. A researcher trying to interpret the words of members of an underclass from a position of relative power may on the one hand be more able to fabricate some kind of empathy with them; on the other hand it may just be easier to delude oneself about the insight one has developed when the researched are less likely to answer back. This leads to my next point.

It is also a notably frequent feature of sociological studies that their subjects are less socially powerful than the researcher. The difference may only be one of level of education, but this is a real difference of status. Of course one cannot weigh up one kind of social hierarchy against another in any general sense, but on the relevant variable of gender the men I interviewed were all in the powerful group and this placed me in an unusual position.

The effect was that I was aware of the interviewing and the research process generally as a power struggle in a way that most researchers seem not to be. Perhaps I mean more exactly that I was aware of the need in myself to exert what power I could over my 'subjects'. After spending days transcribing the men's group discussion I wrote that I felt upset and angry, 'ground down' by the process: 'I have somehow to reduce them to "data", use them for my own ends' (Journal 8.4.83).

The aggression in this statement runs totally counter to most of what has been written on feminist research. A large part of this discourse has concerned research ethics, and has been aimed at democratising the research process, seeing 'normal' research as exploitative. Sometimes the actual proposals have been minimal, for instance that researchers should confess to having answered their interviewees' questions (Oakley 1981), but other writers have seemed to be proposing a more radical form of powersharing with those researched.

The problem here is that writers tend to generalise from the particular experience of a feminist researcher interviewing women. General positions are then constructed, which may lose sight of the very particular *politics* of the specific research in question.

It remains an open question in my mind what ethics a feminist researcher can follow in dealing with men. I have stuck closely to the contract I made with each of my interviewees and with the group. They voluntarily agreed to be interviewed, and I agreed to protect their identities. I do not feel that I owe them anything more, and have not given them privileged access to my research results.

Basically my ethics in the research situation derive from my political principles and not from any abstract or general ideas about research ethics. I cannot treat all people indifferently, 'without prejudice', when what I am dealing in is sexual politics. I make no apology for this as I believe that what I have done is precisely what all researchers do.

The very notion of the need for special professional ethics enshrines the idea that the particular social status of the professional creates specific ethical problems. It is all about power, and my view is that the only way to guard against the abuse of power is to be as fully conscious as possible of all the relevant power dynamics in any given situation.

SELF-REVELATION AND SOCIAL STATUS

This brings me to another neglected methodological issue: the effect on methods used of the researcher's particular social location. I came to consider this question originally through the observation that while ethnomethodology (a phenomenological approach where one's own culture is approached as if it were 'anthropologically strange') would seem to be in many ways a philosophy and practice well suited to feminism it seems mainly to be practised by white middle- and upper-class men. (There are some exceptions to this rule: Smith 1974, 1978; Stanley and Wise 1983.)

From time to time, I have attempted to insert into my accounts of my work some reflective observations about my own experience of the research. Each time I have done this my reactions have been challenged, the accuracy of my perceptions questioned. Stanley and Wise (1979) describe a similar experience. Now this ability to challenge researchers' perceptions should be normal practice, and in a sense it is the reason for revealing one's subjectivity in this way – precisely to make it open to comment and criticism. But each time it occurred, in practice, I felt intensely personally undermined.

What becomes clear is that revealing one's personal feelings as part of the research project is a different matter when one is of the group whose perspective generally constitutes the accepted social view, from when one's perspective is in any sense deviant. My view is seen as an opinion, and a questionable one, while a white middle-class man's is more likely to be taken for granted as reflecting how a person *would* feel in such and such a situation.

Thus self-revelation for a lesbian radical feminist makes one vulnerable in a special way – she knows that her view of reality is not shared by the whole society, indeed is at odds with much that is taken for granted by many people. If she describes her view of society openly *as* her personal perspective, she opens herself to attack on who she is as much as on what she thinks. The oppressed, I would argue, are always, 'naturally', self-reflective in the sense that they are necessarily aware that their particular view *is* a particular view and not a universal one, much less can ever be 'taken for granted'.

Perhaps this explains why ethnomethodology has not appealed especially to oppressed people. It takes tremendous confidence to reveal one's own perceptions *as* individual perceptions, and it is hardly surprising that women have tended rather to want to make universalistic claims. In a sense it is one of the things that women must fight for, that women's points of view should be accepted as real, not always marginalised as 'the woman's angle'.

Certainly it explains something of the compromise which will be apparent in the methodology of my own study. I have tried to be self-reflective but have at the same time wanted to make claims for my analysis which inevitably go beyond describing it simply as one woman's view.

The stress I have felt upon my own status within this research derives partly from the fact that I cannot fall back on the testimony of a group of other women for support. Although I have referred to women's experience in various ways, the picture I present of the society will inevitably emphasise men's power and men's ideas more than women's power and resistance. I have allowed this to occur because I trust that my study is only part of the process and that women will use the information I have gathered and the ideas I offer to assert their own power to create new definitions and to refuse to accept men's version of reality.

Bibliography

Abraham, Suzanne F., 'The Challenges of Adolescence' in Lorraine Dennerstein and Graham Burrows (eds), *Handbook of Psychosomatic Obstetrics and Gynaecology* (Amsterdam and New York: Elsevier Biomedical Press, 1983).

Alther, Lisa, *Kinflicks* (Harmondsworth: Penguin, 1977).

Ardener, Shirley, 'Social Insult and Female Militancy' in Shirley Ardener (ed.), *Perceiving Women* (London: Malaby Press, 1975).

——————, (ed.), *Women and Space* (London: Croom Helm, 1981).

Armstrong, David, 'Developments in medical thought and practice in the 20th century: towards the construction of a sociology of medical knowledge', Chapter 1, (Bedford College, London: PhD thesis, 1982).

Ashley-Montagu, M. F., 'Physiology and Origins of the Menstrual Prohibitions', *Quarterly Review of Biology*, 15 (1940), 211–20.

Barker-Benfield, Ben, 'Sexual Surgery in Late Nineteenth Century America', *International Journal of Health Services*, 5 (1975), 287.

Barnes, Josephine, *Lecture Notes on Gynaecology* (Oxford: Blackwell, 1966; 4th edn 1980).

Barry, Kathleen, *Female Sexual Slavery* (New Jersey: Prentice Hall, 1979).

Bart, Pauline B. and Scully, Diana H., 'The Politics of Hysteria: The Case of the Wandering Womb' in E. S. Gomberg and V. Franks (eds), *Gender and Disordered Behaviour: Sex Differences in Psychopathology* (New York: Brunner & Mazel, 1979).

Bartelmez, G. W., 'Menstruation', *Physiological Reviews*, 17 (1937), 28–72.

Beard, R. W. 'Preface' to Annabel Broome and Louise Wallace (eds), *Psychology and Gynaecological Problems* (London and New York: Tavistock Publications, 1984).

——————, Belsey, E. M., Lieberman, B. A., and Wilkinson, J. C. M., 'Pelvic Pain in Women', *American Journal of Obstetrics and Gynaecology*, 128 (1977), 566.

Berger, P. and Luckman, T., *The Social Construction of Reality: A Treatise in the Sociology of Knowledge* (New York: Doubleday, 1967).

Bettelheim, Bruno, *Symbolic Wounds: Puberty Rites and the Envious Male* (New York: Collier, 1968).

Birke, Lynda and Best, Sandy, 'The Tyrannical Womb: Menstruation and the Menopause' in Brighton Women and Science Group (eds), *Alice Through the Microscope* (London: Virago, 1980).

Blumer, H., *Symbolic Interactionism: Perspective and Method* (New Jersey: Prentice-Hall, 1969).

Bondfield, Margaret, preface to: Women's Group on Public Welfare and Hygiene Committee, *Our Towns: A Close Up* (Oxford: Oxford University Press, 1943).

Boone, Lalia P., 'The Vernacular of Menstruation', *American Speech*, 129 (1954), 297–8.

Boserup, Esther, *Women's role in economic development* (London: St Martin, 1970).

Boston Women's Health Book Collective, *Our Bodies, Ourselves* (New York: Simon & Schuster, 1973).

Bradshaw, Jan, 'Now what are they up to? Men in the "Men's Movement"' in Scarlet Friedman and Elizabeth Sarah, (eds), *On the Problem of Men* (London: Women's Press, 1982).

Briffault, Robert, *The Mothers: A study of the origins of sentiments and institutions*, Vol. II (London: George Allen & Unwin, 1927).

Brighton Women and Science Group (eds), *Alice Through the Microscope: the power of science over women's lives* (London: Virago, 1980).

Brooks-Gunn, Jeanne, and Ruble, Diane, N., The Menstrual Attitude Questionnaire, *Psychosomatic Medicine*, 42, 5 (September 1980), 503–11.

Brush, M. G., *Premenstrual Syndrome and Period Pains* (London: Women's Health Concern, 1981).

Budoff, Penny Wise, *No More Menstrual Cramps and Other Good News* (New York: Penguin Books, 1980).

Bullough, V. and Voght, M., 'Women, Menstruation and Nineteenth Century Medicine', *Bulletin of the History of Medicine*, 47 (1973), 66–83.

Burstyn, Joan N., *Victorian Education and the Ideal of Womanhood* (London: Croom Helm, 1980).

Busfield, Joan, 'Gender, Mental Illness, and Psychiatry' in Mary Evans and Clare Ungerson (eds), *Sexual Divisions: Patterns and Processes* (London and New York: Tavistock, 1983).

Carney, M. W. P., 'Menstrual Disturbance: a Psychogenic Disorder?', *Clinics in Obstetrics and Gynaecology*, 8, 1 (April 1981), 103–9.

Chafetz, J., *A Primer on the Construction and Testing of Theories in Sociology* (IL, USA: F. E. Peacock, 1978).

Chern, M. Myra, Gatewood, Laual C., and Anderson, V. Elving, 'The Inheritance of Menstrual Traits' in Dan *et al* (eds), *The Menstrual Cycle* Vol. 1 (New York: Springer, 1980).

Clark, Heather J. P., 'Women Coming On: Menstruation and Self Definition' BA Dissertation (Liverpool University, 1983).

Clarke, Edward H., *Sex in Education* (Boston: 1873).

Clayton, Sir Stanley and Newton, J. R., *A Pocket Gynaecology*, (Edinburgh: Churchill Livingstone, 1948; 9th edn 1979).

Combahee River Collective, 'The Combahee River Collective Statement' in Barbara Smith (ed.), *Home Girls: A Black Feminist Anthology* (New York: Kitchen Table Women of Colour Press, 1983).

Conrad, P., Book review, *Observer* (London), 8 April 1984.

Consensus Research Pty Ltd., 'A quantitative survey of dysmenorrhoea and menorrhagia amongst women 15 to 54 years of age', prepared for Parke, Davis and Company, 1978.

Cooper, A. and Kessell, N., 'Menstruation and Personality', *British Journal of Psychiatry*, 109 (1963), 711–21.

Coulter, Angela, 'Hysterectomy – a Surgical Fashion', paper to BSA Human Reproduction Study Group (Warwick University, 24 March 1984).

Crawford, Patricia, 'Attitudes to Menstruation in 17th Century England', *Past and Present*, 91 (November 1981), 47–73.

Crawford, Robert, 'You are dangerous to your health: the ideology and politics of victim blaming', *International Journal of Health Services*, 7 (1977), 663.

Crawley, Ernest, *The Mystic Rose: A study of primitive marriage and of primitive thought in its bearing on marriage* (London: Methuen, 1902).

Culpepper, Emily E., 'Exploring Menstrual Attitudes' in Ruth Hubbard, Mary Sue Henefin and Barbara Fried (eds), *Women looking at Biology looking at Women* (Cambridge, Mass.: Shenckman Publishing Co., 1979).

Dalton, Katharina, *The Menstrual Cycle* (Harmondsworth: Penguin, 1969).

————, *The Premenstrual Syndrome and Progesterone Therapy* (London: Heinemann Year Book Medical Publishers, 1977).

————, 'Legal Implications of Premenstrual Syndrome', *World Medicine* (17 April 1982), 93–4.

Daly, Mary *Gyn/Ecology* (Boston: Beacon Press, 1978). (English edn, London: The Women's Press, 1979).

Dan, Alice J., Graham, Effie A., Beecher, Carol P. (eds), *The Menstrual Cycle* Vol. 1 *A Synthesis of Interdisciplinary Research* (New York: Springer, 1980).

Davis, Geoffrey, 'Menstrual Toxin and Human Fertility', letter to *Lancet* (8 June 1974), 1172–3.

Delaney, J., Lupton, M. J. and Toth, E., *The Curse: A Cultural History of Menstruation* (New York: E. P. Dalton, 1976).

Delphy, Christine and Leonard, Diana, 'Marxism, the Division of

Labour and Women's Oppression', paper to BSA Conference on 'Gender and Society' (Manchester 1983).

Dennerstein, Lorraine and Burrows, Graham D., 'Hormones and Female Sexuality' in Lorraine Dennerstein and M. de Senarclens (eds), *The Young Woman: Psychosomatic Aspects of Obstetrics and Gynaecology* (Amsterdam/New York: Elsevier Scientific Publishers, 1983).

Dennerstein, Lorraine and Burrows, Graham D. (eds), *Handbook of Psychosomatic Obstetrics and Gynaecology* (Amsterdam/New York: Elsevier, 1983).

Denzin, Norman K., *The Research Act in Sociology* (Chicago: Aldine, 1970).

Dewhurst, Sir C. J. (ed.), *Integrated Obstetrics and Gynaecology for Postgraduates* (Oxford: Blackwells, 1972; 3rd edn 1981).

Dickens, Linda, Davies, Celia, Homans, Hilary, Laws, Sophie and Rocheron, Yvette, 'Is Feminist Methodology a Red Herring?', letter to the editor of *Network* (BSA Newsletter), 26 (May 1983).

Dingwall, R. *et al* (eds), *Health Care and Health Knowledge* (London: Croom Helm, 1977).

Douglas, Mary, *Purity and Danger* (London: Routledge & Kegan Paul, 1966).

——————, 'Couvade and Menstruation: The Relevance of Tribal Studies' in *Implicit Meanings* (London: Routledge & Kegan Paul, 1975).

Durkheim, Emile, 'Incest: The Nature and Origin of the Taboo' (New York: Lyle Stuart, 1963; first published 1898).

Dworkin, Andrea, *Pornography: Men Possessing Women* (New York: G. P. Putnam, 1979).

Eccles, Audrey, *Obstetrics & Gynaecology in Tudor and Stuart England* (London: Croom Helm, 1982).

Ehrenreich, Barbara and English, Deirdre, *For Her Own Good: 150 Years of Experts' Advice to Women* (London: Pluto Press, 1979).

Ehrlich, Carol, *The Conditions of Feminist Research*, Research Group One Report, 21, (pamphlet), (USA, 1976).

Eichler, Margrit, *The Double Standard* (London: Croom Helm, 1980).

Ellis, Havelock, 'Love and Pain', (1898; republished within *Studies in the Psychology of Sex*, 1913).

——————, *Studies in the Psychology of Sex*, 7 Vols; (Philadelphia: F. A. Davis, in 2 Vols, 1913).

Elston, Mary Ann, 'Medicine as "old husband's tales": the impact of feminism' in Dale Spender (ed.), *Men's Studies Modified* (Oxford: Pergamon Press, 1981), 189–211.

Ernster, Virginia L., 'American Menstrual Expressions', *Sex Roles*, 1, 1 (1975).

Fildes, Sarah, 'The Inevitability of Theory', *Feminist Review*, 14 (September 1983).

Finch, Janet, 'It's great to have someone to talk to: the ethics and politics of interviewing women' in Colin Bell and Helen Roberts, *Social Researching* (London: Routledge & Kegan Paul, 1984).

Firestone, Shulamith, *The Dialectic of Sex* (London: Jonathan Cape, 1971).

Fontanus, Nicholas, *The Woman's Doctour: or an exact and distinct Explanation of all such Diseases as are peculiar to that Sex with Choise and Experimentall Remedies against the same*, 1652. (Quoted in Hilda Smith, 1976).

Frankfort, Ellen, *Vaginal Politics* (New York: Bantam Books, 1972).

Gannon, Linda, 'Evidence for a Psychological Etiology of Menstrual Disorders – A Critical Review', *Psychological Reports*, 48, 1 (1981), 287–93.

Garrey, Matthew M., Govan, A. D. T., Hodge, Colin, and Callander, Robin, *Gynaecology Illustrated* (Edinburgh: Churchill Livingstone, 1972; 2nd edn 1978).

Geer, Blanche, 'First Days in the Field' in Phillip E. Hammond (ed.), *Sociologists at Work* (New York: Basic Books, 1964), 322–44.

Golub, Sharon, 'Sex differences in Attitudes and Beliefs Regarding Menstruation' in Komnenich *et al* (eds), *The Menstrual Cycle*, Vol. 2 (New York: Springer, 1981).

—————, (ed.), 'Lifting the curse of Menstruation: A feminist appraisal of the influence of menstruation on women's lives', *Women & Health* Special Issue, 8, 2 & 3 (New York: The Haworth Press, 1983).

Gould Davis, Elizabeth, *The First Sex* (Harmondsworth: Penguin, 1971).

Grafstein, Rina, 'Menstruation and Sexuality: An Attitudinal Study', *Canadian Women's Studies*, 3 Pt 2 (1981), 14–16.

Graham, Hilary and Oakley, Ann, 'Competing ideologies of reproduction: medical and maternal perspectives on pregnancy' in Helen Roberts (ed.), *Women, Health and Reproduction* (London: Routledge & Kegan Paul, 1981).

Greer, Germaine, *The Female Eunuch* (London: MacGibbon and Kee, 1970).

Gregory, Pat, 'On the grey days, it's comforting to wear a towel that feels this safe', *Peace News*, 2190 (4 March 1983), 10–11.

Gruba, G. H. and Rohrbargh, M., 'MMPI correlates of menstrual distress', *Psychosomatic Medicine*, 37 (1975), 265–73.

Hage, Per and Hararay, Frank, 'Pollution beliefs in Highland New

Guinea', *Man*, 16, 3 (September 1981).

Hanmer, Jalna, 'Violence and the Social Control of Women' in Gary Littlejohn *et al* (eds), *Power and the State* (London: Croom Helm, 1977).

Hartman, Mary and Banner, Lois (eds), *Clio's Consciousness Raised* (New York: Harper & Row, 1974).

Haynes, P. J., 'Current aspects of dysmenorrhoea', *British Journal of Sexual Medicine*, 9, 83 (April 1982).

Heczey, Maria Doros, 'Effects of Biofeedback and Autogenic Training on Dysmenorrhoea' in Dan *et al* (eds), *The Menstrual Cycle*, Vol. 1 (New York: Springer, 1980), 283–91.

Henley, Nancy, *Body Politics* (New Jersey: Prentice Hall, 1977).

Hey, Valerie, 'Getting away with murder: PMT and the Press' in Sophie Laws, Valerie Hey and Andrea Eagan, *Seeing Red: the Politics of PMT* (London: Hutchinson, 1985).

Hite, Shere, *The Hite Report: A Nationwide Study of Female Sexuality* (Tamly Franklyn, GB, 1977).

——————, *Hite Report on Male Sexuality* (London: Macdonald, 1981).

Horney, Karen, *Feminine Psychology* (New York: W. W. Norton & Co., 1967).

Howell, Mary, 'What Medical Schools teach about Women', *New England Journal of Medicine*, 291 (August 1974), 304–7.

Hubbard, Ruth, Henefin, Mary Sue and Fried, Barbara, *Women looking at Biology looking at Women*, (Schenkman Publishing Company, 1979).

Illich, Ivan, *Limits to Medicine* (London: Marion Boyers: Open Forum, 1976).

Imray, Linda and Middleton, Audrey, 'Public and Private: Marking the Boundaries' in Eva Gamarnikov (ed.), *The Public and the private: social patterns of gender relations* (London: Heinemann, 1983).

Jackson, Margaret, 'Sexual Liberation or Social Control? Some Aspects of the Relationship between Feminism and the Social Construction of Sexual Knowledge in the Early 20th century', *Women's Studies International Forum*, 6 (January 1983).

Jeffcoate, T. N. A., 'Pelvic Pain', *British Medical Journal* 3, (1969), 431–5.

Jeffcoate, Sir Norman, *Principles of Gynaecology* (London: Butterworths, 1957; 4th edn 1975).

Jeffreys, Sheila, 'Free from all Uninvited Touch of Man: Women's Campaigns around Sexuality 1880–1914', *Women's Studies International Forum*, 5 (June 1982).

Jeffreys, Sheila, 'Sex reform and anti-feminism in the 1920s' in

London Feminist History Group, *The Sexual Dynamics of History* (London: Pluto Press, 1983).

Joffe, N. F., 'The Vernacular of Menstruation', *Word 4* (1948), 181–6.

John, Hari and Hadley, Janet, 'Depo Provera: Control of Fertility – two feminist views', *Spare Rib* (March 1982), 116.

Jordanova, Ludmilla, 'Natural facets: a historical perspective on science and sexuality' in C. MacCormack and M. Strathern (eds), *Nature, Culture and Gender* (Cambridge: Cambridge University Press, 1980).

Kay, Margarita Artschwager, 'Meanings of Menstruation to Mexican American Women' in Komnenich *et al* (eds), *The Menstrual Cycle*, Vol. 2 (New York: Springer, 1981).

Kelly, Liz, 'Some thoughts on feminist experience in research on male sexual violence' in Olivia Butler (ed.), *Feminist Experience in Feminist Research*, Studies in Sexual Politics No. 2 (Department of Sociology, University of Manchester, 1984).

Kelly, R., 'Witchcraft and sexual relations: an exploration of the social and semantic implications of the structure of belief' in P. Brown and C. Buchbinder (eds), *Man and Woman in the New Guinea Highlands*, Spec. Pub. American Anthropological Association, 8 (1976), 35–53.

King, A. F. A., 'A New Basis for Uterine Pathology', *American Journal of Obstetrics, VIII* (1875/6), 242–3.

King, Aileen, 'Return of the Curse', letter to *Peace News*, 2192 (1 April 1983), 15.

Kingston, Beryl, *Lifting the Curse* (London: Ebury Press, 1980).

Koeske, R. and Koeske, G., 'An Attributional Approach to Moods and the Menstrual Cycle', *Journal of Personality and Social Psychology*, 31, 3 (1975), 473–8.

Koeske, Randi, K. D., 'Theoretical Perspectives on Menstrual Cycle Research: The Relevance of Attributional Approaches for the Perception and Explanation of Premenstrual Emotionality' in Alice Dan *et al* (eds), *The Menstrual Cycle*, Vol. 1 (New York: Springer, 1980).

Komnenich P., McSweeney, M., Noack, J. A. and Elder, N. (eds), *The Menstrual Cycle*, Vol 2, *Research and Implications for Women's Health* (New York: Springer, 1981).

Kupfermann, Jeanette, *The MsTaken Body* (St Albans: Granada, 1979).

The Lancet, 'Premenstrual syndrome', editorial, 2, 8260–1 (19–26 December 1981), 1393–4.

The Lancet, 'Premenstrual uncertainties', editorial, 2, 8356 (22 October 1983), 950–1.

Larsen, V. L., 'Psychological study of colloquial menstrual expressions', *Northwest Medicine*, 62 (1963), 874–7.

Laws, Sophie, 'The Sexual Politics of Premenstrual Tension', *Women's Studies International Forum*, 6, 1 (January 1983), 19–31.

——————— (with Valerie Hey and Andrea Eagan), *Seeing Red: the politics of premenstrual tension* (London: Hutchinson, 1985).

Lee, Rosemary, 'Blood, Blood, Glorious Blood', *Workers Educational Association Women's Studies Newsletter*, n.s. 2, (November 1984), 8.

Leeds Revolutionary Feminist Group, 'Every single academic feminist owes her livelihood to the WLM' (Bradford: Women's Research and Resources Centre Summer School, unpublished paper, 1979).

Legman, G., *The Rationale of the Dirty Joke* (London: Jonathan Cape, 1969; reprinted by Panther Books in 2 vols, 1972).

Lennane, Jean and Lennane, John, 'Alleged psychogenic disorders in women: a possible manifestation of sexual prejudice', *New England Journal of Medicine*, 288 (6 February 1973), 288–92.

Lessing, Doris, *The Golden Notebook* (London: Michael Joseph, 1962).

Lever, Judy, *PMT: the unrecognised illness* (London: New English Library, 1979).

Levitt, E and Lubin, B., 'Some personality factors associated with menstrual complaints and menstrual attitudes', *Journal of Psychosomatic Research*, 11 (1967), 267–70.

Lewis, Gilbert, *Day of Shining Red* (Oxford: Oxford University Press, 1980).

Lewis, I. M., *Ecstatic Religion* (Harmondsworth: Penguin, 1971).

Liddington, Jill, *The Life and Times of a Respectable Rebel: Selina Cooper* (1864–1946) (London: Virago, 1984).

Llewellyn-Jones, Derek, *Fundamentals of Obstetrics and Gynaecology*, Vol. 2, *Gynaecology* (London: Faber & Faber, 1970; 3rd edn 1982).

McClure Browne, J. C., *Postgraduate Obstetrics and Gynaecology* (London: Butterworths, 1950; 4th edn 1973).

MacKinnon, Catharine A., 'Feminism, Marxism, Method and the State: An Agenda for Theory, *Signs*, 7, 2 (1982).

McRobbie, Angela, 'The Politics of Feminist Research: Between Talk, Text and Action', *Feminist Review*, 12 (1982), 46–58.

Macht, David I., 'Further historical and experimental studies on menstrual toxin', *American Journal of Medical Science*, 206 (1943), 281–305.

Madge, John, *The Tools of Social Science* (London: Longman, 1953).

Mahoney, Pat, 'How Alice's chin really came to be pressed against her foot: sexist processes of interaction in mixed-sex classrooms',

Women's Studies International Forum, 6, 1 (1983).

Marieskind, Helen, 'The Women's Health Movement' in *International Journal of Health Services*, 5 (Spring 1973(a)), 271–323.

——————, 'Restructuring Ob/Gyn', *Social Policy*, 6 (September/October 1975(b)), 48–9.

Marshall, Paule, *Brown Girl, Brownstones* (London: W. H. Allen & Co., 1960).

Matriarchy Study Group, *Menstrual Taboos* (Self published, undated (a) ?1975/76).

——————, *Politics of Matriarchy* (Self published, undated (b) ?1979).

Maudsley, Henry, 'Sex in Mind and in Education', *Fortnightly Review*, n.s., 15 (1874), 466–83.

Mayer, Jessica, 'Pollution as an Analytic Category for the study of Gender Ideology: A Critical Review', paper to BMAS meeting 'Women as Healers: Women as Polluters' (Bristol: 1 October 1983).

Mead, Margaret, *Male and Female* (Harmondsworth: Penguin Books, 1950).

Meigs, Dr Charles, *Woman: Her Diseases and Remedies* (Philadelphia: Blanchard & Lee, 1851).

Merskey, H. and Spear, F. G., *Pain, Psychological and Psychiatric Aspects* (London: Bailliere, Tindall and Cassell, 1967).

Merves, Esther, *The Social Management of Menstruation*, MA Thesis (Ohio State University, 1983).

Moos, R. H., 'The development of the Menstrual Distress Questionnaire', *Psychosomatic Medicine*, 30 (1968), 853.

Moraga, Cherrie and Anzaldua, Gloria (eds), *This Bridge called my Back* (USA: Persephone Press, 1981).

Morgan, Susanne, 'Hysterectomy', Feminist History Research Project (Topanga California: Boston Women's Health Book Collective Inc., 1978).

Morrison, Tonia, *The Bluest Eye* (New York: Pocket Books, 1970).

Moscucci, Ornella, 'Separate Spheres: Anthropology and Gynaecology in the second half of the 19th Century', paper to BSA Medical Sociology Conference (Durham, September 1982).

——————, 'The Science of Woman: British Gynaecology 1849–1890', PhD thesis (Oxford University 1984).

Mosher, Clelia Duel, *Women's Physical Freedom*, (New York: The Women's Press, 1923).

——————, *The Mosher Survey: Sexual Attitudes of 45 Victorian Women*, edited by Jane Mahood and Kristine Wenburg (New York: Arno Press (NYT), 1980).

Norbeck, Edward, 'A Sanction for Authority: Etiquette' in R. D. Fogelson and R. N. Adams (eds), *The Anthropology of Power* (New York: Academic Press, 1977).

Oakley, Ann, 'Interviewing Women: a Contradiction in Terms' in Helen Roberts (ed.), *Doing Feminist Research* (London: Routledge & Kegan Paul, 1981), 30–61.

O'Brien, Maggie and McKee, Laura, 'Interviewing Men: Taking Gender Seriously', paper to BSA Conference on 'Gender and Society' (Manchester, April 1982).

O'Brien, Mary, *The Politics of Reproduction* (London: Routledge & Kegan Paul, 1981).

Okeley, Judith, *The Traveller-Gypsies* (Cambridge: Cambridge University Press, 1983).

O'Sullivan, Sue, 'Love and the unmarried woman', *Spare Rib*, 141 (April 1984), 13.

Paige, Karen Erikson and Paige, Jeffrey, *The Politics of Reproductive Ritual* (Berkeley and Los Angeles, California: University of California Press, 1981).

Pankhurst, Christabel, *Plain Facts about a Great Evil* (London: Women's Social and Political Union, 1913).

Parlee, Mary Brown, 'The Premenstrual Syndrome', *Psychological Bulletin*, 80, 6 (1973), 454–65.

————, 'Stereotypic Beliefs about Menstruation: A Methodological Note on the Moos MDQ and some new data', *Psychosomatic Medicine*, 36, 3 (May–June 1974).

Parry, Odette, 'Decent Exposure: Body Presentation in the Naturist Club', paper to BSA Medical Sociology Conference (Durham, September 1982).

Pemberton-Jones, Patricia, 'Tidal Wage', *WEA Women's Studies Newsletter*, n.s., 1 (May 1984), 17–18.

Pfeffer, Naomi, Unpublished paper read to BSA Human Reproduction Study Group (1983).

————, 'The Hidden Pathology of the Male Reproductive System' in Hilary Homans (ed.), *The Sexual Politics of Reproduction* (London: Gower Press, 1985).

Polhemus, Ted (ed.), *Social Aspects of the Human Body* (Harmondsworth: Penguin, 1978).

Prendergast, Shirley, Jim Davis and Prout, Alan, '"This is the time to grow up ..." A Case Study of 15 year old students' knowledge about menstruation', unpublished paper, Health Education Studies Unit (Cambridge: Hughes Hall, 1982).

Prendergast, Shirley, '"Tell me why you can't do games"; girls' accounts of housekeeping the body in school', paper to BSA Medical Sociology Conference, (York, September 1988).

Price Commission, *'In-depth' studies: Prices of Sanitary Towels and Tampons*, Report No. 9 (London: HMSO, October 1975).

Raymond, Janice G., *The Transsexual Empire: the making of the She-Male* (Boston: Beacon, 1980).

Reed, Evelyn, *Women's Evolution* (Pathfinder Press Inc., 1975).

Reitz, Rosetta, *Menopause: a positive approach* (Hassocks, Sussex: Harvester Press, 1979).

Rich, Adrienne, *Of Woman Born* (London: Virago, 1977).

——————, *Women and Honor* (London: Onlywomen Press, 1980).

——————, 'Compulsory Heterosexuality and Lesbian Existence', *Signs*, 5, 4 (1980).

Richman, Charles L., Patty, Rosemarie A. and Fisher, Terri D., 'Mind-Body Revisited: Every 28 Days', *Psychological Reports*, 39 (1976), 1311–14.

Richman, Joel and Goldthorp, W. O., 'When was your last period: temporal aspects of gynaecological diagnosis' in Robert Dingwall, Christian Heath, Margaret Reid and Margaret Stacey (eds), *Health Care and Health Knowledge* (London: Croom Helm, 1977).

Riley, Denise, *War in the Nursery: Theories of the Child and Mother* (London: Virago, 1983).

Roberts, Elizabeth, *A Woman's Place – An Oral History of Working Class Women 1890–1940* (Oxford: Blackwell, 1984).

Roberts, Helen (ed.), *Doing Feminist Research* (London: Routledge & Kegan Paul, 1981).

Robinson, David, *The Process of Becoming Ill* (London: Routledge & Kegan Paul, 1971).

Rodgers, Silvia, 'Women's Space in a Men's House: The British House of Commons' in Shirley Ardener (ed.), *Women and Space: Ground Rules and Social Maps* (London: Croom Helm, 1981), 50–71.

Root, Jane, 'Only Women Bleed', *Honey* (June 1982).

Rosaldo, M. Z., 'The Use and Abuse of Anthropology: Reflections on Feminism and Cross-Cultural Understanding, *Signs*, 5, 3 (1980), 389–417.

Rowbotham, Sheila, Review of Germain Greer's *The Female Eunuch*, in *Oz*, 31 (November/December 1970), 22. Quoted in Clive Pearson: 'Male Sexual Politics and Men's Gender Practice', *Women's Studies International Forum*, 7, 1 (1984), 29–32.

Rugen, Helen, *The Roots of Marie Stopes: Ideas about Female Sexuality in Britain 1900–1920* PhD Dissertation (in Fawcett Library) (University of Edinburgh, 1979).

Ruzek, Sheryl Burt, *The Women's Health Movement* (New York: Praeger, 1979).

Sadgopal, Mira, 'The Neglected Pain', *Manushi*, 3, 4 (1983).

Sagarin, Edward, *The Anatomy of Dirty Words* (New York: Lyle Stuart Publishing, 1968).

Sarachild, Kathie, 'Consciousness Raising: A Radical Weapon' in Redstockings, *Feminist Revolution* (New York: self-published, 1975), 131–7.

Sayers, Janet, *Biological Politics* (London and New York: Tavistock, 1982).

Scott, Sue, 'Qualitative Methods and Feminist Research', unpublished paper for Qualitative Methodology and the Study of Education Workshop, Whitelands College (London, June 1983).

————, 'The personable and the powerful: gender and status in sociological research' in Colin Bell and Helen Roberts (eds), *Social Researching: Politics, Problems and Practice* (London: Routledge & Kegan Paul, 1984).

Scully, Diana, *Men Who Control Women's Health: The Miseducation of Obstetrician-Gynaecologists* (Boston: Houghton Mifflin, 1980).

———— and Bart, Pauline, 'A Funny Thing Happened on the Way to the Orifice: Women in Gynaecology Textbooks' in John Ehrenreich (ed.), *The Cultural Crisis of Modern Medicine* (New York and London: Monthly Review Press, 1978), 212–26.

Seaman, Barbara and Seaman, Gideon, *Women and the Crisis in Sex Hormones* (New York: Bantam Books, 1977).

Sereny, Gitta, *Into that Darkness: from mercy killing to mass murder* (London: Picador, 1977; first published 1974).

Shangold, Mona M., 'The Pain of Dysmenorrhoea', *American Women's Medical Association Journal*, 38, Pt 1 (1983), 12–17.

Shaw, Wilfred, *Textbook of Gynaecology* (London: J. & A. Churchill Ltd., 5th edn 1948; first edn 1936).

Short, R. V., 'Control of Menstruation' in G. V. P. Chamberlain (ed.), *Contemporary Obstetrics and Gynaecology* (London: Northwood Publishers Ltd., 1977).

Shorter, Edward, *The History of Women's Bodies* (London: Allen Lane, 1983).

Showalter, Elaine and Showalter, English, 'Victorian Women and Menstruation' in Martha Vicinus (ed.), *Suffer and Be Still: Women in the Victorian Age* (Indiana: Indiana University Press, 1972; London: Methuen, 1980).

Shuttle, Penelope and Redgrove, Peter, *The Wise Wound: Menstruation and Everywoman* (London: Victor Gollancz, 1978; Harmondsworth: Penguin, 1980).

Skultans, Vieda, 'The symbolic significance of menstruation and the menopause', *Man*, n.s., 5 (1970), 639–51.

Slavin, Hazel, 'Hidden health messages in advertisements aimed at young women', MSc, Health Education (Chelsea College, 1981).

Sloane, B., 'News in Brief', *National Organisation for Women Times* (January/February 1982), 4.

Smith, Dorothy, 'Women's perspective as a radical critique of sociology', *Sociological Inquiry*, 44 (1974), 7–13.

——————, 'K is mentally ill', *Sociology*, 12 (1978), 23–53.

Smith, Hilda, 'Gynaecology and Ideology in Seventeeth Century England' in Berenice A. Carroll (ed.), *Liberating Women's History* (Urbana, Illinois: University of Illinois Press, 1976).

Smith-Rosenberg, Carroll, 'Puberty to Menopause: the Cycle of Femininity in Nineteenth Century America' in Mary Hartman and Lois Banner (eds), *Clio's Consciousness Raised* (New York: Harper & Row, 1974).

Snow, L. F. and Johnson, S. M., 'Modern Day Menstrual Folklore: Some Clinical Implications', *Journal of the American Medical Association*, 237 (1977), 2736–9.

Snowden, Robert and Christian, Barbara (eds), *Patterns and Perceptions of Menstruation: A World Health Organisation International Study*, published by WHO (London: Croom Helm; New York: St Martin's Press, 1983).

Stacey, Margaret, *Methods of Social Research* (Oxford: Pergamon Press, 1969).

Stanley, Liz and Wise, Sue, 'Feminist research, feminist consciousness and experiences of sexism', *Women's Studies International Quarterly*, 2, 3 (1979), 359.

—————— and ——————, *Breaking Out: feminist consciousness and feminist research* (London: Routledge & Kegan Paul, 1983).

Stephens, W. A., 'A Cross-Cultural Study of Menstrual Taboos', *Genetic Psychology Monographs*, 64 (1961), 385–416.

Sternbeck, Richard A., Sanford R. Wolf, Robert W. Murray, and Wayne H. Akeson, 'Aspects of Chronic Low Back Pain', *Psychosomatics*, 14 (January/February 1973), 52–6.

Stimson, Gerry and Webb, Barbara, *Going to see the Doctor* (London: Routledge & Kegan Paul, 1975).

Strathern, Marilyn, *Women in Between: Female roles in a Male world, Mount Hagen, New Guinea* (London and New York: Seminar Press, 1972).

Styles, William, 'The Update Clinical Guide: Dysmenorrhoea', *Update*, 24, 9 (1 May 1982), 1694.

Szasz, T. S., *Pain and Pleasure: A Study of Bodily Feelings* (London: Tavistock Publications, 1957).

Thornhill, Teresa, 'Other people's revolutions', *Trouble and Strife*, 6 (Summer 1985), 7–14.

Toth, Emily, Delaney, Janice, and Lupton, Mary Jane, 'The

Menstruating Woman in the Popular Imagination' in Komne-nich *et al* (eds), *The Menstrual Cycle*, Vol. 2 (New York: Springer, 1978).

Treneman, Ann, 'Cashing in on the Curse: advertising and the menstrual taboo', in M. Marshment and L. Gamman (eds), *The Female Gaze* (London: Women's Press, 1988).

Turnbull, Colin, *The Forest People* (London: Picador, 1976), cited in Birke and Best, 'The Tyrannical Womb', in Brighton Women and Science Group (eds), *Alice Under the Microscope* (London: Virago, 1980).

Udry, J. R. and Morris, N., 'Distribution of coitus in the menstrual cycle', *Nature*, 220 (1968), 593–596.

Voda, Ann M., Dinnerstein, Myra and O'Donnell, Sheryl R. (eds), *Changing Perspectives on Menopause* (Austin: University of Texas Press, 1982).

Walker, Alice, *The Color Purple* (New York: Harcourt Brace Jovano-vitch, 1982).

Walsh, Mary Roth, *Doctors Wanted: No Women Need Apply* (New Haven, Conn.: Yale University Press, 1977).

Webster, Sandra K., 'Problems of Diagnosis of Spasmodic and Congestive Dysmenorrhoea', in Dan *et al* (eds), *The Menstrual Cycle* (New York: Springer, 1980).

Weideger, Paula, *Female Cycles* (London: Women's Press, 1978).

Weisenberg, Matisyohu, 'Pain and Pain Control', *Psychological Bulletin*, 84, 5 (1977), 1008–44.

Whisnant, L., Brett, E. and Zegans, L., 'Implicit messages concerning menstruation in commercial educational materials prepared for young adolescent girls', *American Journal of Psychiatry*, *132* (1975), 815–20.

———— and Zegans, L., 'A study of attitudes toward menarche in white middle-class American girls', *American Journal of Psychiatry*, *132* (1975), 809–14.

White, Leslie, A., *The Evolution of Culture* (New York: McGraw Hill, 1959).

Whitehead, Anne, 'Sex antagonism in Herefordshire' in Diana Leonard Barker and Sheila Allen (eds), *Dependence and Exploitation in Work and Marriage* (London and New York: Longman, 1976).

Whiting, Pat, 'Menstrual Taboos and their Relationship to Female Sexual Repression' in Matriarchy Study Group (eds), *Menstrual Taboos* (self-published, undated).

Willis, Paul, *Learning to Labour* (Farnborough, Hants: Saxon House, 1977).

Wise, Sue and Stanley, Liz (eds), 'Men and Sex: a case study in "sexual sexual politics"', *Women's Studies International Forum*, Special Issue, 7, 1 (1984).

Women's Medical Association of New York, (eds), *Mary Putnam Jacobi: A Pathfinder in Medicine* (New York, 1925).

Wood, Carl, 'Dysmenorrhoea', in L. Dennerstein and G. D. Burrows (eds), *Handbook of Psychosomatic Obstetrics and Gynaecology* (Amsterdam/New York: Elsevier, 1983).

Wood, Julian, 'Boys' sex talk – groping toward sexism?' (Unpublished Paper, ? 1983).

World Health Organisation, *Research on the Menopause*, Report of a WHO Scientific Group (Geneva: WHO, 1981).

WHO Task Force on Psychological Research in Family Planning, 'A Cross Culture Study of Menstruation: Implications for Contraceptive Development and Use', *Studies in Family Planning*, 12, 1 (January 1981), 3–16.

WHO Task Force on Psychological Research in Family Planning, 'Women's Bleeding Patterns: Ability to Recall and Predict Menstrual Events', *Studies in Family Planning*, 12, 1 (1981), 17–27.

Wright Mills, C., *The Sociological Imagination* (New York: Oxford University Press, 1959; London: Pelican, 1970).

Young, Frank W. and Bacdayan, Albert A., 'Menstrual Taboos and Social Rigidity' in S. Ford-Clellan (ed.), *Cross-Cultural Approaches: Readings in Comparative Research* (New Haven, Conn.: HRAF Press, 1967).

Zola, Irving Kenneth, 'Culture and Symptoms – an analysis of patients' presenting symptoms', *American Sociological Review*, 31 (1966), 615.

Index

237

240

Index

jokes about menstruation
children's, 71–3
men's, *see under* male culture
women's, 66–7

Kay, Margarita Artschwager, 136, 173
Kelly, Liz, 131
Kelly, R., 18
King, A. F. A., 136
Kingston, Beryl, 203
Koeske, Randi K. D., and Koeske, G., 189
Kraft-Ebbing, 185
Kupfermann, Jeanette, 20, 27

Lancet, The, 35, 204
Larsen, V. L., 80
Laws, S., *et al*, 188
Lee, Rosemary, 54, 55, 81
Legman, G., 83–4, 88
Lennane, Jean, and Lennane, John, 152, 166
lesbians, 20, 95, 106, 108, 125, 220
see also heterosexuality; sexuality, female
Lessing, Doris, 120
Lestor, Joan, MP, 52
Lever, Judy, 6, 201, 203
Levitt, E., and Lubin, B., 167
Lewis, Gilbert, 104–5
Lewis, I. M., 21
Liddington, Jill, 120
Llewellyn-Jones, Derek, 134–59, 169, 171–2, 177, 203
Loskiel, G. H., 24

MacKinnon, Catharine A., 40
Madge, John, 11
Macht, David I., 35
Mahoney, Pat, 69
male culture, 29, 30–1, 69–93, 107–8, 110, 124, 133, 209, 213–14
on menstrual pain, 162–3, 182
on premenstrual tension, 190–3, 205–6
male reproductive system, medical representations of, 158
Marieskind, Helen, 157

Marshall, Paule, 120
masochism, 185
matriarchalist theories, 15, 22–8, 93–4, 119
Matriarchy Study Group, 15, 19, 22
Maudsley, Henry, 157
Mayer, Jessica, 20–1
McClure Browne, J. C., 137, 153
McRobbie, Angela, 13
Mead, Margaret, 19, 27, 152
medical attitudes towards menstruation, 2, 8–9, 29, 93–4, 102–3, 118, 133–59, 213–14
Indian, 170–1
and menstrual pain, 160–87
and premenstrual tension, 201–6
see also historical
Meigs, Charles, 158–9
men
as individuals, 6–8, 29, 67–8, 207, 212–14
in intimate relationships with women, 39–40, 178–81, 194–200; *see also* heterosexuality
their knowledge of menstruation, 32–4, 37–42, 72
as subjects of research, 89, 215–19
see also boys; fathers; male culture, patriarchy
men's group, nature of, 8, 57–8
menarche (first menstruation), 1, 19, 23–5, 53–6, 129
menopause, 4, 49–50, 135, 141
menstrual cycle
length of, 140–1, 142
mood change, *see under* mood change, menstrual cycle
menstrual problems, 4, 29, 148–52, 171
see under amenorrhoea; heavy bleeding; neurosis; mood change, menstrual cycle; pain, menstrual; premenstrual tension
menstrual toxin, 35–6
menstruation
abolition of, 102